FACING A DEATH IN THE FAMILY

*Caring for Someone Through Illness
and Dying, Arranging the Funeral,
Dealing with the Will and Estate*

MARGARET KERR & JOANN KURTZ

JOHN WILEY & SONS

Toronto • New York • Chichester • Weinheim • Brisbane • Singapore

John Wiley & Sons Canada Limited
22 Worcester Road
Etobicoke, Ontario
M9W1L1

Canadian Cataloguing in Publication Data

Kerr, Margaret Helen, 1954–   .
    Facing a death in the family : caring for someone through illness and dying, arranging the funeral, dealing with the will and estate

(A Wiley legal and practical guide)
Includes index.
ISBN 0-471-64396-3

1. Death—Handbooks, manuals, etc. 2. Wills—Canada—Popular works.
3. Decedents' estates—Canada—Popular works. I. Kurtz, JoAnn, 1951–   .
II. Title. III. Series.

GT3150.K47 1999   306.9   C99–930437-2

PRODUCTION CREDITS

Cover Design: Interrobang Graphic Design
Printer: Tri-Graphic Printing
Printed in Canada
Electronic Formatting: Heidy Lawrance Associates

10 9 8 7 6 5 4 3 2 1

Also available in the Wiley Legal and Practical Guide Series:

The Complete Guide to Buying, Owning and Selling a Home in Canada
by Margaret Kerr and JoAnn Kurtz (ISBN: 0-471-64191-X)

Surviving Your Divorce: A Guide to Canadian Family Law, Second Edition,
by Michael G. Cochrane (ISBN: 0-471-64399-8)

*Surviving Your Parents' Divorce: A Guide for Young Canadians, Second
Edition,* by Michael G. Cochrane (ISBN: 0-471-64398-X)

*For Better or For Worse: The Canadian Guide to Marriage Contracts and
Cohabitation Agreements* by Michael G. Cochrane (ISBN: 0-471-64206-1)

*You Be The Judge: The Complete Canadian Guide to Resolving Legal
Disputes Out of Court* by Norman A. Ross (ISBN: 0-471-64199-5)

Life is pleasant. Death is peaceful.
It's the transition that's troublesome.

Attributed to Isaac Asimov

To Michael M. Sheehan
and
To Jacob Feinberg, who lived a
full life and died in his sleep

CONTENTS

ACKNOWLEDGEMENTS

We would like to thank the following people who read chapters for us and provided a critical appraisal: Mary Jane Woods, Dr. Cameron Guest, Dr. Laurence Librach, Rosalie Mednick Nepom, Marsha Skain, Michael Kerr. We would also like to thank the following people and organizations who generously gave us help and information: Maria Martin, Dr. James Young, Judith Wahl, Hilary Pearson, Wendy Brook Hooper, Bonnie Wasser, Gail Carson, Gilda Jubas, Jim Osborne, Dr. Lynn Fulton, Matt Drown, Dr. John Bonn, Bob Carson, Alzheimer Society for Metro Toronto, Heart and Stroke Foundation of Ontario, Toronto Humane Society, College of Nurses of Ontario, Canadian Association for Community Care, Ontario Board of Funeral Services, Concerned Friends of Ontario Citizens in Care Facilities.

1 FACING A DEATH IN THE FAMILY

This is probably the last book in the world you want to read...in a way. If someone in your family or a close friend is terminally ill or on a downward path because of frailty or injury, you don't really want to think more than you already *are* thinking about all the problems and decisions you have to face.

This is probably the book you've been hoping for...in a way. You know that looking after a family member or friend through illness and dying, arranging the funeral, and dealing with the will and estate mean a lot of hard work for you and others in your family—and there's not a lot of help out there for you. Especially not all in one place. You may have run yourself ragged by now looking for information about what to do next.

For most of human history, people have died in their homes. Babies died in infancy, young women in childbirth, young men of work injuries, old people of strokes and heart attacks, people of all ages of disease. Everyone grew up with death, nursed family members who were dying, assisted with burial preparations, took over the possessions of the person who died according to his or her deathbed wishes and to local customs. Dying and death were part of everyday life. In this century we have finally gained the ability to fight death—with sanitation and vaccines and antibiotics and surgery and other things—and now dying is no longer an ordinary part of living. Instead, it's hidden away and not discussed. Most of us know very little about how to handle dying and death from a practical point of view, but we're still expected to make all the arrangements, learning as we go. Everyone has to make the rounds, all alone, of doctors and lawyers, nursing homes and funeral homes, court offices and government offices, to figure out what needs to be done and how to do it, how to get help, and how to pay for it all.

When you realize that a family member is going to die, you can't just ignore the situation and hope it will go away. And once you admit that you're facing a death in the family, you also have to admit that there's a lot to do—so you might as well find out exactly what it is and how to do it as well as possible. We wrote this book because we wanted to know what to do and there was no easy way to find out everything. So we went to work, researching and interviewing—and living through our own experiences—to find out as much as we could. And now we're ready to share it with you.

WHAT THIS BOOK IS ABOUT

We had a lot of trouble finding the title for this book—a title that would immediately give people the right idea of what it was about, at least in fewer than 25 words. We know that a death in the family involves a whole lot more than finding a nursing home, talking to doctors, coping with your grief, making funeral arrangements, or acting as an executor. There are books and pamphlets about these things, but separate books and pamphlets for each one, as though there's no relationship between grief and estate administration, or between a hospital and a funeral home. In the real world, all of these things flow together, sometimes happening all at once or overlapping. When you're looking after a dying family member or trying to figure out financial affairs after the person is gone, you don't have time to run to the bookstore or library every time a new problem or issue comes up. That's why we set this book up to cover pretty much everything you need to know about caring for a person who is seriously ill or dying, making all the arrangements surrounding death, and looking after the business matters that follow death.

Here are some of the things that this book deals with:

About Advance Planning That Will Make Things Easier

- having your family member make a will and a living will
- getting a power of attorney that will let you look after your family member's financial affairs when she can no longer do it herself
- arranging a living will that will let you make health care decisions for your family member when he can no longer make his own
- making financial arrangements to cover the cost of care

About Caring for a Family Member

- finding the right kind of care, at home, in an extended care facility such as a nursing home, or in a hospital
- getting a family member out of legal messes caused by failing mental or physical health
- paying for care
- getting tax deductions for care
- talking to doctors
- dealing with the staff in a facility
- controlling pain

About Death

- accepting or refusing life-prolonging treatment
- getting "comfort care" for a dying person
- preventing suffering and thereby hastening death
- recognizing the signs of approaching death
- being with someone who is in the process of dying

About What Happens (in This World) after Death

- consenting to organ donation
- dealing with autopsies and inquests
- getting a death certificate

About Funeral Arrangements

- planning or preplanning a funeral, burial or cremation
- paying for funeral arrangements
- shipping a body home
- travelling to a funeral
- getting time off work

About Going on with Your Life

- finding money to pay the bills
- looking after the dependants and pets of the person who has died
- grieving

About Dealing with the Property of a Person Who Has Died

- acting as the personal representative who handles the estate
- paying debts and taxes of the estate
- giving the property to the beneficiaries

About Legal Matters

- knowing when you need a lawyer, and what kind of lawyer
- dealing with lawyers and legal fees
- going to court

WE DON'T HAVE ALL THE ANSWERS

Nobody has all the answers to questions that arise about illness and death, and we're no exception. However, the questions we can't answer go beyond "Why?" and "Why now?" to things like "Exactly what will this cost?" and "What does the legislation say in *my* province?" We've written this book not just to cover every issue we can think of but also to cover all of Canada. On the legal matters we discuss, the law is slightly different in every single province and territory, so we usually talk generally rather than specifically about the law and try to direct you to a source inside your province or territory for the details. We also try to tell you when you need to see a lawyer about a problem that arises. On money matters, we try to give a general idea about the cost of things, but costs often vary from province to province, and are subject to change without notice. You'll need to check out the price of things for yourself.

We hope this book will give you the help you need during this difficult time.

PART I

THE ROAD AHEAD

2 | THINKING THE UNTHINKABLE

$\mathbf{Y}$ou have just realized that your family member is going to die. Perhaps he has recently been diagnosed with a terminal illness. Or she may have a long-term illness that is clearly reaching its final stages. Or he may be elderly and is becoming increasingly frail. Now there are many matters that you and your family member will have to deal with, and few, if any, are pleasant. One thing is to make sure that your family member makes adequate financial and legal plans to see him or her through the dying process.

You and your family member need to make plans about:

- how medical and personal care will be paid for
- how his property will be shared among family members, friends or charitable organizations after he dies
- how her financial affairs will be handled if she can no longer look after them
- how decisions about his medical treatment are to be made if he becomes unable to make the decisions
- whether she would like to donate her organs and/or tissue after death

Your family member may already have his affairs in order, or may be under the age of majority (18 or 19, depending on the province) and so, generally speaking, not have any affairs to put in order. But, more likely, your family member is an adult who has put matters off, never wanting to face the possibility of dying. These matters can't be put off any longer if your family member wants to have a say in how decisions will be made when he is no longer able to make them himself. That's because by law a person must be mentally capable of understanding the issues and the consequences of his decisions in order to make most advance preparations. If he waits too long, his illness may progress to the point where he no longer has that mental capability.

This chapter will tell you about the financial and legal planning that a dying person needs to do, so that you can talk about these issues with your family member, and encourage her to do what is necessary. In later chapters we'll deal with putting these plans into effect.

HOW TO RAISE THE SUBJECT

Before we talk about what you should talk about, let's think about *how* you should talk about it. We do not want to mislead you: discussing this kind of planning can be very difficult, both for you and your family member. For one thing, neither one of you may want to think about dying. For another, you may be afraid that your family member will misinterpret your intentions and suspect that you're trying to take control or, worse, that you're after his money. And, in fact, your family member *may* be suspicious of your motives. We wish we could give you some fail-safe advice, but we can't. You will have to take an approach tailored to your personality, your family member's personality and your relationship with each other. You may find it helpful to give your family member a book about estate planning. A good book on the subject is *You Can't Take It With You*, by Sandra Foster, published by John Wiley & Sons Canada Ltd. If you just can't raise the topic yourself, maybe a friend or another family member can.

PAYING FOR MEDICAL AND PERSONAL CARE

Canadians have good health care coverage: medical care by a doctor or in a hospital is paid for, and home care and care in a facility are subsidized. But dying can still be expensive, especially if it takes a while and the dying person needs to be looked after in a nursing home or other facility, or by a family member who would otherwise be working, or by health care workers (whether at home or in a facility) who have to be paid by the patient or family. It is also expensive if treatment involves frequent travel to a medical centre, or costly drugs not covered under a drug benefit plan, or if special modifications have to be made or special equipment has to be bought so that the dying person can stay at home as long as possible. And as a final blow, a funeral costs several thousand dollars. Sometimes a death in the family—particularly a death after a long illness—is followed immediately by bankruptcy.

By the time you read this, you are probably facing the situation of a terminal illness in the family, and it is probably too late to take steps to ease the financial burden if they haven't already been taken. For example, if the family member who is ill is the main money-earner in the family, at this point he won't be able to take out **disability insurance** so that there will still be an income when he can no longer work, or to buy **mortgage disability insurance** so that the mortgage will still be paid, or to take out **life insurance** so that there will be some money for the family later on. However, it may not be too late to get **extended health care insurance** to supplement your provincial health insurance.

As soon as you realize that a family member is failing, you should take stock of the family's financial situation so you know where the money for care will come from.

- Is there a home or cottage that can be mortgaged (or carry a larger mortgage) or sold if necessary? Are there investments that can be sold? Are there things you can do without, like an extra car or a yearly vacation, if there's a financial crunch?

- Are there existing life insurance or disability insurance policies? Once someone has been diagnosed with a serious illness, it will be impossible or prohibitively expensive to take out insurance. Also note that life insurance policies end or the premiums become extremely expensive when the insured reaches a certain age, such as 65 or 70—when the risk of death gets too high for an insurer to stomach.

- At work, check out the benefits such as extended health care and drug plans available through your or your family member's employer.

- Find out from your employer whether you could arrange flexible work hours, or be allowed to do some work from home, or could take early retirement if you had to care for a sick family member.

- Investigate government resources, such as home care and care in a subsidized facility and special drug plans for certain conditions. You'll be able to get financial help with some but not usually all of the care your family member needs. You may also be able to get help through your provincial government or through the Canada Mortgage and Housing Corporation (CMHC) to adapt housing to the needs of your family member.

- Investigate resources in the community. Volunteers working with the Canadian Cancer Society, Alzheimer's Canada, hospice, and so on, or your local religious organization, may be able to help with meals, transportation or personal care for your family member.

- Find out whether any charitable groups could give you financial support. You may belong to an organization or club that helps members in need, or you may be able to apply to a registered charity for assistance (for example, if your family member is a child, Easter Seals and the Children's Wish Starlight Foundation).

- Speak to your bank manager about what loan arrangements might be available.

GIVING AWAY PROPERTY ON DEATH

The old saying *is* true—you can't take it with you. So after your family member's death, her property will be given away to others.

Last Will and Testament

If your family member wants to control to whom his property is given, he must have a **last will and testament**, or, simply called, a will. A will is a written, signed document that sets out how the person making the will (called the **testator**) wants his property given away after his death. A will also usually appoints someone (called an **executor** in most provinces) to look after the property or **estate** of the person who died, and may deal with other matters such as naming a **guardian** (in Québec, a **tutor**) to look after children under the age of majority, and giving instructions about funeral arrangements.

What Happens If There Is No Will?

If a person dies without having made a will, her property will be given away according to rules set out by provincial law, and so the property may not go to the people she would have chosen. There are other reasons why it's not wise to delay making a will. For example, if a person dies without a will,

- instead of the executor named in the will automatically taking care of the estate, a court will have to appoint an **administrator** to look after the estate, and this process may take some time

- it will be slower and more expensive to take care of the estate because there are more restrictions on what an administrator can do than on what an executor can do

- it's difficult to plan to reduce taxes payable by the estate of the person who died without going through the process of making a will

- there will be problems if any of the people who are to receive property from the estate are under the age of majority, because property given to them will have to be managed by the provincial government until they reach the age of majority

What Does a Will Say?

A formal will can be very short or can go on for pages and pages. But it is usually at least several pages long and contains a number of paragraphs. Each will is unique, but a will prepared by a lawyer or notary often has standard clauses, including clauses

- identifying the testator
- **revoking** (cancelling) all previous wills—in case there was an earlier will, this makes it clear that the most recent will is meant to replace the old will
- naming the executor (but before choosing an executor, the testator should make sure that the person is willing to act). A testator can name one individual or two or more, and/or can name a trust company.
- leaving all of the testator's property to the executor in **trust**—the executor, as **trustee**, is given ownership of the property not for her own benefit, but for the benefit of the people who will eventually receive the property: first those to whom the testator owed money, and then to the **beneficiaries** (the people to whom the testator made gifts in the will).
- directing the executor to pay all legitimate debts, claims and taxes of the estate
- directing the executor to give the remaining property to the beneficiaries after the debts, claims and taxes have been paid
- giving the executor certain powers to deal with the estate, such as the power to keep property of the estate in its current form instead of turning it into cash; the power to invest the estate's cash as the executor thinks best; the power to borrow money on behalf of the estate; and the power to buy property from the estate

What's Involved in Making a Will?

A person can have a will formally prepared by a lawyer or, in British Columbia and Québec, by a notary. Or he may prepare his own will, either by filling in a pre-printed form or by typing or handwriting it.

Who Is Legally Capable of Making a Will?

For a will to be valid, the testator must, with some exceptions, be over the age of majority. The testator must also be mentally competent to

- understand what a will is and what it does

- know and appreciate how much property she has
- appreciate which people might have a claim to share in the estate

The lawyer or notary who prepares a will should be satisfied that the testator is mentally competent and also that the testator's instructions are truly his own, and that the testator is not signing the will as a result of any **duress** (violence or threats of violence) or **undue influence** (pressure exerted by someone in a dominant relationship with the testator). If the will does not represent the free wishes of the testator, it can be set aside after the testator's death.

Are There Any Formalities about Making a Will?

With the exception of a **holograph will** (discussed below), a will must be properly signed and witnessed in order to be valid. The testator must sign the will in the presence of two witnesses, and the two witnesses must also sign the will, in the presence of the testator and each other. In other words, the testator and the two witnesses must all be present and must all watch each other sign the will.

A beneficiary under the will (and in most provinces, a spouse of a beneficiary) should not be a witness to the will, because a witness to a will is not allowed to receive any gifts under the will.

What Is a Holograph Will?

A holograph will is a will that is completely written out in the testator's own handwriting. In most provinces, holograph wills are valid as long as they are dated and signed by the testator. A holograph will does not have to be signed in the presence of witnesses. In fact, in some provinces, a holograph will doesn't even have to be signed by the testator.

A holograph will should only be used in emergency situations because

- the will is probably incomplete or unclear if a lawyer or notary was not involved
- it can be challenged more easily by someone claiming that the testator was mentally incompetent, or acted under duress or undue influence

If the testator types out a will or fills in blanks on a pre-printed form, it will probably not be considered to be a holograph will. That means it is not valid unless it has been signed by the testator and two witnesses, all in each others' presence.

A do-it-yourself will can cause lots of problems down the road, so, if possible, your family member should have a lawyer (or, in Québec and British Columbia, a notary) prepare the will. A lawyer or notary should

- give the testator advice on how to plan her estate

- draft the will so that the testator's instructions are clear and not open to dispute
- make sure that the testator is legally capable of preparing a will, and is making it freely
- see to it that the will is properly signed and witnessed

Once the Will Has Been Prepared

After a will has been prepared, your family member should give the executor the original will or at least tell him where it can be found. Storing it in a safety deposit box is not a good idea, because it may be hard for the executor to get access to the safety deposit box after the death. Your family member should also give the executor information about her property and debts, and where her papers are kept.

HANDLING THE DYING PERSON'S FINANCIAL AFFAIRS IN CASE OF INCAPACITY

At some point during the dying process, your family member may no longer be able to handle his own financial affairs. If your family member wants to choose who will look after his financial affairs when he no longer can, he will have to have a **power of attorney** prepared. Depending on the province, this document may instead be called a **power of attorney for personal property**, a **power of attorney for financial decisions**, a **mandate**, or a **representation agreement**. For convenience, we'll just call it a power of attorney.

Power of Attorney

A power of attorney is a written, signed and witnessed document that gives another person (called the **attorney, attorney in fact, agent, donee, mandatary** or **representative**, depending on the province—we'll use the term attorney) authority to handle the legal and financial affairs of the person who signed the power of attorney (called the **principal, donor** or **grantor**— we'll use the term principal). A power of attorney gives the attorney the power to make financial decisions on behalf of the principal. The attorney can't make just any decisions she chooses, though. She must make decisions that are in the principal's best interests. The attorney must also keep records of all the financial decisions made on the principal's behalf.

A power of attorney can be general or specific. A **general power of attorney** gives the attorney all power to make financial and legal decisions on the principal's behalf. A **specific power of attorney** is limited to transactions specified in the document such as

- doing the principal's banking
- dealing with the principal's Old Age Security or Canada Pension Plan cheques
- selling the principal's home or other real estate

A power of attorney is not restricted to use in situations where the principal is mentally incapable of handling his financial affairs. For example, a person who is leaving the country for several weeks might give his lawyer a power of attorney to sell his cottage, or a person who has trouble getting out of the house might give her housekeeper a power of attorney to do her banking.

Enduring or Continuing Power of Attorney

An ordinary power of attorney ends when the principal becomes mentally incompetent. A power of attorney that is intended to continue in effect even after the principal becomes mentally incompetent is called an **enduring** or **continuing power of attorney**, and the document must specifically say that it is intended to continue after the mental incompetence of the principal. A power of attorney, no matter what kind it is, ends as soon as the principal dies.

Banking Power of Attorney

If your family member prepares a general power of attorney, he does not need a power of attorney for banking. However, banks often have their own form of power of attorney to allow one person to do another's banking, and some banks insist on getting a power of attorney in their own form even after they are shown a general power of attorney. You or your family member should be able to convince the bank that a power of attorney for banking is not necessary (although you may have to go fairly high up in the bank's management to do it). If the bank refuses to accept the general power of attorney, however, the bank's form must be checked over carefully before being signed to make sure that its wording does not cancel the general power of attorney.

What Happens If There Is No Power of Attorney?

If a person becomes incapable of handling her financial affairs and does not have a properly prepared power of attorney, someone will have to apply to the court for authority to handle the financial affairs, or—horror of horrors—the provincial government will look after them. The court may give the person making the application only limited powers to handle financial affairs, and may require that person to **post security** with the court (usually by buying a bond from an insurance or guarantee company and leaving it with the court) in case he does not carry out his duties properly. If your family member has become mentally unable to deal with her finances and has not prepared a power of attorney, see Chapter 6 at p. 60, about what to do next.

What Does a Power of Attorney Say?

While the form differs from province to province, a power of attorney usually contains provisions

- naming the attorney(s)—if more than one attorney is being appointed, the document should state whether the attorneys may make decisions individually or whether they must agree on all decisions. Some powers of attorney appoint a substitute attorney who takes over if the original attorney is unable or unwilling to carry out the duties.

- revoking previous powers of attorney—most power of attorney documents contain a clause that revokes (cancels) previous powers of attorney. If there is an earlier power of attorney that the principal wants to continue in effect, the wording of the more recent power of attorney must reflect that.

- setting out the powers the attorney is to have—the document may give the attorney power to do anything the principal could do, or it may limit powers to certain types of transactions (such as banking) and/or certain types of property (such as real estate or investments or cash)

- indicating whether the power of attorney remains in effect after the principal becomes mentally incompetent—if it is to continue in effect, the power of attorney must specifically say so in the exact language required by the law of the province in which the power of attorney is to be used

- stating when the power of attorney comes into effect: immediately or at some future time—in some provinces the power of attorney comes into effect as soon as it has been signed and witnessed. In other provinces, the principal can decide if it is to come into effect on a fixed date or on the happening of a specific event (usually the incapacity of the principal). If the power of attorney is to come into effect only if the principal becomes incapacitated, in some provinces the document can describe how incapacity is to be determined. For example, it could say that the principal's doctor or lawyer is to decide when the principal is incapacitated. If the document does not say how the person's incapacity is to be determined, the provincial statute governing powers of attorney will state how the determination is to be made. In some provinces, the evidence of two doctors is required; in others, determination by a court is necessary.

- saying whether the attorney is to be paid—in most provinces, the attorney is not entitled to receive any compensation for her services unless the power of attorney says so. In some provinces, the attorney must handle the principal's affairs with a higher level of care and competence if she is receiving compensation.

- setting additional conditions on the way in which the attorney is to exercise his power—for example, the power of attorney may require the attorney to

  – maintain financial records in a specified manner

  – consult with or report to family members, financial advisors or others at certain times

  – invest the principal's money in specific types of investments

What's Involved in Preparing a Power of Attorney?

A person can have a power of attorney formally prepared by a lawyer or, in British Columbia and Québec, by a notary. Or, a person may try to prepare her own power of attorney, either by filling in a pre-printed form or by writing out her own version. We strongly discourage a do-it-yourself approach for the following reasons:

- If the principal wants the power of attorney to continue in effect after he becomes mentally incompetent, the document must use specific wording or it may come to an end just when it is needed.

- The attorney may need professional help to figure out when the power of attorney comes into effect. In some provinces, the power of attorney can be written so that it comes into effect only when a specific event (such as the incapacity of the principal) occurs, but if the event is defined too strictly, the result may be a delay before the attorney can start to use the document. In other provinces, the power of attorney is effective as soon as it is signed, but the principal may want to give a lawyer written instructions to hold the power of attorney and not to give it to the attorney until the principal can no longer handle her own financial affairs.

- Special wording and signing procedures may be required if the power of attorney is intended to be used to deal with real property.

- In some provinces, if the attorney is the spouse of the principal, the attorney cannot sign on behalf of the principal to give consent to the sale or other transfer or mortgage of the family residence.

- The power of attorney must be written in a certain way if the principal wants another, earlier power of attorney to continue in effect. For example, the principal may have given a specific power of attorney to his housekeeper to allow her to make withdrawals from one bank account, and may want that arrangement to continue even though the principal is giving a general power of attorney to his daughter.

- The power of attorney must be written in a certain way if there is to be more than one attorney.
- If the principal has property in another province, an additional power of attorney that is valid in the other province may be necessary.
- The principal may want to include some limitations on the attorney's powers or to require the attorney to submit financial records for review by some other person or by the court.
- A lawyer should make sure that the principal is mentally competent to give a power of attorney (see below).
- The power of attorney must be properly signed and witnessed (see below).

Who Is Legally Capable of Giving a Power of Attorney?

To make a valid power of attorney, the principal must have reached the age of majority. The principal must also be mentally competent—she must be capable of knowing the value and kind of property that she has and of understanding the powers that she is giving to the attorney.

Who Can Be Appointed as an Attorney?

The principal can appoint anyone to act as attorney, as long as the attorney has reached the age of majority and is mentally competent. Or the principal can appoint a trust company.

Are There Any Formalities about Making a Power of Attorney?

A power of attorney must be signed by the principal, and it must be witnessed when it is signed. In most provinces two witnesses must be present when the principal signs the document and then the witnesses must also sign the document. The principal and witnesses must all be present to watch each other sign. In some provinces, the witnesses may have to swear an oath before a commissioner (usually a lawyer or law clerk) or a notary public that they are in fact the witnesses—especially if the power of attorney can be used to deal with real estate.

There are restrictions on who may witness a power of attorney. In every province the witnesses must *not* be

- the attorney
- the attorney's spouse
- the principal's spouse

• the principal's child

In some provinces, only a very limited group of people such as judges, justices of the peace, lawyers and doctors can witness a power of attorney.

Once the Power of Attorney Has Been Prepared

In addition to having the power of attorney prepared, the principal should give the attorney the original power of attorney, or at least tell him where it can be found. A safety deposit box is not recommended because it may be hard for the attorney to get access to the box after the principal is incapacitated. If the principal decides not to give the power of attorney document to the attorney immediately but to have someone else hold it until a particular event happens, the principal should give the holder written instructions explaining in detail when the power of attorney is to be given to the attorney. If it is not to be given to the attorney until the principal is mentally incompetent, the principal may want to set out how mental incompetence is to be determined (for example, by a letter from the family doctor).

The principal may want to leave written instructions for the attorney, explaining how to exercise his powers. Even though these instructions will not be legally binding on the attorney, they will give him some sense of the principal's wishes.

MAKING DECISIONS ABOUT MEDICAL TREATMENT IN CASE OF INCAPACITY

As your family member's health declines, at some point she may no longer be able to make decisions about health care. The consent of the person being treated is necessary before any medical treatment can be given (for more on consent to treatment, see Chapter 7 at p. 80). If your family member wants to have a say in the medical treatment that she will receive after she has lost the ability to decide for herself, or wants to choose the person who will have the authority to make medical decisions for her then, she should prepare a **living will**.

Living Wills

A living will sets out the person's wishes about his health care, and takes effect only when the person is unable to consent to medical treatment. A living will may do two things:

• it may appoint someone to make health care decisions for a person when he is unable to make those decisions himself

- it may tell the appointed decision maker what decisions the person would like made

In some provinces, a living will may deal only with health care decisions, and in other provinces it may also deal with personal care decisions, such as decisions about housing, nutrition, health, safety, hygiene or clothing.

Most provinces have passed statutes that legally recognize living wills. Depending on the province, the living will may be called a **personal directive, representation agreement, health care directive, power of attorney for personal care, mandate, directive** or **authorization**. The decision maker may be called an **attorney for personal care, proxy, agent, representative, substitute decision maker** or **mandatary** (in our discussion, we'll use the term substitute decision maker). The legislation in most provinces allows a person both to appoint a substitute decision maker and to give instructions to the decision maker. In most of the provinces that allow instructions to be given, those instructions must be followed. (Even in provinces that don't specifically recognize the validity of living wills, there is a good chance that the instructions in a living will will be followed.) These instructions take precedence over the wishes of the person's family and friends.

What Happens If There Is No Living Will?

What if a person is incapable of giving or refusing consent to medical treatment, and has not made a living will? In emergency situations, doctors have the right, without getting anyone's consent, to give treatment that is urgently needed to save a person's life or maintain a person's health. In such situations doctors will usually consult with the person's family members, but they are not legally required to do so.

In non-emergency situations, doctors or other health care workers must get consent from someone acting on behalf of the person who is incapable of giving consent. Some provinces have a statute that says that the closest relative, in a stated order (spouse first, then an adult child, and so on), has the power to give consent if the person has not appointed a substitute decision maker and there has been no court order appointing a **guardian for the person** (see Chapter 6 at p. 65). The courts have also approved of this approach. The relative can't make whatever decision *she* likes, though. When deciding whether to consent to medical treatment on behalf of an incapacitated person, the decision maker is supposed to follow the wishes that the person expressed before he became incapable of making his own decision. If the person never expressed any wishes, the decision maker is supposed to do what she believes the person would have done.

What Does a Living Will Say?

While the form varies from province to province, living wills contain provisions

- naming the substitute decision maker(s)—if more than one substitute decision maker is named, the living will should say whether they may make decisions individually or whether they must agree on all decisions. Some living wills appoint a back-up substitute decision maker in case the original substitute decision maker is unable or unwilling to carry out his duties.

- revoking (cancelling) previous living wills

- listing the kinds of health care decisions that the substitute decision maker can make—the living will may give the substitute decision maker power over all health care decisions, or only over some types of decisions such as nutrition, safety and hygiene

- instructing the substitute decision maker about the kind of medical treatment the person would or would not want in certain health care situations. (For example, a living will might say that the substitute decision maker should not consent to the use of a ventilator if the person is in a permanent coma.) If the living will contains instructions about the decisions that are to be made, it should state how much leeway the substitute decision maker has in following those instructions. (For example, the living will may give the substitute decision maker discretion to consent to a particular medical treatment if advances have been made in the treatment of the person's disease.) The living will may also set out the person's general wishes about health care decisions to help the substitute decision maker make decisions in situations not specifically addressed in the instructions.

What's Involved in Making a Living Will?

Although do-it-yourself forms are available, it is better to have a living will prepared by a lawyer. A lawyer will

- make sure that the person is legally mentally capable of making a living will
- use the language required by provincial law when writing the living will
- make sure that the person chosen as a substitute decision maker is eligible under provincial law
- make sure that the living will is properly signed and witnessed according to provincial law
- help sort out disagreements between the family and the substitute decision maker

Who Is Legally Capable of Making a Living Will?

The minimum age for making a living will varies from province to province, from 16 (and possibly younger in some provinces) to 19. In addition, the person making the living will must be mentally capable of making a living will: in some provinces, the person must be able to "understand the nature and effect of the living will"; in others, the person must be able to "make health care decisions by being able to understand and appreciate the consequences of treatment choices." If you have any doubt about your family member's legal ability to make a living will, speak to her doctor and/or lawyer beforehand.

Who Can Be Appointed as a Substitute Decision Maker?

There are very few restrictions on who can be a substitute decision maker. In some provinces, a person as young as 16 can be named a substitute decision maker, while in others the person must have reached the age of majority. The substitute decision maker must be mentally capable of understanding and appreciating the consequences of medical treatment choices and decisions. In Ontario, a person who is being paid to provide health care or residential, social, training or support services for a person cannot be appointed as substitute decision maker for that person.

Are There Any Formalities in Making a Living Will?

A living will must be signed by the person making it (or if he is physically unable to sign, by someone on his behalf), and dated. In some provinces, a living will must also be witnessed—by either one or two witnesses, depending on the province. In other provinces, no witnesses are necessary unless someone signed the living will on the person's behalf. If witnesses are required, they must not be the substitute decision maker or his spouse, nor the spouse of the person making the living will. In some provinces, the substitute decision maker must agree in writing to act.

Before Your Family Member Makes a Living Will

Before you and your family member rush off to a lawyer to have a living will prepared, do some work in advance. Your family member should think carefully about who would be the best person to appoint as substitute decision maker. The substitute decision maker should be someone who your family member believes will be best able to carry out her wishes. Your family member should not choose someone who will feel overwhelmed by the burden of making decisions that may turn out to be very difficult, that may in fact be decisions of life and death. Your family member should discuss her wishes with the family and the substitute decision maker so everyone clearly understands what your family member wants and why—and so your family member will know whether anyone agrees to carry out her wishes. Discussion in advance will reduce the chances of disagreement when the time comes for decisions to be made, and will give your family member confidence that her wishes will be respected.

If the living will is to contain instructions to the substitute decision maker, your family member must understand the various choices of treatment that may be available to treat his condition, what these treatments involve, and their rate of success. Your family member should discuss these issues with his doctor. Your family member should also understand what life-prolonging measures are generally available and what they involve. (See Chapter 12 at p. 130.) A good source of information about different treatment options is the University of Toronto Joint Centre for Bioethics, which is a partnership among the University of Toronto and several Toronto hospitals and medical facilities. The Centre provides information on the Internet at www.utoronto.ca/jcb/jcblw.htm. This site also includes a living will form that will take you and your family member through a number of health care situations and the available treatments.

After the Living Will Has Been Made

Once the living will has been made your family member should give copies to his doctor and to the substitute decision maker (or at least tell her where to find it), and may also want to give copies to his lawyer and other family members. Your family member should not leave the living will in a safety deposit box, because it may be hard for the substitute decision maker to get access to the box when your family member is incapacitated.

If possible, your family member should keep up-to-date on medical advances in combating her particular illness or condition and on available treatments, so that she knows whether to revise her living will.

TIP: PLAN AHEAD

Encourage your family member to prepare:

• a will

• a power of attorney

• a living will

ORGAN AND TISSUE DONATION

Adults in every province (and in Québec, children over the age of 14) can agree in advance to organ and tissue donation by giving written consent (no witnesses are necessary) or by giving oral consent in the presence of two witnesses. If your family member wants to donate his organs or tissue for transplant purposes, or wants to donate all or part of his body for medical education or scientific research, he should sign the consent form on the back of his driver's licence or an organ donation consent card, or should set out his consent in his living will. If your family member gives advance consent, it is binding on the family. In practice, however, most hospitals will not accept an organ donation if other family members are opposed when the time comes.

If a person does not give instructions on organ donation, family members have the right to authorize organ donation at the time of death, in the following order:

• the spouse, if there is one

• if there is no spouse, an adult child

• if there is no adult child, a parent

• if there is no parent, an adult sibling

• if there is no adult sibling, any adult next-of-kin

3 CARING FOR SOMEONE WHO IS SICK

A 1996 Statistics Canada study showed that nearly three million Canadians were caring for someone with long-term health problems—and that most of the caregivers were also holding down jobs. So if you're a caregiver, chances are you could use a little assistance. In this chapter we'll try to lay out the geography of care as simply as possible—to give you the big picture. In later chapters we'll look more closely at hospital care, home care and extended care in a facility, and at making health care decisions for a family member.

MEDICAL CARE

Throughout your family member's illness, she will be cared for by doctors—a family physician, and probably specialists as well. Family physicians are the gateway to the medical treatment system. In most provinces, your family member needs one in order to be referred to a specialist—a doctor who has expertise in treating particular diseases or disorders. Undoubtedly you will want your family member to be treated by a specialist, although your family physician will also be involved in the treatment—and will also be much easier to get an appointment with. Your family member will need a doctor (whether a family physician or specialist) to refer her for laboratory testing for a diagnosis of her condition, or to provide treatment. A doctor is also needed to admit a patient to hospital, except on an emergency basis.

HOSPITAL CARE

Hospital care in an **acute care** hospital is short-term medical and nursing care. Its purpose is to try to cure or reverse a condition—for example, to set a broken leg, remove a tumour, bypass clogged blood vessels leading to the heart, or destroy diseased bone marrow and replace it with healthy transplanted bone marrow. Acute care might include:

- diagnosing an illness or injury
- laboratory and diagnostic services (blood tests, x-rays, electrocardiograms, ultrasound, etc.)
- treating an illness or injury, including medication, surgery, radiation, chemotherapy, etc.
- anesthesia
- emergency services
- nursing care
- rehabilitative care, such as physiotherapy, occupational therapy, speech therapy, audiology

The Canadian health care system is geared toward providing medical care in acute care hospitals. But for most people who have a chronic illness or a terminal illness, a cure is less important than long-term care.

CARE AT HOME

Informal home care is provided by family and friends. You may know all about it by now—making meals, doing laundry, doing the shopping, driving to appointments, sitting and talking, helping with bathing, making check-up phone calls and visits, and lots more. For most families, a time comes when the work and skills required for care get beyond their ability for one reason or another. Perhaps family members don't live close enough or don't have the time (what with work and children to think of) to provide help every single day, or perhaps they aren't trained to give the kind of help that's needed. Then it's time to make formal arrangements for home care.

Formal Home Care

Formal home care is sometimes known as **community care** to distinguish it from informal care by family members. Home care programs offer both health care services (such as nursing, physiotherapy and other kinds of rehabilitation, laboratory services) and support services (such as cleaning, shopping and preparing meals, and helping with bathing and grooming) in the patient's home. (See Chapter 8 for more about services.) Depending on the province and depending on the kind of care, home care may be provided by a branch of the provincial government, by a regional or district health board, by community organizations or not-for-profit agencies, or by for-profit businesses. Formal home care is not intended to replace family care—which is, of course, free to the health care system—but to provide various kinds of help to make the task more manageable. Home care can be a means of preventing frail, incapacitated or disabled people from having to move into an extended care facility, or it can be a substitute for care in a facility or hospital care.

As the Canadian population ages, and as patients are discharged from the hospital sooner (and sicker) than in the past, there is an increasing demand for home care. However, home care is not yet properly integrated into the national health care system and it suffers from lack of funding. People who need home care may be put on waiting lists, or may receive insufficient care for their needs, or may even be turned away altogether and told to look to family and friends for help. Many patients and their families find that government-subsidized home care is simply not enough. So they end up paying for extra care out of their own pockets—paying the workers provided by the regional health care authority to work more hours, or employing workers from a private health care or nursing agency, or hiring other employees to come in on a daily basis or to live in full-time.

Federal and provincial governments have been talking about making changes to home care. No one really knows when or if these changes will happen—and whether they'll improve the system.

EXTENDED CARE FACILITIES

Even with the family pitching in and with hired health care workers, sooner or later the time may come when your family member cannot be properly cared for at home. That time used to come sooner. In the 1970s, almost half of the residents living in extended care facilities required only supervisory care. Many were in their sixties or seventies, and could have remained in their homes if they had had access to the right kind of home care. Things are different now because people are encouraged to stay in their homes as long as possible. The average age of admission to an extended care facility these days is somewhere in the eighties. Over half of the people living in extended care facilities are suffering from dementia such as Alzheimer's disease, even though only about 5 per cent of the elderly population as a whole suffers from Alzheimer's.

Extended care facilities can be privately financed or government subsidized. Some facilities, especially those that offer personal care but little or no nursing care, may be associated with a particular cultural or religious community and provide a cultural setting that is familiar to the residents (for example, attendants who speak their language, ethnic cooking, activities and outings that are geared specifically to the cultural group). Living conditions and care can range from excellent to not so great in any kind of facility, whether government-subsidized or privately funded. In Chapter 9, we'll tell you about some of the specific things to look for—and look out for—in an extended care facility.

Privately Financed Facilities

Extended care facilities that are not government-subsidized include such things as supportive housing (for example, seniors' apartments) and retirement homes. The premises, care and services are not regulated by provincial legislation, although the accommodations fall under the residential tenancy laws of most provinces. These laws govern increases in rent, the right of the resident to give notice and leave, and the right of the owner (landlord) of the home to force the resident to leave. In some large municipalities, retirement homes also come under by-laws that establish minimum requirements for certain services provided to residents. In addition, most provinces have a voluntary association of retirement homes that sets standards for members.

Supportive Housing

Somewhere between home care and institutional care lies supportive housing. Supportive housing is not suitable for people who require a great deal of personal care or nursing care—it works best for people who just need assistance with cooking and cleaning as well as some personal care. People needing supportive housing live in a building (sometimes an apartment building, sometimes a large converted house or a specially designed building) with a number of other people who require care, but have their own living quarters. The living quarters may be a full-sized apartment with a kitchen or something more in the line of a bed-sitting room. There are common areas as well, and a common dining room where residents may eat together (there may also be communal kitchens where residents can do some of their own cooking). The housing is run by full-time staff. A caregiver or even a nurse is available, and the resident can get assistance with such things as bathing, dressing, laundry or housecleaning.

Some supportive housing may not permit pets, overnight guests or the use of alcohol.

Retirement Homes

Retirement homes move a little further along the care continuum than supportive housing, although they can vary considerably in terms of facilities and services. Some offer apartments, while some have rooms similar to hotel rooms, with a range from private rooms (one person) to semi-private rooms (two people sharing) to a ward (with three or more people). Bathrooms may be private or shared. Some retirement homes prefer that residents come into the home still able to manage most of their own needs and able to participate in activities, although the homes do provide services such as meals, housekeeping and laundry, personal care aides, assistance with medication, 24-hour nursing supervision, a doctor on call, and an emergency call system in case a resident falls or is taken ill. Many retirement homes also provide a secure area for people with impaired memories. Some retirement homes can provide care nearly to the nursing home level.

When a resident needs more care than the retirement home normally offers, the home may ask the resident or family to pay extra for more nursing care, or may ask the resident and/or family to make arrangements to transfer to a facility that provides more care. Some retirement homes are actually attached to a government-subsidized extended care facility so that, in theory, a person who eventually needs more care than the retirement home provides can stay in more or less the same place. In most provinces, however, an application for admission to an extended care facility annexed to a retirement home must be made through a regional health care authority, and a retirement home resident may have no better chance of getting into that facility than any other applicant.

A 1998 study of retirement homes in one province suggested that many were not properly equipped and staffed to look after residents who had severe mental or physical disabilities—and that over half of residents did, in fact, have severe mental or physical disabilities.

Government-Subsidized Facilities

A government-subsidized extended care facility might provide one or more of the following kinds of care:

- personal care (assistance with bathing, dressing, grooming)
- nursing care (for example, injections of insulin or other drugs, caring for bedsores, tube feeding, intravenous therapy)

- rehabilitative care such as physiotherapy, occupational therapy, speech therapy
- respiratory (oxygen) therapy
- medical care in the form of a doctor who makes regular rounds and is also on call for problems that arise between rounds

Government-subsidized extended care facilities are not necessarily run by the government. They may be

- government-owned (municipal, provincial or federal government) and operated as a not-for-profit business
- owned by religious groups or ethnic groups, or by lay groups, and operated as a not-for-profit business
- privately owned and operated for profit (in Ontario, over half of all facility beds are in privately owned facilities; in other provinces, the figure is around one-quarter)

Facilities that receive government subsidies must meet detailed government standards and be inspected regularly by provincial authorities. Sometimes people are suspicious of facilities that are privately owned and operated for profit, thinking that the owners will cut corners in order to increase their profits. This is more likely to happen in privately owned facilities that do not receive government subsidies and therefore do not have to be inspected.

An application for government-subsidized extended care is made through the local or regional health care authority, not the facility, and the authority will decide whether the applicant meets the test for admission. (For information about admission criteria, see Chapter 4 at p. 36.) There are usually also criteria to decide which facility is appropriate. For example, the test for admission to a facility that offers only personal care might be that the applicant requires at least one and a half hours of personal care per day or needs supervision or frequent monitoring; for admission to a facility that offers nursing care, the criteria might be that the applicant requires nursing services to be available 24 hours a day, and needs at least two hours of nursing care per day.

Government-subsidized facilities seem to have a different name in every province. Names include **boarding homes, community care facilities, community residences, extended care facilities, homes for the aged, hostels, intermediate care homes, licensed boarding homes, licenced private hospitals, lodges, nursing homes, personal care homes, regional care centres, rest homes, retirement homes** (not to be confused with privately financed retirement homes!), **senior citizens' homes**, and **special homes**.

Chronic Care Facilities

Patients who are chronically ill with a condition such as heart disease, cerebrovascular disease, chronic obstructive pulmonary disease, liver disease or kidney failure might need more than two or three hours' nursing care a day, and might need more medical care than can be provided by a doctor who makes house calls or rounds at an extended care facility. Such patients may be admitted to a chronic care facility, which is often attached to a hospital.

HELP!

Even with all the health care services available through the provincial government, you may find that looking after a chronically or terminally ill family member is a very uphill struggle. One useful thing you can do is to contact an organization that has special knowledge of the illness that your family member is suffering from. There's one for every major disease and many for less well-known diseases too. So look up the local branch of the Canadian Cancer Society, Heart and Stroke Foundation, Alzheimer's Canada, Parkinson Foundation, AIDS Committee, Multiple Sclerosis Society, Amyotrophic Lateral Sclerosis (ALS) Society or Arthritis Society. You'll be able to get information about the disease and about caring for a family member and may be able to get volunteer help with the care, and support and counselling for the caregivers.

If the prospect of finding the right care for your family member all by yourself has got you completely stressed out, you may be able to get help from a consultant who specializes in helping people find appropriate care. These consultants are often nurses or social workers. One may be available at no charge through an employee assistance plan at your workplace (the help you get may be quite limited, though); or you may be able to track one down privately by asking for names from a hospital social worker or discharge planner, a case manager at the regional health care authority, your doctor, or friends or acquaintances who have been through the same process.

CARING FOR THE CAREGIVER

Looking after someone over a long period or during a serious illness is exhausting, often depressing, and can be isolating. You may find yourself withdrawing from friends, losing interest in your work, sleeping badly, losing your appetite or gaining weight, drinking more alcohol or using stimulants, feeling helpless or fearful. These may be symptoms of burn-out.

You need to look after yourself too so that you don't get sick:

- Have a support network—friends, colleagues at work, a caregivers' support group—that understands what you're going through and can give you ideas about how to cope. Some provincial home care programs offer **respite care**: alternative care for the sick person so that the caregiver can have a few hours or a few days off.
- Don't let your world get narrowed down to your work and your caregiving— keep up a hobby, go out and see friends, take regular breaks for a movie or dinner out or something else you enjoy.
- Follow a healthy diet.
- Exercise every day.
- Schedule quiet time for yourself.

ABUSE

Looking after someone who needs a lot of care and attention can tire you out and frazzle your nerves to the point where you're ready to take it out on the person. Try not to let yourself get to that point. You might injure your family member, you'll feel guilty and ashamed when the moment passes, and you're committing a criminal offence. Even if you think it's the only way to get action or reaction from the person you're caring for, don't

- hit or push or shove her
- forcibly confine him to a room, bed or chair, or mistreat him physically in any other way
- shout at her or use abusive language, or humiliate, threaten or frighten her
- deliberately withhold food or health care or anything else that he needs

If you do things of this nature, you could be charged criminally with assault and battery, or neglect, or you could be sued in tort law by the person who's been mistreated. In all provinces, children who are being mistreated can be taken away from the family. In a few provinces, elderly people who are being neglected or abused by their caregivers can be removed from the residence and put into protective care.

If you know someone who is being abused, you can contact the police. If the victim is a child, you can call the Children's Aid Society, or if the victim is elderly, a community organization such as a family shelter or (in Ontario) the Ontario Network for the Prevention of Elder Abuse or the Advocacy Centre for the Elderly; or you can get advice from a doctor, religious advisor or social worker.

4 PAYING FOR HEALTH CARE

Living in Canada, we're very fortunate to have universal access to health care (even though we spend a lot of time complaining about our health care system!). That means that many major expenses are taken care of—but it doesn't mean that they're *all* taken care of. You can still end up paying a considerable amount of money to care for someone who's sick.

MEDICAL CARE

Provincial health insurance covers the cost of care by a physician (whether in a hospital, in an extended care facility, in a clinic or office, or at home). However, the patient or her family may have to pay extra for such things as

- medication or medical supplies provided directly by a physician
- renewal of prescriptions
- telephone advice
- mileage or travel time for care by a physician outside her office or hospital
- preparation of a report or certificate
- an examination for private insurance (such as life or disability insurance)

DRUGS

No universal drug plan exists in Canada, and the cost of drugs can mount if a drug is expensive or if drugs must be taken over a long period. Drugs are usually supplied free of charge to patients in a hospital, but otherwise the patient (or patient's family) must pay for them. You can get help with drug costs through prescription drug insurance plans, which are available privately or through employment benefits packages, and sometimes through provincial programs. In some provinces, the provincial government subsidizes drugs for one or more of the following groups: low-income senior citizens, people receiving social assistance, residents of subsidized extended care facilities or people receiving subsidized home care, and people suffering from specific diseases or conditions (such as AIDS, cystic fibrosis or organ transplants). Contact your provincial ministry of health for information about subsidized drugs.

MEDICAL SUPPLIES AND EQUIPMENT

Your family member may need medical and surgical supplies and equipment (such as wound dressings, ostomy supplies, needles and syringes for diabetics), wheelchairs, walkers, hearing aids, artificial limbs, and respiratory equipment and oxygen. In general, the patient has to pay for these things, although some provinces provide financial assistance to buy or rent necessary supplies and equipment. Again, contact your provincial ministry of health for information.

HOSPITAL CARE

Most hospital care is covered by provincial health insurance, but there may be extra charges for such things as

- ambulance
- private room (one bed) or semi-private room (two beds) instead of standard accommodation (three or more beds)
- telephone, radio or television in the room
- take-home supplies of drugs and dressings

These extra charges may be covered by extended health care insurance carried by the patient or her family, available privately or through an employment benefits package.

In many hospitals, nursing staff has been cut back, and you may not be satisfied with the level of attention and care that your family member is receiving in the hospital. If this is the case, you may be able to arrange to hire (through the hospital itself) a personal care aide or a nurse who will look after your family member exclusively. The cost of some private nursing may also be covered by extended health care insurance.

OUT-OF-PROVINCE AND OUT-OF-COUNTRY HEALTH CARE

If your family member receives medical care or hospital care outside his home province but in another Canadian province or territory, his provincial health insurance plan will cover the cost of care. However, if your family member receives medical care outside Canada, the provincial health insurance plan will usually only pay for part of it. The general rule is that the province will pay the standard rate that it would pay within the province—and in Canadian dollars. In the United States, for example, this would come nowhere near covering the cost of care. For this reason, anyone in your family travelling outside Canada should have out-of-country health insurance.

Joy was on a day trip to Buffalo with her family when she suffered a brain aneurysm. No one had thought of getting out-of-country health insurance just for one day. When she died after spending two weeks in a U.S. hospital, her family was presented with a hospital bill that came to $150,000 Canadian. The provincial health insurance plan paid $6000 of the bill.

If your family member leaves the country to seek medical treatment but wants provincial health insurance to cover the cost of treatment, the provincial health plan must give approval in advance. The plan authorities must be satisfied that the treatment is legitimate and that appropriate treatment is not available in Canada, or is not available fast enough. This kind of approval is usually very difficult to obtain.

GOVERNMENT-SUBSIDIZED CARE AT HOME OR IN AN EXTENDED CARE FACILITY

If you want the government to help pay for home care or care in a facility such as a nursing home, you have to qualify for the care by meeting certain criteria set down by your province. In almost all provinces, the first criterion is that the person needing the care must be a resident of the province. "Residency" is defined differently in different provinces. In some provinces, a person is a resident if she is in the process of moving to the province, while in others a person must have lived in the province for some period of time before she becomes a resident. (In addition, to maintain status as a resident, a person must be physically present in the province for six months of every year—four or five months in the odd province). In most provinces, a person must also be insured under the provincial health insurance plan to be eligible to receive extended care. A person who moves into a province is not eligible for provincial health insurance until she has been physically present in the province for two (in a couple of provinces, three) months. These residency and insurance requirements can cause problems if a family is moving a sick or disabled person from out of the province to take care of her.

Besides the residency and insurance requirements, there are eligibility requirements relating to health for both home care and facility care. The usual requirements for home care include that the person is in ill health or very frail, he can't stay at or return home without help, and the necessary help can be appropriately and safely delivered at home. Because home care is less expensive for the government to provide than facility care, admission to a subsidized facility won't normally be considered unless further eligibility requirements are met—typically that the person can't look after himself in his home because of severe chronic illness or disability, and that neither family (or other informal caregivers) nor formal home care services can provide the necessary care.

However, even passing these eligibility hurdles doesn't usually mean that the government will foot the entire bill for care—the patient (or patient's family) will often have to pay for something too.

Home Care

Many home care services are rationed, and people who need care are only entitled to a certain number of hours of service. After that, they must pay the full cost of the service, either out of their own pocket or through their own extended health insurance (if they have it).

In most provinces, there are limits on the amount of home care a person can receive, or can receive for free. For example, in several provinces there is a limit on the number of hours of home care per week or per month that will be delivered without charge—even to people who genuinely need a lot of care. (In one province this limit is 30 hours per week or 120 hours per month; in another, 35 to 44 hours per week; in another, four nursing visits per day and 80 hours per month for the first month, and 60 hours per month thereafter.) There may also be limits on the total cost of home care (in one province, $2500 to $3000 per month; in another $2000 for any 15-day period, and a maximum of $4000 per month).

Jessica, an 81-year-old woman, injured her back in a fall at home. She did not need to be hospitalized, but she needed constant care and she had no family. She received around-the-clock home care for five days—and then was cut down to two hours a day. The home care authorities told her she would have to find friends to help her because she had used up her home care entitlement. She ended up spending about $5000 for four weeks of private home care.

Some provinces provide support services (that is, non-health care services such as homemaking—see Chapter 8 at p. 87) free of charge (although usually only up to a limit), but in other provinces user fees apply to support services from the beginning. The user fees may reflect the actual cost of support care, may be subsidized by the province, or may be determined according to a sliding scale based on the income of the person who needs care. In a few provinces there is a cap on the amount that a person can be charged monthly for support services. In certain provinces, support services are allotted first to, or even reserved exclusively for, people with low incomes.

Depending on the province, clients may or may not be charged, or charged the full amount, for medication, supplies and equipment needed for home health care.

A few provinces offer "self-managed care." In these provinces the needs of the person who requires care are assessed by the regional health care authority, and funding is provided directly to the patient and his family, who can then use the money to buy the necessary services privately.

Government-subsidized home care does not provide enough care for many people who remain in their homes. When that is the case, the next step may be for family members and friends or community volunteers to take up the slack; or the patient or family members may have to pay the regional health care authority or community organization that provides the subsidized care to provide extra care, or may have to hire home care workers directly (see below at p. 38).

Extended Care Facilities

Health care services in extended care facilities (medical and nursing care, and most personal care) are covered by provincial health insurance plans. Basic accommodation in a facility is subsidized but not completely paid for by the provincial government. Basic accommodation ordinarily includes

• a standard room, which usually means a room with at least three beds. A semi-private room (two beds) or private room (one bed) is an upgrade

• food and dietary services

- laundry and linen service
- housekeeping services
- administrative services
- in some provinces, activities

The resident has to make a **co-payment** or **accommodation payment** to help cover the cost of room and board. The amount of the co-payment is set by the government, not by the facility. In most provinces, this amount is based on the patient's income as well as on whether the room is standard, semi-private or private. Depending on the province or territory, the co-payment may run from about $20 per day ($600 per month) to well over $100 per day ($3000 per month).

On top of the co-payment, the facility will charge for optional services such as

- hairdresser or barber
- dry cleaning, ironing or mending of clothes
- telephone
- cable television
- transportation
- activities and outings
- security bracelet for a patient who wanders

People who cannot afford the co-payment are not turned away, but they will only get a standard room, for which the government makes the co-payment. They may also be entitled to a small "comfort allowance" from the province so that they can get some of the optional services provided by the facility, or buy clothing and personal items.

PRIVATELY FINANCED CARE

Privately financed care includes home care arranged directly by the patient or her family, and facilities such as supportive housing and retirement homes.

Home Care

If you hire a homemaker, or a health care aide through an agency or directly, it will cost about $10 to $15 per hour, while a nurse will cost about $25 to $35 an hour. If you hire live-in help who will be available between 8 and 12 hours a day, that might cost about $1000 to $2000 per month in wages (you can deduct the cost of room and board from the salary, though).

Supportive Housing and Retirement Homes

In shared housing, the resident pays the full rent (which is generally comparable to the rent of ordinary apartments in the city) and also pays the full amount for any services provided.

In a retirement home, monthly fees range in most provinces from about $1500 to $3000, although they can go much higher in some facilities, and services (such as bathing, grooming, dressing, nursing care, etc.) cost extra. Standard personal care provided by the facility may not be enough for the needs of the patient. In that case, the family will either have to provide the extra care themselves, or pay for a special attendant (usually arranged for through the facility) to provide the required additional care. It may be possible to split the cost of an attendant among several patients/families.

Private facilities fall under the residential tenancy laws of most provinces. These laws govern increases in rent, the right of the resident to give notice and leave, and the right of the owner (landlord) of the home to force the resident to leave, but they do not govern amounts that can be charged for care services or meals.

TAX BREAKS FOR CARE

Care of an ill or disabled person is expensive; so it's a lucky thing that there are tax credits and tax deductions for some of the expenses. The person receiving the care can claim deductions or credits himself, and in some cases another family member may be able to claim deductions or credits. Where there is a choice about who may make the claim, the decision should probably be based on reducing tax payable for the family as a unit. This usually means that the person with the higher income will claim the deduction or credit.

The Person Who Is Sick Makes the Claim

The person who needs care may be entitled to claim a deduction for attendant care expenses or to receive a tax credit for a disability amount or for medical expenses.

Attendant Care Expenses

If the sick person paid for care by an attendant, and that care allowed the sick person to earn income, she can deduct the expense from income. The payment may be for

• full-time care at home, if a doctor certifies that the person is dependent on others for care because of a long-term mental or physical infirmity, or

- full-time care in a nursing home, if a doctor certifies that the person is dependent on others for care because of a lack of normal mental capacity, or
- full-time or part-time care in a nursing home or other facility, if a doctor certifies that the person needs such care because of a physical or mental handicap

Disability Amount

A person who has a "severe mental or physical impairment which causes marked restriction in any of the basic activities of daily living" and which has lasted (or is expected to last) a continuous period of at least 12 months, and who has had the appropriate Revenue Canada form signed by a doctor to confirm this, can claim a tax credit of approximately $4200.

A person is markedly restricted in a basic activity of living if he

- is blind
- is unable to feed and dress himself, control bowel and bladder functions, walk, speak, hear, think and remember, or
- takes an extremely long time, even with therapy and appropriate aids and medication, to feed and dress himself, control bowel and bladder functions, walk, speak, hear, think and remember

The marked restriction must exist all or almost all of the time, so a person who is in a state described above only part of the time does not qualify for the disability amount tax credit.

Medical Expenses

A person who has medical expenses can claim a tax credit for the full amount of those expenses less approximately $1600, even if the expenses were not paid in Canada. Examples of allowable medical expenses include

- payments made to a doctor or nurse, or to a public or licensed private hospital (that were not covered by provincial health insurance)
- payments for care by an attendant (see above under "Attendant Care Expenses"), even if the care didn't allow income to be earned
- payments made for prescription drugs
- payments made for the purchase, rental or maintenance of a wheelchair, pacemaker, artificial limb, hearing aid, prescription eyeglasses or contact lenses—and a number of other things
- payments to renovate a home to allow mobility (wheelchair ramps, extra-wide doorways, lower cabinets, and so on)
- most premiums paid to private health insurance plans

Contact Revenue Canada for more information about allowable expenses.

There is a cap of about $10,000 on expenses for care by an attendant if the person is also claiming the disability amount. If attendant-care expenses are high, there may be a tax advantage in not claiming the disability amount at all.

The Caregiver Makes a Claim

A person who is caring for a spouse or a close relative may be able to claim deductions or tax credits.

Equivalent to Spouse Amount

A caregiver may be able to claim a tax credit of approximately $5300 if at any time in the taxation year she was single, divorced, separated or widowed, and supported a dependant who was

• financially dependent on the caregiver

• physically or mentally infirm

• related to the caregiver by blood, marriage or adoption, and

• living in Canada

Amounts for Infirm Dependants over Age 18

A caregiver may be able to claim a tax credit of approximately $2300 if she supported (alone or with others) a dependant who lived in Canada at any time during the taxation year and who was

• the caregiver's or the caregiver's spouse's child, grandchild, parent, grandparent, brother, sister, aunt, uncle, niece or nephew

• 18 or older, and

• physically or mentally infirm

It is possible to claim both the equivalent-to-spouse amount and the amount for an infirm dependant.

Caregiver Credit

If a caregiver lives with and provides in-home care for a parent or grandparent over age 65 or for an infirm dependant relative, he may be able to claim a tax credit of up to $600. This credit is intended to provide a tax break for caregivers who do not qualify for the infirm dependant credit.

Disability Amount

The caregiver may be able to claim the disability amount tax credit (of approximately $4200) if the person who qualifies for a disability amount does not use it or does not use all of it (he would not use all of it if his income is already so low that no deductions are needed to reduce tax payable), and if

• the caregiver claimed an equivalent-to-spouse amount for the person

• the person was financially dependent on the caregiver and was the caregiver's or the caregiver's spouse's child, grandchild, parent or grandparent, or

• the person was dependent on the caregiver and was the caregiver's or the caregiver's spouse's child or grandchild, and the caregiver made a claim for "amounts for infirm dependants age 18 or older"

Medical Expenses

A caregiver can claim a tax credit for medical expenses of more than about $1600 if the person for whom the medical expenses were paid did not claim the expenses or all of the expenses herself (because her income was already so low that no deductions are needed to reduce tax payable). The ill or disabled person must be the caregiver's or the caregiver's spouse's

• child or grandchild who was financially dependent on the caregiver, or

• parent, grandparent, brother, sister, uncle, aunt, niece or nephew who lived in Canada at any time in the year and who was financially dependent on the caregiver

Again, there is a cap of about $10,000 on expenses for attendant care if the ill or disabled person is also claiming the disability amount.

TIP: MINIMIZE YOUR HEALTH CARE EXPENSES

• check your family member's extended health care insurance

• get out-of-country health insurance if your family member is travelling outside of Canada

• check whether your family member is eligible for any government-subsidized care or supplies

• speak to an accountant when preparing tax returns for your family member and yourself

PART II

THE ROAD GETS ROUGH

5 | CLEANING UP LEGAL MESSES

$\mathbf{B}$y the time you realize that your family member is no longer up to looking after himself or running his own affairs, some problems may have already arisen. Your family member may have agreed to buy a new roof or driveway that he didn't need or to support a religious organization you've never heard of. He may have caused an accident at home or while driving. He may even have acquired, out of the blue, a new wife! What are you going to do? Some of these legal messes can be tidied up fairly easily, but others may present serious problems.

GETTING OUT OF A CONTRACT

Your family member may have entered into a contract that will not provide her with any noticeable benefit and may, in fact, cause her serious financial harm. A contract is an agreement between two (or more) parties that each will do something for the other. That sounds pretty harmless, but contracts are backed up by laws that will penalize a party who doesn't do what he, she or it promised. (A party doesn't have to be an individual—it can be a business run as a partnership or corporation, or it can be an arm of government.) The party who won't keep the promise can be sued by the other party, and the court has the power to force the non-performing party to do what it promised, or to pay **damages** (compensation) to the other party that can, in some cases, amount to more than the value of the original promise. It's always a contract situation if one party purchases goods or services from the other, or if one party works for another.

Contracts to Buy Goods or Services

When someone becomes seriously ill, many different areas of her life may be affected. She may no longer need the suit she just bought for work, or the kitchen renovation that's supposed to start next month, or the leased car that still has two years left in the lease. If the person's mind has been affected by the illness but she can still get around enough to answer the door or the phone, she may be victimized by door-to-door salespeople or telemarketers who persuade her to buy unnecessary items, such as a new roof or a vacuum cleaner, or the Encyclopedia Galactica. So before your family member shells out a lot of money or gets sued for not paying for something—is there anything you can do to get the person out of the contract? The answer is maybe yes, maybe no.

- If a purchaser buys something in a retail store, the store has no legal obligation to take it back unless there's something wrong with the product itself. Most stores have refund or exchange policies that allow customers to return unwanted (but unused and unaltered) goods within a stated period of time, often a week or two. If you want to return a product, contact the store it came from and find out about its return policy. Even if you're not within the time period, some stores will take the item back anyway once you've explained the circumstances. Remember that your legal rights are next to none in this situation, so don't try to bully the store—be polite.

- If someone has a written contract that covers a long period of time, such as a car lease, or a loan agreement, or a contract for cable TV, the contract itself governs whether you can get out before the stated date. There may be a clause allowing cancellation of the agreement on payment of a certain amount of money...but if there is, the sum of money that has to be paid is often as much or nearly as much as the amount payable over the full term of the contract if it *isn't* cancelled. If that is the case (and you may need a lawyer to help you figure it out), write or ask your lawyer to write to the other party to the contract and find out if they are willing to allow cancellation on better terms, given the nature of the situation. If they're not, and the contract is for a large amount of money, it may be worthwhile to discuss with a lawyer whether there's any legal loophole that will allow the person to get out of the contract. Or your family member may just have to pay up.

• If the contract is to rent residential premises, most provinces have laws governing residential tenancies, including cancellation of a tenancy by the tenant. A tenant's right to cancel depends on the nature of the lease. If the lease is for a fixed term such as one or two years, the tenant has no automatic right to end the tenancy before the term ends. However, the landlord may agree to let a tenant out of the lease if the landlord can re-rent the apartment to a new tenant. Or the tenant may be able to find someone else to sub-let the apartment or to take over the lease. If the lease is monthly, usually the tenant must give a certain amount of notice to end the tenancy (for example, two months), but does not have to make any more rental payments after the notice period is up and after moving out, even if no one else has offered to rent the apartment.

• If your family member has arranged to have work done in the future, contact the party who is to do the work. There may be no problem with cancellation. If a deposit has been paid, it should be returned in full. A reputable business won't give you a lot of trouble about returning the deposit, but occasionally people have to sue to get deposits back. If the party who was to do the work says that there is a cancellation fee, ask to see the written agreement that says so, if you don't have a copy.

Sometimes, although no work has been done yet, the other party has made preparations to do the work (for example, a contractor who was to do a kitchen renovation may already have ordered custom cabinets as requested by the homeowner, or a landscape architect may have spent time drawing up a plan for the garden). In that case, your family member will probably have to pay for those preparations.

Door-to-Door Sellers and Telemarketers

Door-to-door sellers and telemarketers present special problems because although many of them are honest and reputable, some are scam artists. If your family member has entered into a contract with one of the honest and reputable ones, contacting the seller or telemarketer and explaining the situation may be all you need to do. They don't want to get a reputation for taking advantage of elderly or mentally impaired people, and they'll probably cancel the contract and refund the money without any fuss. However, if it turns out that your family member has been scammed, he probably paid money up front...and you'll never see it again. If the payment was made by cheque, you may be in time to put a stop payment on the cheque; if it was made in cash or by credit card, you can kiss it goodbye. Very few credit card companies are willing to reverse a charge without the agreement of whoever got paid. If you're thinking of suing to get the money back, you should first try to find out whether the seller has any property that you will be able to seize if you win the lawsuit. You may be dealing with a "shell" corporation, which has a name and an address but nothing more—well, maybe a telephone, a desk, and a chair.

Below we discuss some of the things you can try to get the money back, and, more usefully, the steps you can take to prevent your family member from being cheated in the future.

Door-to-Door Sellers

If your family member has bought a product or service from a door-to-door seller, in each province there is legislation that allows the buyer to cancel without any penalty in certain circumstances. Every province has a "cooling-off" period during which the buyer can change his mind and get his money back, as long as the product has not been delivered or the service performed. The cooling-off period varies from province to province—it's ten days in Alberta, Québec, Nova Scotia and Newfoundland; seven days in British Columbia and Prince Edward Island; five days in New Brunswick; four days in Manitoba and Saskatchewan; and just two days in Ontario. That means that you may have to act fast to cancel the contract. In some provinces, the amount involved must be a minimum sum ($25 to $50 depending on the province) before this law applies. The time allowed for cancellation is longer in most provinces if the door-to-door seller was required to register with the government but did not, if the door-to-door seller was required by law to include certain information in the written contract but did not, or if the door-to-door seller does not provide the goods or services within a certain period.

To cancel and get the money back, you must send notice in writing (a letter signed by your family member saying she wants to cancel and wants a refund) to the door-to-door seller within the specified period. Make sure you have some proof of the date of cancellation: within the allowed time period, either deliver the notice personally to the seller and take a witness with you, or send it by registered mail (the seller may, of course, refuse to accept the letter). Keep a photocopy of the notice.

If the product has been delivered and used up or the service has been completely performed, it's not possible to get your money back. If the product has been used but not used up or damaged, or if the service has been partly performed, in some provinces you may be able to get part of your money back—but the door-to-door seller is entitled to keep some money (and, of course, to get the product back) in compensation for the work done or for the use of the product.

In many provinces, under laws prohibiting unfair business practices there is a cancellation period of six months or more if a seller (not just a door-to-door seller) took advantage of the buyer's mental or physical disabilities or language difficulties to get a sale, or pressured the buyer into buying, or made a very unfair contract (for example, by charging far too much), or misrepresented (made untruthful statements about) the product or service. Deliver or mail a notice in writing to the seller, signed by your family member and stating that he wants to cancel the contract and why, and that he wants a refund.

Contact your provincial ministry of consumer affairs for more information about getting a refund. Better yet, try to protect your family member from getting into unwanted contracts of this kind in the first place. Tell her (or her caregivers) not to buy anything from people who come to the door uninvited, and not to let anyone into the house who is trying to sell something (a favourite sellers' tactic is simply to refuse to leave until a contract has been signed).

Telemarketers

In most provinces, telemarketing is not covered under the laws that govern door-to-door sales. That means there's no cooling-off period during which you can cancel the contract without penalty. However, you may be able to cancel under the provincial laws prohibiting unfair business practices (see above). But if this was telephone fraud rather than honest telemarketing, your best bet is to contact either your local police if they have a seniors' fraud unit, or a program run by the Ontario Provincial Police called Phonebusters. Although it's located in North Bay, Ontario, the program covers all of Canada. Their toll-free number is 1-888-495-8501. You could also consider contacting the federal Competition Bureau (Deceptive Telemarketing Practices).

Prevention, though, is better than cure. If you are concerned about telemarketers taking advantage of your family member,

- install a telephone with call display in your family member's home and tell him not to answer the phone unless he recognizes the number
- warn other family members, caregivers, friends, neighbours—anyone who is in frequent contact with your family member—about the possibility of telephone fraud and ask them to keep an ear on telephone conversations and end them if advisable
- speak to the staff at your family member's bank and ask them to alert you if your family member makes large or frequent cash withdrawals

Unsolicited Goods

What happens if goods that were not ordered, such as magazines, CDs or videos, have been delivered to your family member, and someone has used them? Is your family member responsible for paying for them even though no one asked for the goods in the first place? The answer is no. If unsolicited goods are delivered to someone, he does not have to pay for them *and* can do with them whatever he likes. Unsolicited goods can be used or thrown out—or even returned if you want to go to the trouble. But they don't have to be paid for, no matter how alarming the bill or letter demanding payment looks. (Just check to make sure that no one *did* order them! Also, keep in mind that by joining a book-of-the-month club or a CD-of-the-month club, you agree to pay for whatever they send you or else return it.)

Contracts to Provide Services

What if the contract that's worrying you requires your family member to do more than pay for goods or services? What if the contract requires him to perform accounting work, or paint the exterior of a house, or design a wedding gown? These are contracts for personal services that require the skill of the particular individual. The law says that if the person who agreed to perform the services becomes physically incapable of doing so (either through illness, injury or death), the contract is ended. The one party does not have to perform the services, and the other party does not have to pay for them. If your family member received a deposit in advance of performing the service, it may have to be returned.

However, a contract that does not require personal skill (for example, an agreement to sell the dining-room suite for $1000) is not ended. Even if the person who made the original agreement is not physically capable of doing what he promised, the other party has the right to insist on going through with the contract. Someone else, a relative or friend, may have to do what is required (for example, deliver the dining-room suite to the right address, and pick up the money).

Contracts to Sell Property or Goods

Sometimes it appears that someone has taken advantage of a person who is in frail physical or mental health to get her to sell something for less than its value. An acquaintance may persuade an elderly woman to sell her home or her car for half its market value, or a caregiver may offer to buy a valuable coin collection or a piece of art for a few dollars and the owner, who has little idea what anything is worth, agrees. In situations like these, it would be best to speak to a lawyer. The law says that in certain cases a contract can be set aside—but you have to go to court unless the other party voluntarily agrees to return the property and take back his money. The cases in which a contract can be set aside involve circumstances in which one party took advantage of the other, specifically,

- one party made a false statement to the other about an important fact related to the contract, and the other party relied on that statement when deciding to enter into the contract (this is **misrepresentation**); or

- one party used violence or threats of violence or threats of criminal prosecution to persuade the other party to enter into the contract (this is **duress**); or

- one party used her dominant position in a relationship to persuade the other party to enter into the contract—for example, if the person who always looked after a frail patient got the patient to lend her a large sum of money—(this is **undue influence**); or

- one party persuaded another to enter into a contract that was extremely unfair to the other (this is **unconscionability**); or

- one party was physically incapable of reading the contract document and signed it after relying on what someone else told him the document said (this is **non est factum**, Latin for "this is not my act").

In addition, if one party's mental condition made it impossible for her to understand that she was entering into a contract, no contract exists in the first place. However, if the other party insisted on going through with the contract, you might have to start a lawsuit to get a court to rule that the contract never existed.

Where to Go for Help

If you need information about cancelling a contract, or maybe even some help doing it, there are different organizations you can contact. Try your provincial ministry of consumer affairs (some provinces have a consumers' hotline), the Better Business Bureau or the Consumers' Association of Canada (CAC). The CAC's head office is in Ottawa, but provincial offices are located in the capital city of each province. Or you may be able to get help from an organization that has some authority over the individual the contract is with, such as a regional home builders' association, or a local merchants' association. If the contract is for a significant amount of money, you might as well see a lawyer right away.

INJURY OR DAMAGE CAUSED BY AN ILL PERSON

Occasionally people who are unwell, either physically or mentally, cause injury to others or damage the property of others. For example, if a driver has a heart attack or a blackout caused by a medical condition, while driving on a busy street, she may cause an accident that injures others. A person who is suffering from dementia may attack a caregiver. A person whose memory is slipping may leave the stove on and cause a fire, or leave the bath running and cause a flood. If any of these things happen, what are the legal responsibilities of the ill person and the people who look after her?

Whenever one person deliberately or carelessly injures another or damages another's property, in law he has committed a civil wrong (a **tort**), and possibly also a crime. One of the differences between a crime and a tort is that the Crown (government) considers itself the injured party in a crime and prosecutes the crime; a criminal court can convict the wrongdoer and order imprisonment or a fine as punishment. The person who actually suffered the injury or whose property was damaged is the injured party in a tort and must be the one who sues; a civil court can find the wrongdoer liable and order him to pay money damages to compensate the victim for her injury or loss.

Tort or Civil Wrong

If one person hits, grabs or throws something at another (these are some examples of the tort of **battery**), or threatens to hit or throw something at another (these are examples of the tort of **assault**), or damages or destroys another's property (these are examples of the tort of **trespass to property**), the law will look at the person's mental state before deciding whether she is liable to pay compensation. If the person acted without any real intention at all (as an advanced Alzheimer's patient might), then she will not be held liable. If the person intentionally did the act that caused harm, then she will be held liable. So it's no excuse for a sick person to harm another person or another's property just because she is feeling cranky and aggressive from pain or anxiety. She will be held liable if sued and will have to pay money to compensate the injured person. Although a patient with dementia would probably not be held liable, that's not the end of the story. The person who had the duty to look after the patient with dementia might be sued and held liable. Keep reading.

If a person injures another or damages another's property carelessly rather than intentionally, an area of the law of torts called **negligence** comes into the picture. The law of negligence says that if a person performs an act that he knows is likely to cause harm OR that he *should have known* was likely to cause harm because any ordinary person would know that, then that person can be held liable to pay compensation to the injured person. For example, if a person who has suffered a series of minor strokes goes for a drive and suffers a stroke while on the road and causes an accident, he will be held liable if sued because he should have known better than to drive a car when there was a reasonable chance of having a stroke.

Similarly, if a person is caring for a family member who might forget to turn off the stove or who might punch a visiting nurse, that caregiver, if sued, might be held liable to compensate the injured person if there is a fire or a punch. The reasoning is that the caregiver *knew or ought to have known* that the person with mental problems might leave the stove on or might hit someone, but did not take reasonable care to prevent this from happening. If you are caring for someone with mental problems, you have to think about all the harmful things she might do, and take reasonable steps to prevent them. This might just mean having kitchen appliances that shut off automatically after a time, or providing assistance with bathing (and turning off the taps), or it might mean having someone with your family member all the time to watch him. If you are looking after someone who you think might cause harm, make sure each of you has third-party liability insurance as part of your home insurance. The insurance company will pay to defend a lawsuit brought against the insured person, and will pay any compensation that the court orders to be paid, up to the policy limits (usually $1 million, but you can pay extra to get a higher limit). Third-party liability insurance does not cover deliberate harmful acts (the cranky punch), only negligent harmful acts (failing to make sure that a forgetful person turns off the taps).

Offence or Crime

It is also possible that a person who hits, grabs or throws something at another, or threatens to hit or throw something at another, or who damages or destroys another's property could be charged with a crime—the crime of **assault** in the first two cases, the crime of **mischief** or **wilful damage to property** in the case of damaging or destroying property. A person charged with a crime will be found guilty if he intentionally (deliberately) committed the act. A person who didn't know what he was doing would not be convicted of a crime. A person who caused an accident by driving when she had a medical condition that she knew might interfere with her ability to drive safely could be charged with a provincial offence under a highway traffic statute such as careless driving, or with a more serious criminal offence such as dangerous driving or criminal negligence.

CIVIL RIGHTS

Adult Canadian citizens have the right to do many things, such as vote, leave the country and return, rent an apartment, or buy cigarettes. We take most of these rights for granted. But once a person's physical or mental health starts to decline, problems can arise when he tries to engage in activities that most of us look upon as a "right." Two activities in particular come to mind here: driving a car and getting married.

Driving

Many people think of driving as their absolute right, and there's no doubt that it can contribute to self-esteem and feelings of independence and personal freedom. People often resist strongly when told they should not drive. But driving is a privilege, and one way provincial governments decide who is entitled to that privilege is by looking at the health of the driver. In most provinces, the law says that a person who suffers from any mental, emotional, nervous or physical disability that is likely to interfere significantly with his ability to drive cannot hold a driver's licence. Specific conditions that provincial law considers likely to interfere significantly with driving ability include:

• diabetes that requires insulin for control

• taking drugs that could impair the ability to drive

• heart disease

• respiratory problems

• aortic aneurysm

• an established history of loss of consciousness or awareness due to a medical condition

• high blood pressure (hypertension) that results in giddiness even when treated

• disorders of the musculoskeletal or nervous system that interfere with safe driving

• psychotic or psychoneurotic disorders that cannot be controlled with treatment

• poor vision (either short-sightedness or lack of peripheral vision) that is not corrected by lenses

Your family member may voluntarily stop driving, realizing that she is no longer capable of the visual processing, good judgment, complex actions, and fast reactions that are necessary for safe driving. Or she may listen if you discuss the matter openly, and agree that her driving days must come to an end.

But are you prepared to turn your mother or father or wife or husband in to the authorities if he or she won't stop driving? In some provinces, physicians have a legal duty to report to the provincial licensing authority that a person has a condition, whether mental or physical, that affects driving ability. Also, in some provinces, a person over a certain age (for example, 70) who has had an accident may have to take a test to re-qualify for a driver's licence, and people over 80 may have to take a driver's test every two years. So the matter may be taken out of your hands and the hands of the driver. If it's not, though, and you reasonably believe that your family member is endangering the safety of others or his own safety by driving, you may have to confiscate the car keys, or remove the car from the premises, or disable it so that it can't be started.

Once it's impossible for your family member to drive, make sure that she doesn't feel trapped. Be prepared to drive her on errands, or enlist friends to drive, or contact a volunteer driving program in your area, or keep taxi numbers near the phone and make sure that taxi money is always available or open an account with a taxi company. In some cities, there is a special publicly subsidized transit service for the disabled. Service can be ordered in advance, like a taxi, but since several people share the vehicle, it takes longer and delays must be factored in when planning travel time.

Marriage

We've all heard or read about elderly or even senile men who suddenly married a younger (sometimes much younger) woman. Occasionally we hear of a man and a woman who meet as residents in a nursing home and marry. The new wife or husband may suddenly be running the person's life, or helping to make decisions about medical treatment, in a way that the person's children or other relatives think is not appropriate—and in law the wishes of a spouse are generally ranked above the wishes of other family members. Further, marriage cancels any existing will, so the children may be concerned that family property matters that had been settled are now unsettled.

If a family member who is in poor mental or physical health decides to marry, is there anything you can do to cancel a marriage that does not seem to be in his best interest? Well, it's a tough row to hoe. You'll need to discuss the matter with a family law lawyer, but here's a general outline of the law of **annulling** (setting aside) a marriage. A marriage can be annulled if one of the parties does not have the mental capacity at the time of the marriage to understand the basic nature of marriage and its obligations. However, very little understanding is required to satisfy this standard. It may not be much more than understanding that a husband and wife live together and love each other as husband and wife to the exclusion of all others. A marriage can also be annulled if one party is forced into it by pressure such as physical abuse or threats, or if one party is misled about the nature of the ceremony that the parties are going through.

Impotence (the inability to have sexual intercourse in order to consummate the marriage) is not a strong ground to rely on to have someone's marriage annulled because it's up to the spouses, including the spouse who is not impotent, to decide whether to accept the impotence and continue the marriage or to annul the marriage. After one of the spouses dies, it is not possible to have a marriage declared invalid on the ground of impotence.

Richard was a 78-year-old man living in a nursing home because he suffered from periods of mental confusion that made it impossible for him to live alone. He became increasingly anxious to be able to live in his own home, and he announced to his family that he was going to marry a widow whom he had known for several years. Four days before the wedding, he made a new will naming his wife as the sole beneficiary of his estate. Two days after the wedding, he died. The family challenged the validity of the will on the ground that the man was not of sufficiently sound mind to make a valid will. The court agreed, but then another problem arose. Since marriage cancels an existing will, the family could not inherit under the earlier will the man had made. The family therefore asked the court to decide whether the marriage was valid—that is, whether the man had had the necessary mental capacity to enter into a marriage. The court concluded that he did, and that there was therefore no valid will. The man's estate would have to be distributed as if he had made no will at all—instead of having made two.

6

MANAGING THE AFFAIRS OF SOMEONE WHO NO LONGER CAN

In Chapter 2 we looked at how you could help your family member make financial and legal plans to see him through the dying process, including dealing with:

- how your family member's financial affairs will be handled if he becomes unable to handle them personally
- how decisions about your family member's medical treatment will be made if he becomes unable to make the decisions

In this chapter, we assume that your family member's illness has progressed to the point where you now believe that you must make decisions about financial matters or medical matters, or both. This chapter will explain what you can do. If your family member earlier agreed to give you a power of attorney for financial matters and to make a living will for health care matters, your role will be much easier.

FINANCIAL MATTERS

A person is considered to be mentally incapable of making financial decisions when she is not able to understand information that is relevant to making

a decision or is not able to appreciate what is likely to happen as a result
of making the decision. If your family member is no longer able to make
decisions about financial matters, someone will have to make those decisions
on her behalf. Who that person is, and how that person gets the power to
make those decisions, will depend on whether your family member made
advance plans.

If Your Family Member Prepared a Power of Attorney

Your family member may have prepared a power of attorney to give another
person (the attorney) authority to handle legal and financial affairs. (See
Chapter 2 at p. 13.) If you were named as the attorney, what do you do now?

First Things First

You must get the original power of attorney document if you don't already
have it. With good planning—or good luck—your family member previously
told you where it could be found, or is still able to tell you now. Your family
member may have left the power of attorney with a lawyer (or some other
person), with instructions to release the document to you only if he became
incapable of making financial decisions. In that case you will have to speak to
the lawyer. Your family member may have told the lawyer to get the opinion
of your family member's doctor about whether he is incapable before
releasing the power of attorney, or may have instructed the lawyer to decide
whether he is incapable.

Once you have the power of attorney, you must figure out whether it is
in effect. The power of attorney may have come into effect on the date it was
signed. Fine so far. However, now you must determine whether it *remains* in
effect. If your family member is mentally incapacitated, you can't use the
power of attorney unless it specifically says that it is to continue in effect
even after your family member becomes mentally incompetent. On the other
hand, the power of attorney may state that it comes into effect only when
your family member becomes mentally incapacitated. The power of attorney
may also say how mental incapacity is to be determined. For example, it may
say that a named person, such as your family member's doctor or lawyer, is to
decide. If the document does not say how your family member's incapacity
is to be determined, the provincial statute governing powers of attorney will
state how the determination is to be made. In some provinces, the evidence
of two doctors is required; in others, a court must decide. You may need
to see a lawyer.

The Duties of an Attorney

An attorney has a number of duties. First, if you're an attorney you can't make just any financial decisions you choose: you must always act honestly and in your principal's best interests. Second, you must be reasonably careful. Third, you must avoid any conflicts of interest with your principal and must not make any secret profits as a result of handling your principal's financial affairs. Fourth, you must keep records of all your transactions. (If you are an attorney in Ontario, you have other duties as well, such as encouraging your principal to participate to the best of her abilities in decisions, consulting with the principal's "supportive" family and friends, and paying attention to the financial needs of family who are financially dependent on the principal.)

The power of attorney document may place additional duties on you, such as

- maintaining financial records in whatever form the principal specifies
- reporting to another family member
- consulting with a financial planner, stockbroker, banker or other advisor

Exercising Your Powers as Attorney

You must read the power of attorney to see what powers you have been given. In most provinces, unless the power of attorney limits the attorney's powers, you are authorized to make any financial decisions that your principal could make, and perform any financial act that your principal could perform (other than to prepare or change your principal's will). If there are no limitations, you will have complete power to manage your principal's property, bank accounts and investments, including the power to buy and sell property, to receive money due to your principal and to pay your principal's bills.

In Québec, unless the power of attorney (the mandate) gives the attorney (the mandatary) "full administrative powers," the attorney only has the authority to make decisions and take actions necessary to preserve the principal's property, and is very limited in the way she can invest the principal's money. Without full administrative powers, the attorney will need a court order to sell any of the principal's property.

If you were appointed as attorney along with another person, check the power of attorney to see whether the two of you must always act together or whether you may make decisions on your own. In most provinces, if the power of attorney does not give one attorney the power to act alone, either attorney may only act in agreement with the other.

When you exercise the power of attorney on behalf of your principal, you will have to show the original document to anyone you are dealing with, and you may be required to produce identification to prove that you are the attorney named in the document. To make your path smoother, introduce yourself formally to the people you will be dealing with, and give them each a copy of the power of attorney.

- Go to your principal's bank to make arrangements to handle the accounts.
- Make similar arrangements with anyone else you will be dealing with on an ongoing basis, such as stockbrokers.
- If you decide to sell your principal's house or any other real estate, be sure to tell the real estate agent and lawyer that you are acting as attorney under a power of attorney.

Compensation for Your Work as Attorney

In most provinces, you are not entitled to receive any compensation for your services as attorney unless the power of attorney says that you are. The power of attorney may set the amount of your compensation or you may be paid at a rate set by provincial law.

Informal Arrangements When There Is No Power of Attorney

As we told you before, it is much more complicated to manage financial affairs if your family member has not prepared a power of attorney. You may be able to make informal arrangements to manage affairs if they are very simple— that is, if your family member will cooperate with you. You can deposit any cheques payable to your family member directly into his bank account. You don't need any special arrangements to do that. You can also ask your family member to change his bank account into a joint account with you. Once your name is on the account, you can sign cheques on the account and withdraw money to pay your family member's bills. If your family member receives Canada Pension Plan or Old Age Security Payments, you can apply to the Canadian government to be appointed as a trustee to receive the benefits. You will have to fill in government forms in which you certify that your family member is incapable of managing her own affairs and you promise to act on her behalf and to provide financial records of your transactions to the government whenever required.

Becoming Your Family Member's Property Guardian or Committee

You will probably not be able to make informal arrangements to manage your family member's financial affairs if they are more complicated than those discussed above; for example, if your family member has a number of investments that need tending or owns a home or other real estate that must be sold. If power of attorney cannot be given, the only way that anyone can assume control of your family member's financial affairs is by getting formally appointed as his **property guardian** or (in some provinces) **committee**. (By the way, you pronounce "committee" like "jamboree," not like the kind of committee that holds meetings.) In almost every province you will have to start a court proceeding to do this.

The Court Proceeding

Before a court will appoint a property guardian or committee for someone, it must find that the person is incapable of handling her own financial matters—depending on the province, that the person is **mentally incompetent**, **mentally disordered**, **mentally disabled**, or that she is **incapable** of managing her own affairs because of a **mental infirmity**.

The court procedure varies from province to province, but usually the person wanting to be appointed property guardian or committee has to give the court an application plus an **affidavit**—a written statement containing evidence about the matter, sworn under oath. The affidavit must deal with the following matters:

- the mental state of the person who cannot manage her affairs
- the reasons for believing that the person is incapable of managing her affairs
- the nature of the relationship between the person who wants to be appointed and the incapable person, and why this person would be an appropriate choice as property guardian
- the names of (other) family members and whether they are aware of and consent to the appointment as property guardian
- details of the incapable person's property, debts, income and expenses
- the would-be property guardian's plans for managing the incapable person's property, and the rights and powers being requested to deal with the property, such as a right to sell certain property or a right to make certain types of investments
- the property guardian's willingness to **provide security** to the court to ensure that he manages the incapable person's property honestly and carefully

The applicant also usually has to provide affidavits from at least two doctors that

- state the doctor's qualifications
- set out the nature of the doctor's contact with the incapable person
- give the doctor's **diagnosis** (statement of the current medical condition) and **prognosis** (the doctor's prediction as to the future course of the medical condition)

- give a medical opinion that the person is mentally incapable of managing her own affairs.

In certain provinces, the court has the power to order that the incapable person be medically examined if it's necessary for a doctor to give an opinion.

In some provinces the applicant will have to give official notice of the application to the incapable person's spouse, adult children and other adult family members, or give their signed consent to the appointment to the court. In some provinces the applicant also has to give notice to the **Public Trustee**, a government official who is responsible for looking after the interests of people who are mentally incompetent.

The court doesn't have to appoint the applicant, or the court may have two or more applicants to choose between. When deciding whom to appoint as property guardian or committee,

- the court may appoint more than one property guardian

- if the court must choose between a family member and a non-family member, the court will generally appoint a family member to be property guardian

- the court will take into consideration the incapable person's preference if she has stated one

- if only one person is being appointed, usually the property guardian must reside in the same province as the incapable person

In most cases, the court will require the property guardian to post security with the court, as a guarantee that the guardian will be careful and honest.

The Powers of a Property Guardian

The powers of the property guardian depend on the wording of the court order making the appointment and on the province in which the order was made. In some provinces, a property guardian is given all of the rights and powers that the incapable person would have, except as limited by the court order. In other provinces, a property guardian is given a range of powers that he can exercise without getting the approval of the court, and other powers that can be exercised only if the court approves the action in advance. In yet other provinces, a property guardian is given only those powers that are specifically set out in the court order. In most provinces, a property guardian has the power to invest money, although only in the safest investments. In a few provinces, a property guardian must hand over to the court any money not needed to meet the expenses of the incapable person and her dependants. The court will hold the money unless and until it is needed to pay expenses. In most provinces, a property guardian cannot sell any property without first getting permission from the court.

By law, a property guardian should change the nature of the incapable person's property as little as possible when exercising his powers. That's so that if the person becomes capable again, his financial affairs will not have changed too much. As a result, the courts are reluctant to permit a property guardian to sell any property unless it's property that will go down in value, such as a car, or unless cash is needed to pay expenses.

The Duties of a Property Guardian

A property guardian must exercise her powers in the best interests of the incapable person and be reasonably careful in managing the property. The property guardian must always act honestly and avoid any conflicts of interest with the incapable person (for example, by trying to buy the person's property). The property guardian must not make any secret profits as a result of handling the incapable person's financial affairs (for example, by charging a secret commission for selling the property).

A property guardian is also required within a specified time, usually six months, to make an inventory (a list) of all the property and debts of the incapable person and to give a copy to the court. The property guardian must also give financial records of all transactions for the incapable person to the court at regular intervals, usually once every year or two.

Compensation of the Property Guardian

A property guardian is entitled to receive fair and reasonable compensation, which is paid out of the incapable person's property and income. The court sets the amount of compensation. The property guardian is also entitled to be repaid for any proper and reasonable expenses related to managing the financial affairs.

MEDICAL MATTERS

A person is considered to be mentally incapable of making medical decisions when he is not able to understand information that is relevant to making a decision or is not able to appreciate what is likely to happen as a result of making the decision. If your family member is no longer able to make rational decisions about his medical treatment, someone else will have to make those decisions on his behalf. Who that person is, and how that person gets the power to make those decisions, will depend on whether advance plans were made.

If There's a Living Will

Your family member may have prepared a living will and appointed a substitute decision maker (see Chapter 2 at p. 19).

When Does the Living Will Come into Effect?

A living will comes into effect only when the patient is incapable of making medical decisions. Usually it is a health care practitioner, such as a doctor or nurse, who will conclude that the patient is incapable, probably when some form of medical treatment is proposed for which the hospital or doctor needs consent. Once the doctor or hospital concludes that the patient is not capable of giving the necessary consent, in most situations the substitute decision maker will either be asked to consent to or refuse the proposed treatment.

How the Substitute Decision Maker Makes Decisions

When all eyes turn to the substitute decision maker, what should she do? First, she should get the original living will if she doesn't already have it. The incapable person may have said where it can be found. If not, he may still be able to say where it is now, or perhaps his doctor or other health care provider may know where it is.

The living will may not only name the substitute decision maker, but may also set out instructions about what decisions the substitute decision maker should make. If so, in most provinces the substitute decision maker as a rule must follow those instructions, even if the instructions are not what the substitute decision maker would personally choose to do for the patient. In other provinces, the substitute decision maker must consider the patient's instructions, but can make her own final decision.

If the patient did not give instructions in the living will, the substitute decision maker must follow any wishes that the patient expressed in the past (if the substitute decision maker knows of them). If the patient did not make his wishes known, the substitute decision maker must decide whether to consent to the treatment based on the decision that she believes the patient would make in the circumstances. If the substitute decision maker doesn't know what the patient would decide, or if it's impossible to follow the patient's wishes, the substitute decision maker must make her own decision after considering whether the proposed treatment will improve or maintain the patient's quality of life, and whether the benefits of the proposed treatment outweigh the risks.

Informal Arrangements If There Is No Living Will

In emergency situations, a doctor or hospital does not need a patient's consent to give treatment. (See Chapter 7 at p. 81.) If the situation is not an emergency, a doctor or other health practitioner must get consent from either the patient or someone on the patient's behalf before giving any medical treatment. If the patient is not capable of consenting and did not appoint a substitute decision maker, doctors in most provinces will look to his closest relatives to consent to or refuse treatment. (See Chapter 2 at p. 19) If you are asked to consent to medical treatment under these circumstances, you should follow any wishes stated by your family member before he became incapacitated. If you don't know your family member's wishes, try to make the decision that your family member would have made. If you don't know what your family member would have decided, or you know but it's impossible to do, you must make your decision by considering whether the proposed treatment will improve or maintain your family member's quality of life, and whether the benefits of the proposed treatment outweigh the risks.

Guardian of the Person

An incapable person may need a **guardian of the person** if his need for assistance in decision making goes beyond medical matters to matters affecting his personal welfare, such as decisions about where to live, what food to eat and what clothing to wear.

The procedure for appointing a guardian of the person is similar to the procedure for appointing a property guardian. The court must agree that the incapable person is mentally incompetent or incapable of caring for himself on a continuing basis. The court considers the same factors in choosing a guardian of the person as it would in choosing a property guardian; in fact, if a property guardian has been appointed, most courts prefer to appoint the same person as guardian of the person.

In a few provinces, the powers of a guardian of the person are set out in detail, and include the power to decide:

• where and with whom the person should live

• what social activities the person should participate in

• what sort of health care the person should receive

• what sort of food the person should eat

In the other provinces, the guardian of the person is simply given **custody** of the incapable person, and is therefore given the same rights that a parent would have over a child.

The guardian of the person must make reasonable arrangements for the care and maintenance of the person. She must always act in the person's best interests and be reasonably careful in the decisions that she makes.

PART III

GETTING THE BEST CARE

7 DOCTORS AND HOSPITALS

Doctors and hospitals will probably occupy a lot of your time and attention when someone in your family is very ill. If you understand how doctors and hospitals work, you may get better care for your family member *and* save yourself some frustration.

DOCTORS

A **family physician** is the doctor most people deal with on a regular basis, and go to for a check-up or when they're feeling sick. Family physicians are generalists—they know a lot about common health problems and also something about a wide range of less common ones. If a problem arises that the family physician needs help diagnosing or treating, she may refer the patient to a **specialist,** a doctor who has had additional training to deal with a specific area of medicine such as neurology (treatment of the brain and nerves), oncology (treatment of cancer) or cardiology (treatment of heart problems). Most specialists will not accept a patient without a referral from a family physician. In some provinces, this is because specialists are allowed to see a patient only if he has been referred by a family physician. In other provinces, it's because specialists are paid more by the government health plan when a patient is referred by a family physician.

You may think that it's easy for a family physician to choose the right specialty when referring a patient to a specialist—but it isn't always. For example, a family physician might refer someone with back pain to an orthopedic surgeon (a specialist in bone surgery), a rheumatologist (a specialist in auto-immune disorders such as arthritis), a neurosurgeon (a surgeon specializing in the brain and spinal cord), an oncologist (a specialist in cancer), and a chronic pain specialist before the root of the problem is found, because back pain can have several different causes. Some conditions require referral to a doctor who specializes in a very narrow area. For example, a patient may need to be referred not to an ophthalmologist (an eye specialist) but to a vitreo-retinal specialist or a neuro-ophthalmologist.

The family physician will probably have a specialist to whom he ordinarily sends his patients, but your family member may want to be referred to someone else. Before choosing a specialist, consider

• whether that specialist is an expert in the field and has a good reputation in the medical community

• how long your family member will have to wait for an appointment with that specialist—the wait for an appointment with a specialist (and then for treatment) can be very long—sometimes longer than medical standards recommend, even for life-threatening conditions

When dealing with a life-threatening illness, these are the two most critical factors. However, you may also want to think about

• how the specialist deals with her patients—whether she is easy to talk to, spends time with each patient, and explains things to patients in easy-to-understand language

• what hospital the specialist is affiliated with, because that's the hospital your family member will be admitted to if hospital treatment is required. Does the hospital have a good reputation? Is it located reasonably close to home?

But, as a rule, you want the specialist who knows the most about your family member's condition, even if she is grumpy and is affiliated with a hospital in an inconvenient location. You should even consider travelling to another city to see a specialist with particular expertise in your family member's illness. The specialist may be able to develop a treatment plan that can be carried out by the family physician, so that there's not too much travel.

Talking to a Doctor

Your family member will have questions for his doctors and will want to report any changes in his condition. In an ideal world, your family member should just be able to pick up the phone and talk to the doctor any time he has a concern. As you are no doubt unhappily aware by now, this is not an ideal world. Before a patient can talk to his doctor, he first has to get past a secretary (whose job it is to protect the doctor from interruptions)— and that's if the patient is lucky enough to get through to the secretary! Often a patient can only reach a recorded message. What should your family member do?

Start by leaving a detailed message with the doctor's secretary or on the doctor's voice-mail or answering machine. The secretary may be able to answer the question (many doctors' secretaries are also nurses and can respond to commonly asked questions). If the secretary can't answer the question herself, she may be able to ask the doctor and get back with an answer. This will usually take less time than waiting for the doctor to call so that you can ask the question yourself. If the secretary doesn't return calls, try sending a fax to the doctor's office. For some reason faxes seem to get answered faster than telephone calls.

If your family member has more than a quick question or two for the doctor, she should make an appointment to see the doctor. If you're dealing with a specialist, the wait for follow-up appointments is usually not nearly as long as the wait for the first appointment, although it can still be a matter of days or weeks (unless the patient has what the doctor considers to be an urgent problem). If your family member can't get a timely appointment with the specialist, then she should speak to her family physician. The family physician may be able to answer the question himself. If not, he will have an easier time getting through to the specialist than the patient will.

Getting to speak to the doctor is just the first problem. Understanding what the doctor says is the next. Doctors often use medical jargon, especially if the news they have to give is bad. Doctors are human too—they don't like telling people that they're very sick or are going to die—and so they may hide behind technical language that a patient can't easily understand. The patient and family should keep asking the doctor to explain until they do understand. Your family member should consider taking someone along to appointments to listen to what the doctor has to say and to make it understandable. It is useful to write down the questions for the doctor, and the answers. Bad news is not just difficult to deliver; it's also difficult to absorb.

If more than one doctor is treating your family member, each may stick to her own specialty when talking about what's going to happen. For example, if your family member is in hospital with a very serious head injury and a broken ankle, the orthopedic surgeon who fixed the ankle may be quite optimistic about how the ankle will heal, but the neurosurgeon who is treating the head injury may say that your family member is not likely to live. Your family physician may be able to help you get the "big picture."

Diagnostic Testing

The family physician or specialist may want your family member to have tests done, such as blood tests, urine tests, x-rays, CAT scans and so on. The doctor will give the patient a form directing the laboratory or facility to perform the test(s). Ask the doctor whether there are any special instructions to be followed before having the test. Your doctor may send your family member to a hospital lab or x-ray facility, or may suggest that your family member go to an independent facility—perhaps one located near the doctor's office. If it's more convenient to go to a facility closer to home, ask if the test can be carried out there instead. Depending on the test and the facility, your family member may have to make an appointment to have the test carried out. Even if the doctor is sending your family member to a lab or facility in a hospital, many, if not most, tests can be done on an outpatient basis.

HOSPITALS

At some point during your family member's illness, he will probably need to receive medical treatment in a hospital.

Admission to a Hospital

A patient may be admitted to the hospital in one of the following ways:
- on an outpatient basis
- by a doctor
- through the emergency department

On an Outpatient Basis

A person admitted to the hospital as an outpatient receives treatment (such as diagnostic tests or minor surgery) at the hospital during the day, but does not stay overnight. Treatment on an outpatient basis can continue over many days; for example, rehabilitation or other therapy.

By a Doctor

A patient's doctor may recommend admission to the hospital for extensive diagnostic testing, for surgery, or for active treatment. In that case the doctor arranges for the patient to be admitted to the hospital where the doctor has treatment privileges (has the right to admit patients). The doctor makes a treatment plan for the patient, and instructs the hospital staff about what treatment to provide.

Through the Emergency Department

Not all admissions to the hospital are pre-planned. All too often they occur on an emergency basis. If an emergency arises and there is time, call your family member's doctor for instructions on what to do and where to go. After hours, most doctors leave emergency instructions for their patients with an answering service or on an answering machine. Again, if there is time, you should go to the hospital where your family member has been treated (because that's where her treatment records are) or the one with which her doctor is affiliated if your family member hasn't been in the hospital before. If you have spoken to the doctor first, he may call the emergency department to tell them that you are on the way. If you don't have time to get to that hospital, go to the nearest hospital with an emergency department. Call ahead to make sure that it's open—in this age of government cutbacks you can't just assume it will be. An emergency department may be open only during specified hours, or it may be closed at any particular time because it has too many patients. If the emergency department has too many patients, all but the most serious cases (and sometimes *all* cases) will be re-directed to other hospitals.

In an extreme emergency, you should call an ambulance. Not only will it be able to get your family member to the hospital more quickly, but ambulance attendants are trained to administer emergency treatment on the scene and to continue providing treatment en route to the hospital. Keep in mind, however, that the ambulance attendants have to transport the patient to the nearest hospital with an open emergency room. Your family member may not end up in the hospital where his treatment records are or where his doctor has privileges.

TIP: PLAN AHEAD FOR EMERGENCIES

• Ask your family member's doctor well **before** an emergency comes up what you should do and where you should go in case of an emergency.

• Know the location and telephone number of the nearest hospital with an emergency department and know the hours the emergency department is open.

• When an emergency happens, call the hospital to make sure the emergency department is open and if there's time, call your family member's doctor before you go to the hospital.

When you arrive at the emergency department, you may find that lots of other people are already there, and you may face a very long wait to be seen. Treatment in an emergency department is not on a first-come, first-served basis. Instead, all incoming patients are seen briefly by a **triage** nurse, who determines which patient should be treated first. Patients with life-threatening conditions, such as heart attack, stroke, serious breathing difficulties, seizures, and heavy bleeding, will be seen first.

After emergency treatment is administered, your family member may be released, admitted to the hospital as an inpatient or transferred to another hospital.

A Room with a View...of the Nursing Station

If your family member is admitted to the hospital as an inpatient, she will be assigned a room as soon as one is available (which you hope is immediately. Occasionally patients in crowded hospitals just get a bed in a corridor.), unless she goes straight to the intensive care unit (see below at p. 76). Standard hospital accommodation, which is covered under provincial health insurance, is considered to be a room with three or more beds, although some hospitals only have rooms with two beds. A semi-private room (two beds) or a private room (one bed) is usually considered an upgrade for which you will have to pay extra. Extended health care insurance plans will usually pay for the upgrade, at least to semi-private accommodation. Telephone and television service are usually available for an additional daily fee.

TIP: WHAT TO BRING FOR A HOSPITAL PATIENT

- Bathrobe and/or nightclothes, if the patient is able to wear them—hospital gowns are supplied, but patients usually hate them
- Toothbrush, toothpaste, razor, comb and/or hairbrush
- Mild soap and/or skin lotions
- Books, magazines
- An inexpensive radio
- DON'T BRING anything that your family member cares about losing, such as jewellery or expensive electronic equipment

---

There's an old joke that a hospital is the last place to go if you want to get any rest. But it's no joke. The hospital floor can be both noisy and busy. There may be very little privacy, especially if your family member is sharing a room. Nurses may come into the room throughout the day and night to check on your family member and/or other patients. Other patients may be very ill and in pain, and may moan and cry, or they may be deranged and make a lot of noise. Your family member may not get much sleep and may become exhausted. In fact, patients often feel more pain in a hospital than when they are at home, possibly because they're tired and agitated all the time.

Many patients also become disoriented in the hospital's unfamiliar surroundings. This is especially true of older patients, particularly after surgery, and of patients in intensive care units. Your family member may become confused about where he is and what has happened to him and may even hallucinate and/or become suspicious of everyone. This can be very upsetting to witness. If your family member is hallucinating or doesn't know where he is, don't argue with him. It will only make him worse. Instead, keep reminding him as gently as possible that he is in the hospital and how he came to be there. It may also be helpful to bring in pictures of family and familiar surroundings to help him re-orient himself. If your family member becomes very agitated, staff may have to sedate him.

Another old joke says that a hospital is a good place to get sick. Again, this is no joke. There are diseases in hospitals—other patients may have contagious diseases, or a patient, especially one weakened by surgery or illness, may pick up an infection (sometimes an antibiotic-resistant bacterial infection) from being touched by staff or from touching furniture or equipment. It's not unknown for a patient to come down sick with something she picked up in the hospital, and it's also not unknown for a patient, especially a weak one, to die of such a sickness.

As a result of government cutbacks, there are often not enough nursing staff to attend to all the needs of all the patients. If your family member is disoriented or unable to look after her personal needs, then you or other relatives may have to spend a lot of time (including nights) with her or else hire someone to look after her. If you are thinking of hiring someone to stay with your family member, speak to the nurse who is on duty. The nurse will tell you what kind of help you need—a registered nurse, registered practical nurse, health care aide or just a sitter. In addition, the hospital may only allow certain pre-approved people to work at the hospital, in which case the nurse can tell you how to make the necessary arrangements. Or the nurse may be able to give you the names of employment agencies through which you can hire someone.

TIP: EXTRA NURSING HELP

If you want to hire someone to sit with your family member overnight, don't wait too late in the day to make arrangements. There may be no one available at the last minute.

Intensive Care

Your family member may be too ill to be in a standard room and may require treatment in the intensive care unit. Patients are placed in intensive care when they are so ill that they require careful monitoring and one-on-one nursing. Brace yourself before you enter the intensive care unit. It's all bright lights and activity. There may be many patients and they will be hooked up to lots of machines with blinking lights and beeping sounds. There is no privacy whatsoever in intensive care. The patients in intensive care are placed so that the nurses can constantly observe them.

The number of visitors is strictly limited. Sometimes only the closest family members are allowed to visit and you may be allowed to stay for only short periods at a time. You may be asked to leave if your family member or some other patient requires emergency treatment.

TIP: PREPARE YOURSELF FOR INTENSIVE CARE

If your family member is in intensive care, prepare yourself before going in for the first time. Ask a nurse what you can expect. Can your family member hear you? Can he speak to you? What equipment will your family member be hooked up to? What does it mean when the equipment beeps? When should you call for a nurse?

Hospitals have other units, sometimes called **step-down units**, for patients who do not need the level of nursing offered in the intensive care unit, but who need more intensive nursing than is available on an ordinary floor.

But Is There a Doctor in the House?

You may visit your family member every day and still go days without ever seeing her doctor. You may even wonder whether there are any doctors in the hospital at all. While many doctors do rounds on a daily basis, rounds may take place very early in the morning. A doctor may check on his patients, or may just check in with the nurses. Doctors leave orders with the nurses about medication and treatment, and rely on them to manage everything throughout the day—to carry out their orders and to contact the doctor if further instructions are needed. If you want to speak to your family member's doctor, ask the nurses when the doctor is usually around to see patients and then arrange to be there at that time. Or make an appointment to see the doctor at the hospital or in her office.

If your family member is in a teaching hospital, not all the doctors there are created equal. During their fourth year of medical school, medical students (called **clerks** at that point) work in the hospital, rotating through various departments. Medical-school graduates become **residents** for up to five years, depending on the area of medicine they're studying. Doctors who do additional specialist training after the fifth year of residency are called **fellows**. In a teaching hospital, the doctors you see are usually residents and fellows. (And if your family member is in the hospital in July, the first-year resident was merely a clerk just days before.) There are often advantages to dealing with residents and fellows. They are educated in the newest developments, and are often more willing and have more time to talk to patients and family members than do more senior doctors. However, if you don't feel confident about the way a resident is handling your family member's case, ask to speak to the fellow or chief resident. If you are still not satisfied, ask to speak to the doctor on staff.

Visitors

Every hospital has rules about visitors. Check with the hospital to find out:

- what the visiting hours are
- how many visitors are allowed at any time
- whether and when children are allowed to visit

Think about your family member's condition before you encourage lots of visitors. The patient may be too ill or tired to have visitors, or may not want to see a lot of people in his present condition. Also, consider any other patients in your family member's room. The other patient may be very ill and may be really bothered by your family member's visitors. If the other patient in the room has constant visitors and they are annoying your family member, speak to the nursing staff.

A limited number of family members who are actively looking after the patient may be allowed to stay beyond regular visiting hours—even overnight. If you stay overnight, be prepared to sleep (or to try to sleep) sitting up in a chair, although if you're lucky, the nursing staff may be able to arrange for a cot to be set up in the patient's room.

How to Treat Hospital Staff

To make sure that your family member gets the very best care while in the hospital, it's important to let the staff know that you care how he is treated. But do it by being helpful to the patient and staff, and by thanking the staff for doing a good job. As the old expression goes, you'll catch more flies with honey than with vinegar—and you'll get more from the hospital staff by being pleasant with them than by complaining and being nasty.

Most nursing staff are overworked because of government funding cutbacks. Instead of calling for nursing staff for every little thing, do the small jobs yourself when you're there. Once they see that you are not calling them constantly for trivial things, they are more likely to come right away when you really do need them, and possibly to pay more attention to your family member when you're not there. Keep in mind that your family member may not be at her best. Let the staff know (by your behaviour) that your family member is a loved and valued person, so that they will value her too. And while you're at it, let the staff know that *they're* valued people. They appreciate recognition for a job well done, even if it's as simple as a smile and a thank you. If the nursing staff have been kind and helpful, bring them a card and cookies or candies when your family member leaves the hospital.

The Patient's Family

If you're from out of town, you will need a place to stay while your family member is in the hospital. Call the hospital for suggestions about places to stay, or contact the municipal tourist office for information about hotels, and especially about bed-and-breakfast establishments, which tend to be less expensive and more home-like. Some children's hospitals have a Ronald McDonalds House nearby, where families of children can stay.

Give some thought to where you will eat and park your car. These things can be expensive over time. Find out whether the hospital has a long-term parking rate, and if staff can recommend a local restaurant with decent food at a good price.

If your family member is in intensive care, you may want to stay at the hospital, even if you're not from out of town. Some hospitals will allow family members to stay overnight in surgical waiting rooms or other areas of the hospital—some even provide pillows and blankets.

SURGERY

Your family member may require surgery at some time during her illness. Unless it is an emergency, she may have to wait for surgery, and sometimes the wait, even for urgently needed surgery, can be quite long.

Risks of Surgery

There are risks attached to any surgery—general risks such as infection or complications from the anesthesia, and specific risks of a particular operation.

The surgeon is required to tell you about these risks (see below at p. 81), but if you have further questions, ask them. The surgeon will want your family member's medical history in order to assess and reduce the risks of surgery. Be prepared to answer questions about your family member's present medications and past illnesses and operations. The surgeon will be particularly interested in information about heart, breathing and bleeding conditions, and about previous reactions to drugs. The surgeon will also want to know what medication your family member is presently taking. If possible, bring all of your family member's pill bottles to the doctor. Then there won't be any mistakes about names of medications or dosages.

Preparation for Surgery

Except in the most dire emergency, a patient must not eat for at least six hours before surgery (although clear liquids are usually allowed until three hours before surgery). This is because the patient might vomit while under anesthesia and breathe stomach contents into his lungs, and this can be deadly. If the surgery is pre-planned, the patient will usually be required to fast from midnight the night before.

At some point before the surgery, the surgeon or anesthetist will discuss the risks and benefits of the surgery and ask the patient (or someone on his behalf) to sign a consent form. (See below at p. 80.)

Additional Questions before Surgery

You will want to know what to expect after the surgery, so ask the doctor or nurse:

• where you should wait during surgery

• how long the surgery is likely to take

• will the surgeon speak to you after the surgery, and if so where?—Hospitals often have "quiet rooms" with lots of tissues where surgeons take families to deliver bad news. But some surgeons always use the quiet rooms, for good news or bad, to talk to family members. Knowing that your surgeon does that may save you from an unnecessary fright if you're directed to the quiet room after surgery just to hear a report on how things went.

• where your family member will be taken after surgery—to a surgical recovery room or intensive care? Will anyone be able to visit with the family member there?

• what your family member will look like after surgery—Will he be attached to any special equipment?

- what the immediate after-effects of the surgery are likely to be; for example, from the anesthesia, from the surgery itself, from any drugs given during or after surgery, from drugs stopped before surgery
- how much pain the patient is likely to be in, and what painkiller will be used
- how soon after surgery you can expect your family member to be gotten up out of bed—the longer a patient remains in bed the more likely it is that she will develop complications such as breathing difficulties and bedsores
- how long your family member will be in the hospital, and whether he can go home after discharge—will he require further treatment in a rehabilitation hospital or other facility?

Outpatient Surgery

More and more surgery is being performed on an outpatient basis. In outpatient surgery, the patient is sent home as soon as the effects of the anesthesia have worn off. The patient will need someone to take her home, and may need someone to stay with her for the rest of the day or for several days. Depending on the surgery and the hospital, the patient may have to return to the hospital within the next day or two for examination. If you've come from out of town, you may need to arrange for accommodation nearby. The hospital may have suggestions.

CONSENT TO MEDICAL TREATMENT

Whatever the treatment and whatever the treatment setting, a patient's consent is necessary before any medical treatment can be given. This requirement doesn't apply just to medical procedures such as surgery and diagnostic tests, but to every touch by a doctor, nurse or other health care practitioner.

Form of Consent

A patient's consent to medical treatment can be oral, such as when she asks for a particular treatment or agrees when her doctor suggests it. Or it can be written; for example, a consent form signed by the patient. A patient's consent can even be implied from his conduct; for example, when a patient opens his mouth to allow the doctor to examine his throat or rolls up his sleeve to allow a nurse to take a blood sample.

Informed Consent

However consent is given, the patient must understand the treatment proposed before she can give true consent, and must be given enough information about a proposed medical treatment to make an informed decision. Without being asked, a doctor must tell his patient:

• the nature of the proposed treatment

• the significant risks of the treatment

• any alternatives to the proposed treatment

• what is likely to happen if the treatment is not given

In addition, the doctor must answer any of the patient's questions.

Ability to Give Consent

A patient over the age of majority (18 or 19 depending on the province) is legally capable of consenting to or refusing medical treatment, as in most provinces is an older child who has the ability to appreciate the nature and consequences of medical treatment. A patient is legally capable of giving or refusing consent if she is able to understand information that is relevant to making a medical decision and is able to appreciate what is likely to happen as a result of making the decision.

A patient may be capable of giving or refusing consent on an on-again off-again basis. For example, a patient may be capable when discussing surgery with his doctor, then incapable during or immediately after surgery, then capable again once he is conscious and rational following surgery.

When a Patient Is Unable to Consent

In an emergency situation, a doctor or hospital does not need a patient's consent to give treatment that is urgent and needed to save her life or maintain her health. Doctors will usually consult first with the person's family or substitute decision maker, but they are not legally required to do so.

If a patient is unable to consent but the situation is not an emergency, a doctor or other health practitioner must get consent from someone on the patient's behalf. If the patient is a child, a parent can consent. If the patient is an adult, consent can be given by:

• the patient's guardian of the person, if there is one

• if there is no guardian of the person, by the patient's substitute decision maker if the patient has appointed one

• if the patient has not appointed a substitute decision maker, by the patient's closest relatives

See Chapter 6 at p. 63 for a discussion of how the decision to consent to or refuse treatment should be made.

The Right to Refuse Treatment

A patient who is mentally competent has the right to refuse life-saving or life-prolonging treatment or request that the treatment be stopped, even if the decision is not one that the doctor agrees with. A patient cannot be given medical treatment against his wishes as long as he understands his condition, the nature of the proposed treatment and what is likely to happen if he decides against the treatment.

In certain cases, the doctor or hospital may *ask* a patient or patient's family to refuse treatment—specifically, to refuse resuscitation if the patient's heart or breathing stops. In many hospitals, resuscitation is automatic unless the patient or family agrees to an order DNR (Do Not Resuscitate), or to a "no code" (the same thing as DNR), or the more precise "No CPR" (No Cardiopulmonary Resucitation) being put on the patient's chart. A doctor would suggest the order DNR in the belief that resuscitation would be of no benefit to the patient because the patient would be in really terrible shape after being resuscitated—for example, if she had suffered extremely serious brain damage in an accident and was unlikely ever to recover consciousness, or was in the final stages of dying of cancer or another disease. On the other hand, in some hospitals DNR might be written on a patient's chart without consulting the patient or family if doctors were convinced that resuscitation would not benefit the patient. If you ever have to discuss with the doctor whether your family member should be resuscitated, be sure that you fully understand what resuscitation involves and get an explanation of the condition your family member would be in following resuscitation. (See Chapter 12 at p. 130.)

If the Hospital and the Family Don't Agree

A hospital may disagree with the family's decision about medical treatment for the patient (whether it's a decision to withhold treatment or insist on treatment) because the doctors believe that the decision is not in the patient's best interest. Although doctors and hospitals have the right to refuse to give treatment to a patient if the patient will get no benefit from it, in practice the hospital will usually try to explain the situation to the family so they understand why the hospital is taking this position. A hospital would probably be reluctant to withhold treatment that the family wanted—although staff would try to explain to the family why it would be better for the patient to withhold treatment. If a hospital can't get the family to come around to its way of thinking, it might go ahead and do what it wants anyway; or it may ask the provincial Public Trustee to step in in place of the family and make treatment decisions for the patient; or it might ask a court to make a decision about the treatment. The family could also ask the court to make a ruling about treatment. If a court is called upon to decide, it will make its decision on the basis of the best interests of the patient—so it might side with the family or the hospital, depending on the facts in the case.

PATIENT INFORMATION

Doctors have a duty to keep information about a patient confidential. That means that a doctor cannot disclose information about a patient to anyone but the patient. A doctor can tell others about a patient's medical condition if the patient consents directly or by implication. In most circumstances, there is an implied consent for a doctor to answer reasonable questions about the patient's condition asked by the patient's immediate family. For example, if a woman has an operation and while she is still unconscious her worried husband asks the surgeon how she is, the surgeon may and probably will answer. A patient can, however, expressly forbid her doctor from giving information to a particular family member or members. A patient would have to give direct consent for her doctor to give information to another doctor, an insurance company or an employer. Most doctors want the patient's consent or request to disclose the information to be in writing.

A doctor has the right to withhold information about a patient from the patient himself, even if a patient directly asks for it, if it is the doctor's medical judgment that disclosing the information will do the patient more harm than good. There have been instances of doctors not telling patients that they had a fatal disease, in the belief that the patient would be mentally unable to cope with the news.

Medical records, whether in a doctor's office or a hospital, contain medical information and are also confidential. Medical records are not to be disclosed to anyone other than the patient unless the patient consents. A patient has a right to her medical records. The doctor or hospital owns the physical record, but the patient owns the information. So a patient has the right to get information from her records, including the right to get photocopies of the records, although not to take away the original records.

HOME CARE

It's not always easy to get the best care at home, but the health care system encourages people to stay in their homes as long as possible. And, in fact, most people *want* to stay in their homes.

If your family member is going to be looked after at home, as a first step you may need to make some changes around the house to keep him safe and comfortable. For example, you may need to

- have a ramp installed so he can get in and out of the house
- have doorways widened so that a wheelchair can easily go through
- install handrails in the bathroom and perhaps in the hall
- put down non-skid flooring
- put a special high seat on the toilet if your family member has trouble sitting down and standing up
- replace the usual bed with a hospital bed

Special equipment can be bought or rented from stores that deal in home health care supplies. You may also want to enroll your family member in a service that provides a medical alarm, a pendant or hand-held device that the person can use to summon help if he falls or otherwise can't get to a phone.

PUBLICLY FUNDED HOME CARE

People who are in poor health usually start off with informal home care given by family and friends. That's rarely enough for the long term—and then the patient looks to publicly funded home care ("community care"). Home care services vary considerably across the country. In some provinces, all services are available through the provincial authority responsible for home care (usually a branch of the provincial health or social service department, or a district or regional health board); in others, they are divided up and some services are provided directly by the provincial authority and others by community organizations or not-for-profit agencies.

What Kind of Services Are Available through Home Care?

Health care and home support are the two kinds of services provided by home care programs. In most provinces, medical care from a doctor must be arranged by the patient or patient's family (it may not always be easy to find a doctor who is willing to make house calls, though).

Health Care Services

Below is a list of almost all the possible health care services available through home care. At the moment, probably no province provides every single one of these services; some provide most of them, some just a few of them. The services include

- nursing care—including wound care, administration of medication, catheterization, IV (intravenous) therapy with chemotherapy chemicals and antibiotics, health teaching, mental health nursing
- medication assessment, management and monitoring
- palliative care (pain control)
- chemotherapy
- HIV therapy
- dialysis
- diabetes management
- post-operative rehabilitation
- physiotherapy
- occupational therapy
- respiration therapy (including support for people on home ventilators) and home oxygen therapy programs

- speech-language pathology
- audiology
- social work
- nutrition counselling or dietetics
- laboratory testing (of blood and specimens)
- health information (a telephone service staffed by nurses 24 hours a day, seven days a week—in some cases the nurses have access to client files for home care patients)

Health care supplies may also be provided—drugs, medical supplies (such as wound dressings, oxygen, needles and syringes), and health care equipment (such as hospital beds, wheelchairs, walkers, respirators and so on). In some provinces, supplies are provided at no charge, in others at a full charge.

Support Services

Support services available in your province may include some or all of the following:

- personal care—assistance with bathing, grooming, dressing, etc.
- homemaking services—such as cleaning, shopping and meal preparation, and laundry, ironing and mending
- banking and paying bills
- child care
- meals on wheels and wheels to meals
- home maintenance—such as installing special equipment (for example, handrails, and non-skid surfaces) and performing indoor and outdoor tasks necessary for safety
- transportation to and from medical appointments
- friendly visiting
- security calls (telephone calls to the person in home care at certain times of the day to make sure he is all right—for example, a call first thing in the morning, last thing at night)
- respite care to relieve family caregivers—who are often exhausted and stressed from looking after the ill person. Respite care can take several forms, including
  - sitting services (a volunteer comes and stays with the patient for a few hours while the family gets out of the house)
  - organized group activities

- adult day care centres, where a home care patient can be sent for several hours (either on a regular basis, ranging from every day to once a week, or on an irregular basis as the family needs a rest)
- facility placement—the patient is admitted to an extended care facility for a few days or weeks while the family takes a break
• information about community resources

Availability of Services

The range of services available is different in every province, so you will have to contact the regional health care authority responsible for home care to find out what services might be available to you—the more money the province has to put into the home care program, the more services are available. In addition, not all kinds of services are available in every region of the province (typically, large urban areas have the best home care programs). Moreover, certain services are only available from 9 a.m. to 5 p.m., Monday to Friday; others are only available if arranged a reasonable time in advance. However, some services are available 24 hours a day, without pre-arrangement —these are usually palliative care and home IV services, and sometimes other nursing care.

Quality of Services

The competence and usefulness of home care workers can vary widely. Health care workers (especially those employed directly by the provincial authority) are often run off their feet with heavy caseloads and barely have time to perform the one task they came for, much less to stop and chat about general health or other matters. Although national standards for home care and an accreditation program were developed in 1997, practically speaking there is often no one except the patient and the family to oversee the quality of care provided.

Support workers usually have little formal training in their duties and are usually underpaid. Some of them are wonderful workers and wonderful human beings anyway; others are a nightmare. (The grandmother of one of the authors, although dead several years, is probably still fuming about the support worker who ruined her silver tea service by polishing it with brass cleaner.)

Joan is a 63-year-old woman with ALS (Lou Gehrig's disease, a disease that progressively paralyzes the entire body). She has had the disease for several years and now cannot move her arms or legs. She needs someone to bathe and clothe her in the morning, feed her during the day, take her to the toilet, and put her to bed. She has had many home care workers. Sometimes she has seen a new worker every day, but even the ones who are with her for a while know or care very little about her disease. For two years she was fortunate to have a worker who learned all she could about ALS, but that worker is now moving to another city.

Whom Should You Contact to Arrange for Home Care?

If your family member is being discharged from a hospital or is an outpatient in a hospital, speak to the hospital social worker or discharge planner about arranging home care. If the person is still in her home, speak to your family physician or any other health professional you are in contact with (physiotherapist, speech therapist, social worker, etc.). A professional will be able to give you the right number to call for the regional home care authority. The case manager you deal with there will be able to give you information about the conditions for eligibility (see Chapter 4 at p. 36), the services available, which services are free, and when user fees are charged and what they will amount to.

PRIVATE HOME CARE

Kathleen was determined to live in her home until the day of her death. She lived to be 95, and needed 24-hour supervision in her home for the last 10 years of her life. The cost of the care was about $70,000 a year, of which her provincial home care program only covered a very small part. (She did not need 24-hour nursing care, which would have been much more expensive, only occasional nursing visits.) Fortunately, she was independently wealthy—but there was not much money left when she died. If she had lived a couple of years longer, she would not have been able to stay in her home.

Publicly subsidized home care does not provide enough care for many people who remain in their homes. When that is the case, family members and friends or community volunteers have to take up the slack, or else extra care has to be purchased from the regional authority or community organization that provides the subsidized care. When even that is not enough—or not good enough—it's time to hire your own health care worker.

Home Health Care Staffing Agencies

You can hire home health care workers privately through businesses that provide them on a contract basis. You can find these businesses listed in the yellow pages under "nurses," "home health services," or "employment agencies — domestic help." You can contract with these agencies for the services of registered nurses, registered practical nurses, health care aides, personal attendants, homemakers and companions. The workers are employees of the agency, and are paid by the agency. You pay the agency for the services on an hourly basis (although you may be required to pay for a minimum number of hours). One of the advantages of using these agencies is that you do not have the legal responsibilities of an employer (see below at p. 92). The major disadvantage, however, is that you may not have direct control over how many different workers get sent to care for your family member, or how good they are.

Before using an agency, ask its representative questions about

- the workers that the agency uses: what are their qualifications? how much experience do they have? does the agency screen the workers and check their references? how long have the workers been employed by the agency? are the workers insured and/or bonded?

- how much choice you will have about the worker who cares for your family member: can you interview a proposed worker first, or will she simply be assigned to the job? will the same worker care for your family member or will there be different workers all the time?

- work hours: are workers available 24 hours a day? can you get a worker who will meet your time needs—by the hour, by shift, or around the clock? how much notice do you need to give if you want a worker to come?

- what will the agency do if you are not satisfied with the worker who is assigned to the job: will the agency send someone else instead? will the agency accept responsibility if the worker steals anything or causes any damage?

Establishing a Good Relationship with a Health Care Worker

If your family member isn't used to being cared for by people outside the family, having a stranger come in may be an uncomfortable experience. Here are some suggestions for starting the relationship off on the right footing, and keeping it that way.

- Be honest about the care needed. Don't let your family member's or your embarrassment prevent the health care worker from doing a good job. And if there are any unusual family circumstances that the worker should know about (say an all-out war between a couple of the people living in the house), be honest about them too if they might affect how the health care worker does his job.

- Be specific about things you want done or don't want done. For example, tell the worker that no smoking is permitted in the house if that's a concern, point out your family member's preferred clothing or lotions or soap if the worker will be bathing and dressing her, show the worker what dishes and cookware to use if she will be in the kitchen.

- Tell the worker about your family member's routine. Let the worker know what time your family member gets up, breakfasts, bathes, takes medication, has a nap, watches a favourite TV program, goes out for medical or other appointments. Tell the worker about your own routine if necessary. ("The bathroom is mine, *mine*, MINE while I'm getting ready for work!")

- Don't micromanage the worker, but keep in regular touch with her and let her know how she is doing. Tell her when you're pleased with the care or with how she gets along with your family member. Also tell her when things aren't right. If being critical to someone's face bothers you, speak to the supervisor at the agency, and he will speak to the worker for you. If you continue to have problems with a worker, ask the agency to send someone else.

Employing Someone to Look after Your Family Member at Home

If you do not want to use the services of an agency—for example, if you are looking for a full-time live-in caregiver—you will have to consider hiring someone directly to do the job. This will bring you into a completely new world, the world of employment law.

The Hiring Process

You will have to find candidates for the job of caring for your family member, interview those you are interested in, and finally choose someone for the job.

You can find candidates yourself by advertising in the newspaper or by posting notices at a community college or university that has a nursing program, an Employment Insurance office, your workplace, or in local stores that accept community notices. You can ask for recommendations from doctors, social workers, agencies or charitable organizations you have dealt with, or acquaintances who have gone through the same thing. Or you can go to an employment agency that specializes in health care or domestic help. If you use an agency, you will have to pay a fee, which is often equal to one month's salary of the person you are hiring. Some agencies pre-screen job candidates by interviewing them and checking their references, and will guarantee to find a replacement if you hire someone who does not work out after a short time.

Interview the most qualified candidates. The purpose of the interview is to find out whether the person has the skill and ability to do the job, will be caring, honest and reliable, and is someone your family member can get along with. If you find a candidate you are interested in, check the person's references before offering him the job. Do this even if the candidate came from an agency. You want to confirm the candidate's qualifications and employment history and to find out as much as you can about the candidate's personal skills.

Being an Employer

Once you hire someone, you have many responsibilities as an employer. You should contact your provincial Employment Standards office for detailed information about what's required in your province, but the following will give you the general idea. You have to:

- Pay your employee—in most provinces, you must pay your employee at least the minimum wage, pay overtime (usually at the rate of one and a half times the usual pay) if she works extra hours, and allow your employee to take a paid vacation after completing one full year of employment. If the employee lives with your family member, you may be entitled to deduct an amount (set by law) from her pay for room and board.

- Remit taxes on behalf of your employee—you must deduct income taxes, Canada Pension Plan contributions and Employment Insurance contributions from your employee's wages and remit them to Revenue Canada. You must also contribute to CPP and EI on your employee's behalf. You may also have to pay employment-related provincial taxes, such as a payroll tax or health insurance tax.

- Provide a safe workplace for your employee—you must take reasonable steps to provide a safe and healthy workplace for your employee, and you may have to pay for coverage of your employee under your provincial workers' compensation legislation.

Firing an Employee

If you want to fire your employee, you can only fire him on the spot if you have **just cause**. The following are commonly considered just cause for firing an employee:

- dishonesty toward the employer, such as theft from the employer
- disobedience or insubordination, such as refusing to obey reasonable orders or talking back
- drunkenness or drug abuse that affects the employee's work
- repeated absences or lateness without a reasonable medical or personal excuse
- incompetence or carelessness

If you don't have just cause, you must either give the employee **reasonable notice** that her employment will end (that is, tell her that she must leave at the end of a stated period) or else give her **pay in lieu of notice** (that is, tell her that she must leave immediately, but pay her what she would have earned during a notice period). Every province has legislation setting out the minimum notice that you must give an employee, often amounting to one week for every year the employee has worked for the employer. (Again, contact your Employment Standards office.) An employee you have fired may decide to sue you for **wrongful dismissal**. If this happens, speak to a litigation lawyer.

9 EXTENDED CARE FACILITIES

When home care is not or is no longer an option, you'll have to find your family member a facility where she can get the kind of care she needs. Your family member may qualify for a government-subsidized facility (see Chapter 4 at p. 38), or she may have to or may choose to live in a private facility such as supportive housing or a retirement home. Whatever kind of extended care facility your family member is headed for, you need to know how to choose the best of what's available.

HOW TO CHOOSE A PRIVATELY FINANCED FACILITY

You'll want to look over a private facility, whether it's a seniors' apartment building or a retirement home, to see whether it suits your family member. Think about its location, what the rooms and common rooms are like, the general atmosphere, the state the other residents are in, whether the food is good. Ask the managers of the facility:

• What different types of accommodation are available and what is the rental charge for each type?

- What provincial landlord and tenant laws apply to the facility?
- What packages of care services and meals are available, and what is the charge for each package?
- What services and meals are available on a pay-for-use basis?
- How often can charges for accommodation or services and meals be increased?
- Can residents bring their own furniture?
- Is there a secure storage area for residents' belongings?
- How many staff are available during the day? during the night? How many residents are they responsible for? What are the staff's qualifications?
- Is there an emergency call system?
- What are the security arrangements for people who may suffer from confusion or memory impairment?
- What emergency plans are in place?
- What will happen if your family member needs more care after a while?
- Are there any activities?
- What are the rules about visitors and visiting hours?
- Is the facility a member of a provincial organization that sets standards for accommodation and care?
- What is their procedure for dealing with complaints?

In some provinces, the owners of private facilities are required by law to provide prospective residents with an information package that they can examine before they sign the agreement. The package answers some of the questions listed above, but not necessarily all of them.

Before your family member moves in, he (or you if you are managing his affairs) will have to enter into a written contract with the facility. It would probably be wise to have a lawyer who is familiar with private care facilities, or at least with landlord and tenant law, look over any agreement before you sign it. Or contact the provincial bureau that deals with landlord and tenant matters, or a local community organization that has information about private care facilities and experience in dealing with related issues, or the provincial organization (such as a provincial nursing homes association) that sets voluntary standards for private facilities.

HOW TO CHOOSE A GOVERNMENT-SUBSIDIZED FACILITY

When a person is found to be eligible for a place in a government-subsidized facility, the regional health care authority usually provides her and her family with a list of facilities in the region. Unless there's only one publicly subsidized facility in your area, or only one facility that can provide the necessary level of care, you and your family member will be asked to choose several of the listed facilities and your family member will be put on a waiting list for the first bed that becomes available in one of those facilities. In some large urban areas, you may have to choose among 15 or 20 facilities. The facilities may be spread out over quite a wide area, and you will probably know absolutely nothing about them, unless you know people who are or have been in them. How do you make your choice?

You'll have to make an investigation. You may be able to get help to do this. The case manager at the regional authority, or the social worker at the hospital (if your family member is going from the hospital to the facility), or your family doctor may be able to tell you something about each facility. Or you may be able to hire a consultant who specializes in helping people find appropriate care for themselves or a family member (see Chapter 3 at p. 31). Whether you're choosing a facility on your own or with more experienced help, here are the kinds of things to look for to help you narrow the choice.

- Location—Is the facility easy for visiting family and friends to reach? Is it close to home? Is it accessible by public transit?

- The doctor—Can a resident continue to be looked after by his family doctor, or are all residents expected to use the facility's doctor? If the latter, what is the doctor's reputation among staff and patients? Is the doctor available on a regular basis? Is the doctor on 24-hour call to the facility? Is the doctor willing to consult with a patient's family?

- The nursing staff—Is a registered nurse on the premises 24 hours a day, or only available part of the day? What is the ratio of nursing staff to patients—in the daytime, in the evening, and at night? What ongoing training do the nursing staff get (for example, in dealing with Alzheimer's patients, if your family member has Alzheimer's)?

- Other professionals—Can physiotherapy or occupational therapy or speech therapy (or whatever other services your family member may require) be easily arranged?

- The health care aides—Do there seem to be enough aides to look after all the residents? Do patients look well cared for? How do the aides treat the patients—are they pleasant and efficient, or are they rough or short-tempered or hurried or patronizing with them? What is the ratio of health care aides to residents—in the daytime, in the evening, and at night?

- The other residents—Are there residents wandering around who look disoriented, or dirty or uncared for? Are there residents who appear to be aggressive? Are there many residents in restraints (for example, tied into wheelchairs or chairs)? What is the facility's policy on restraints? (See below at p. 102.) Do people needing different levels of care seem to be mixed together—are people with all their wits about them mingling with people who are seriously mentally impaired?

- The common areas—Are they bright or well lit without glare, clean, pleasantly and comfortably furnished? Is there enough room in the dining room for all residents, or are some served in their rooms or in corridors? Are there handrails, ramps, non-skid floors? Are there bathrooms nearby? Are exits well marked? Is there a garden that residents can enjoy in good weather? Is there a pleasant view from any of the common rooms?

- The atmosphere—Generally, does the facility seem comfortable and (if possible) home-like, or does it seem, well, institutional? Does everything smell fresh? Is there a lot of noise? Is there no noise or movement at all?

- The bedrooms—Are they large enough for the number of people in each? If rooms are shared, are there privacy dividers or curtains? Are rooms large enough to manoeuvre a wheelchair or walker? Is there adequate closet and drawer space? Is there good lighting (a 70-year-old needs a lot more light than a 20-year-old), and will a resident be able to see to read in bed? Is there a telephone or telephone jack? Is there a TV hook-up in the bedroom, or only in the common rooms? Is there a nurse call bell within easy reach of the bed? Does the facility's paging system blare into the bedrooms? Can residents bring in some of their own furniture—how much and how large? Can residents put up pictures or other decorations on the walls, or have plants?

- Moves—Under what circumstances would a person be moved out of his room to another room or another floor or wing? Will you and your family member be notified beforehand? If it is likely that your family member won't remain in the room or section he starts out in, look at rooms in the other sections or floors as well.

- The bathrooms—How many residents share a bathroom—is there one for each room? One between rooms? Only a communal bathroom—if so, how far is it from the farthest rooms? Are there grab bars, raised toilet seats, non-slip surfaces in tub and shower, nurse call bells, plenty of room for a wheelchair or walker plus a health care aide or two? Is there special equipment for people who are disabled, such as shower chairs and chair lifts?

- The food—Is there good food, plenty of it, and is it attractively served? Is the menu varied? Is there a qualified dietician in charge of the menu? Are special diets available? If your family member needs a meal supplement, who pays for it? Is room service available if necessary? Can family or friends bring in food for the resident? Can family and friends arrange to eat with the resident in the dining room? (If possible, eat a meal at the facility as part of your investigation.)

- Security—If your family member is confused and likely to wander, are doors to dangerous places (street, parking lot, kitchen, boiler room, equipment room) secured? Is it still easy for staff to get patients out of the building if there's an emergency such as a fire? Do staff watch the patients carefully?

- Activities—What social activities and recreational programs (including shopping) are there that your family member might participate in? Do residents look as though they're enjoying the activities? Are there any activities for those who cannot leave their beds, or who are confused? Are there religious services? Are there volunteers who come in, and are family members welcome to act as volunteers?

- Personal grooming—Is there a hairdresser available? A barber? A manicurist or pedicurist?

- Visitors—What are the visiting hours? Who may visit (are children and pets allowed)? Can alcohol be brought in? Is smoking allowed? Ask if there is a brochure about visitors' rules.

- Personal belongings—What arrangements are there for safe-keeping of money and other valuable items? Do staff recommend that no valuables be brought in? Is it possible to make arrangements for safe storage of larger items such as suitcases or pieces of furniture?

- Language—Are there staff, volunteers or other residents who speak your family member's language?

- Hospitalization or vacation—How long can the resident leave the facility for and still be guaranteed a space and preferably the same room?

- Laundry—Are laundry services available? Is there an extra charge? Do staff recommend sending only indestructible clothing to it?

- Financial matters—What are the rates for the room your family member would prefer? What additional charges are there? Does the facility issue an itemized account along with the monthly bill?

- Ownership of the facility—Who owns the facility—the municipal government, the provincial government, a religious group, a charitable organization, a private owner?

Waiting Lists

Most facilities have waiting lists—usually fairly long ones. It may be a matter of several months before *any* of your choices (much less your first
choice) has available space. In some regions, a central agency may keep an
up-to-date waiting list for all publicly subsidized facilities and will notify
you when one of your chosen facilities comes up; in other regions, you may
have to keep in regular touch with each facility you are interested in—if
they have lots of potential customers, they may not care whether the first
who came was the first served. When a bed does become available, your
family member may have to move in immediately (within two or three
days) or lose the space. If it's not possible to move in that quickly, you may
be able to keep the space for a short time by making the co-payment (see
Chapter 4 at p. 38) for the month.

If your family member could not get into the facility that was your first
or second choice and had to accept a bed in a less desirable facility, ask the
facilities you prefer or the regional authority if they will keep your family
member on the waiting list and accept a transfer if a bed becomes available
later. However, a second move will be just as traumatic as the first, so you may
want to hang on until you can get into your first choice.

If your family member is in a hospital, there may be a "first available bed"
policy under which a person is supposed to go to the first facility with an
opening. If it's really, really the wrong facility, stick to your guns and wait for
the right one. The hospital will threaten to bill the patient and family a large
amount for staying when the patient could have left. There's a legal limit to
what they can charge and it may be quite a bit less than they say. Get more
information about the hospital's legal rights from your doctor, a health care
consultant, a social worker, your provincial ministry of health, an organization like the Advocacy Centre for the Elderly (Toronto), or a lawyer if necessary. Reason with the hospital administration and explain why it's not
acceptable for your family member to go to the offered facility.

Contract with the Facility

On admission, the resident or family may be asked to sign an agreement with
the facility. As with a private facility, it's a good idea to have a lawyer who is
familiar with extended care facilities look over any agreement before you
sign it. Or contact the provincial ministry of health's extended or long-term
care division, or a local community organization that has information about
contracts with these facilities, or the provincial nursing homes association.

DEALING WITH PROBLEMS IN EXTENDED CARE FACILITIES

The care in some facilities is great. But it's not great in every facility, or not great all the time, and you may find that you face some problems. Residents in institutions and families of residents are often very reluctant to complain about conditions—and perhaps with reason. They're afraid of retaliation against the resident, and the family can't be there 24 hours a day to make sure that the resident isn't ignored or neglected or insulted or treated roughly. If the problem is serious enough that you might think of taking legal action, that requires time, money and your attention, and if you're looking after a family member who is very unwell, you probably have none of these to spare. So what do you do if there's a problem? There are a number of things to try, and what you do must depend on the situation and your own judgment.

Advance Decisions about Hospitalization

When a patient is admitted to a facility, he may be asked to decide in advance about whether he wants to be hospitalized if he becomes seriously ill. The patient or his substitute decision maker may be asked to sign a **non-treatment document** headed "Do Not Hospitalize" (DNH) or "Do Not Transfer." (In some facilities, the patient or family may be asked to sign a "Do Not Resuscitate" (DNR) document, but this is rather pointless in most extended care facilities since they do not normally have the equipment required to resuscitate a dying patient. See Chapter 12 at p. 130.) Signing these documents indicates that the patient (or substitute decision maker) does not want aggressive care to prolong his life if he becomes very ill but only wants palliative care (pain control) to keep him comfortable until he dies. If your family member doesn't want to make a blanket decision like that in advance, he should not sign the documents. There may come a time later when he wants to tell the facility that he should be allowed to stay there to die and not be rushed to the hospital. Indeed, some people have a horror of being taken from the place they're accustomed to and put in a hospital, and they're more than willing to agree to a DNH order. Some provinces have "Degree of Intervention" orders, which cover a wider range of possibilities according to the kind of illness or injury that potentially may occur, from palliative care in the facility to care in a hospital to resuscitation in a hospital.

A doctor usually also has to sign a non-treatment order and may raise objections because of personal moral or religious feelings, or because of concern about her own legal position if a patient dies after refusing treatment. You and your family member and the facility and the doctor may need to have a discussion to resolve this problem; you may have to get another doctor. Some doctors, however, may take the opposite view and issue DNR or DNH orders about a patient without speaking to the resident or family members. After you and your family member (or you alone if you are the substitute decision maker) have decided what you want, make sure you know what's on your family member's chart about treatment.

Personal Care Attendants

There are many more personal care attendants than nurses in extended care facilities, and provincial regulations may not require a trained nurse to be on the premises at all times. Because personal care attendants do not have the legal right to perform certain kinds of procedures—in particular, do not have the right to give injections—you may sometimes run into a problem with administration of medication, especially painkillers. If your family member is in pain or needs an injection for another reason, the facility staff may tell you that they can't give injections. If this happens, insist that a trained nurse who can give injections be located and give the medication. Note that the medication must have been prescribed by a doctor—nurses cannot prescribe drugs—so you may have to get the facility's doctor involved too.

Restraint of Patients

Facilities restrain patients to prevent them from wandering if they are confused and to prevent falls. Restraints are any restrictions on a person's freedom to move around the facility. These restrictions might include

- locked doors
- elevators that can only be operated by staff
- refusal of permission to leave the facility or part of the facility
- removal of power from a motorized wheelchair
- bed rails that lock in the "up" position
- restraining belts that keep a patient in a chair, wheelchair or bed
- a geri-chair or a chair with a table across it
- restraining vests or "posie jackets"
- sedative drugs

Facilities may claim that restraining patients with bedrails and belts and tables across chairs prevents falls, but some studies have indicated that these kinds of restraints do not prevent injuries from falls very effectively and in fact *cause* fall-related injuries—because the patient is trying to get out of the restraint to go somewhere (often the toilet). If the facility wants to restrain your family member, make sure that the staff keep a close watch on restrained patients and don't just go away and leave them for extended periods.

Several provinces have passed laws about restraints. They usually specify that a restraint is only to be used when it is necessary to protect the resident from injury to herself or others, that a doctor must have given a written order approving the restraint, that the restraint must not cause injury or discomfort, and that any patient who is restrained must be checked by staff (in some provinces by a nurse) regularly. Depending on the province, "regularly" can mean from every half hour to every two hours. In one province, family members must be consulted before restraints are used.

If you do not want the facility to use restraints, the facility will probably require you to sign a document saying that it will not be held liable in the event that the patient injures himself in a fall. (The patient and/or family may still be able to sue the facility if there's a fall, especially if the facility didn't reach a minimum standard of care in looking after the patient.) If your family member poses a danger to other residents because of her behaviour and you don't want restraints, the facility might refuse to accept your family member in the first place or might, once she is living in the facility, take action to evict her if she is putting other residents at risk.

Other Problems

There are a number of other problems that can arise in facilities:

- The food isn't very good, or there may not be very much of it.

- Thefts of personal property occur—the thieves may be other patients, or staff members, or even outsiders who manage to slip in.

- The facility is understaffed, so staff members never have time to attend to residents properly. Residents who aren't mobile enough to get to a bathroom by themselves may be kept in diapers, or may end up sitting or lying in their own urine because staff members don't come promptly when called. Residents' clothes may be put on inside out, or their hair may not be brushed and their teeth cleaned.

- There is little privacy—residents' doors are not usually lockable and other patients (particularly those with mental problems) may wander in uninvited and unannounced, even in the middle of the night; staff may not bother to close doors when assisting residents with toilet or bathing activities.

- Group activities may be geared to the ability levels of the least functional patients, and therefore be excruciatingly boring to those residents who still have their wits; there may be pressure on residents to join in activities that they would rather pass up.

- Patients with dementia may not be properly supervised and may attack and injure other patients.
- There may be inadequate air conditioning during a hot summer.
- The rooms and common areas may not be attractive, and may not even be very clean; equipment may be in a bad state of repair.
- Everyone may have to receive care from the facility's doctor (rather than their own family doctor) and you may not find this doctor satisfactory.

What to Do about Problems

You have to accept that a facility is not your home and it's not run exactly as you would run your home, and that the staff are not your family member's personal staff and have many other patients to look after. However, you should not ignore problems that are more than an inconvenience.

First Try to Prevent Problems

- Choose the facility as carefully as you can in the first place.
- Spend plenty of time at the facility with your family member and show that you care how your family member is treated. Get to know the staff. Be pleasant with them, and compliment them when they're doing a good job with your family member. Gently bring minor problems to their attention so they don't get the idea that they can cut corners with your family member—and thank them when the problem is corrected.
- Don't leave anything at the facility that you don't want to get lost, stolen or damaged. (This may include dentures!) Some provinces require facilities to open a trust account in a bank or trust company to hold residents' personal funds. Whether or not this is the case in your province, the patient should keep little or no money in her room in the facility.

Then Try to Correct Problems

- Take more care of your family member yourself. Bring meals. Help with bathing and grooming. Take the laundry home and do it yourself. Entertain your family member.
- Hire a personal care aide to provide more care for your family member. You may be able to find another family with someone in the facility who will share the aide and the cost with you.
- Put the problem before the residents' council—if provincial legislation requires a residents' council in the facility and if the council is active—or before the family advisory committee or family council if there is such a group.

- Find out when staff meetings concerning residents' care are held and attend a meeting to raise your concerns (calmly and rationally). Take a supporter with you if you're afraid of feeling completely outnumbered.
- Complain. If you make the complaint in person or over the phone, follow up with a letter. If you start with a letter, follow up with a telephone call or a meeting.
  - Identify the problem area or person involved—is it a nurse or nursing aide or nursing care generally? Is it the food? Is it the activities? Then find out who is in charge of that area (who's director of nursing? of nutrition? of activities?) and speak to that person. It's best to be reasonable and polite during your discussion.
  - If speaking to the director responsible for the problem area doesn't solve the problem, then go to the administrator of the facility. Continue to be reasonable and to keep your temper.
  - If the problem is one that affects many residents and not just your family member, organize other families to talk to administration as well.
  - If it appears that you're not getting anywhere yourself, consider bringing in an advocate to represent you—your family doctor, a health care consultant, a friend who's more imposing and a better speaker, or a lawyer if the problem really causes you concern.
  - Go over the administrator's head. In a privately owned facility that's run on a for-profit basis, go to the owner of the facility. In a non-profit facility, go to the board of directors.
  - Contact the provincial Ministry of Health. If you make a complaint, the ministry has an obligation to investigate.
  - If the problem revolves around the actions of a nurse, contact the provincial College of Nurses, which will investigate your complaint. If it's a doctor, contact the provincial College of Physicians and Surgeons. Some other health professionals, such as physiotherapists and occupational therapists, also have governing colleges in most provinces.
- Call the police if the problem is theft of something valuable, or an assault on your family member by another resident or by staff, or abuse or neglect by the staff that is not immediately dealt with by administration.

Get Your Family Member Out of There

If your attempts to solve the problem aren't working, get in touch with the regional health care authority that deals with admissions to facilities, and start looking for another facility.

LIABILITY OF A FACILITY

A facility is responsible for keeping its residents safe and (insofar as their pre-existing state of health allows) well, and to keep their personal property safe. If the facility doesn't fulfill its responsibility, because it

- does not supervise patients with the result, for example, that a patient falls down stairs or is attacked by another patient

- does not supervise staff with the result, for example, that a staff member abuses or attacks a patient

- does not supervise work on the premises with the result, for example, that residents suffer food poisoning or inhale irritating paint fumes

- does not maintain the premises and equipment with the result, for example, that a resident is injured when a bed collapses or a stair rail gives way

- does not safeguard residents' property with the result, for example, that it is lost, destroyed or stolen

then the facility can be sued by the resident (or, in some cases by her estate after the resident dies), and in some cases by the resident's family, for compensation. (For more about lawsuits, see Chapter 23.)

BILL OF RIGHTS

A few provinces have a "bill of rights" for the residents of extended care facilities. Some of the rights in these bills exist anyway (such as the rights to be free from abuse, to give or refuse consent to treatment, to have medical records kept confidential, to exercise the rights of a citizen), whether the province has a bill of rights or not, because they are part of the common law or are included in the *Canadian Charter of Rights and Freedoms*; other rights may be almost impossible to enforce. Perhaps a bill of rights is mostly useful simply for reminding the facility owners, administrators and staff how to treat residents. Ontario's bill of rights is enforceable as a contract between the resident and the facility. This means that if the facility does not act in accordance with the bill of rights, the resident has the right to start a lawsuit either to get damages in compensation, or to make the facility act in the way the bill of rights says it must. If this seems like a difficult way to get the facility to take proper care of your family member, you're not alone in thinking that.

BILL OF RIGHTS (ONTARIO)

1. Every resident has the right to be treated with courtesy and respect and in a way that fully recognizes the resident's dignity and individuality and to be free from mental and physical abuse.
2. Every resident has the right to be properly sheltered, fed, clothed, groomed and cared for in a manner consistent with his or her needs.
3. Every resident has the right to be told who is responsible for and who is providing the resident's direct care.
4. Every resident has the right to be afforded privacy in treatment and in caring for his or her personal needs.
5. Every resident has the right to keep in his or her room and display personal possessions, pictures and furnishings in keeping with safety requirements and other residents' rights.
6. Every resident has the right,
    i) to be informed of his or her medical condition, treatment and proposed course of treatment,
    ii) to give or refuse consent to treatment, including medication, in accordance with the law and to be informed of the consequences of giving or refusing consent,
    iii) to have the opportunity to participate fully in making any decision and obtaining an independent medical opinion concerning any aspect of his or her care, including any decision concerning his or her admission, discharge or transfer to or from a nursing home, and
    iv) to have his or her medical records kept confidential in accordance with the law.
7. Every resident has the right to receive reactivation and assistance towards independence consistent with his or her requirements.
8. Every resident who is being considered for restraints has the right to be fully informed about the procedures and the consequences of receiving or refusing them.
9. Every resident has the right to communicate in confidence, to receive visitors of his or her choice and to consult in private with any person without interference.
10. Every resident whose death is likely to be imminent has the right to have members of the resident's family present twenty-four hours per day.
11. Every resident has the right to designate a person to receive information concerning any transfer or emergency hospitalization of the resident and where a person is so designated to have that person so informed forthwith.
12. Every resident has the right to exercise the rights of a citizen and to raise concerns or recommend changes in policies and services on behalf of himself or herself or others to the residents' council, nursing home staff, government

officials or any other person inside or outside the nursing home, without fear of restraint, interference, coercion, discrimination or reprisal.

13. Every resident has the right to form friendships, to enjoy relationships and to participate in the residents' council.

14. Every resident has the right to meet privately with his or her spouse in a room that assures privacy and where both spouses are residents in the same nursing home, they have a right to share a room according to their wishes, if an appropriate room is available.

15. Every resident has a right to pursue social, cultural, religious and other interests, to develop his or her potential and to be given reasonable provisions by the nursing home to accommodate these pursuits.

16. Every resident has the right to be informed in writing of any law, rule or policy affecting the operation of the long-term care facility and of the procedures for initiating complaints.

17. Every resident has the right to manage his or her own financial affairs where the resident is able to do so, and where the resident's financial affairs are managed by the nursing home, to receive a quarterly accounting of any transactions undertaken on his or her behalf and to be assured that the resident's property is managed solely on the resident's behalf.

18. Every resident has the right to live in a safe and clean environment.

19. Every resident has the right to be given access to protected areas outside the nursing home in order to enjoy outdoor activity, unless the physical setting makes this impossible.

PART IV

DARK HOURS

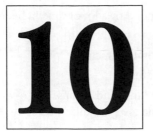

PAIN CONTROL

Most people fear dying because they think it involves great pain. You may have looked into this chapter expecting to be scared out of your wits. You may think you'll hear that dying means unbearable, unrelievable pain, and that legalizing euthanasia or physician-assisted suicide is the only thing we can do to save ourselves and the people we love. Well, that's not what this chapter is going to say at all. In fact, this chapter is fairly encouraging.

In North America, and perhaps in western society as a whole, we have almost no images of a peaceful death. We read the news, we watch television, we go to the movies, and we come away from all of them thinking that most people die horribly by being blown up or by suffering long drawn-out agonies from terrible diseases. But in reality, many people—maybe as many as half or even two-thirds—go through the dying process with no pain. The others experience pain (it is common with cancer) but it can almost always be either completely relieved or made bearable if the right steps are taken.

WHAT KIND OF PAIN?

Kinds of pain that terminally ill people have may include

• in cancer, pain at the site of the cancer

- muscle spasms, leg cramps, and backaches from spending a lot of time in bed
- bedsores (raw patches where the bed puts pressure on the skin)

    In addition, there may be other kinds of discomfort such as

- nausea and vomiting, from the disease or from drugs
- breathing problems, as secretions build up in the lungs and as muscles grow weaker; people with lung cancer and emphysema are particularly likely to have breathing difficulties
- increasing muscle weakness and inability to control the muscles
- incontinence of bladder and bowels as muscles weaken, constipation caused by painkillers and other drugs or by the breakdown of the body
- loss of appetite
- insomnia and nightmares

DYING DOESN'T HAVE TO BE PAINFUL

Here's the part where we're going to scare you. People—lots of them—do suffer pain in the dying process and that pain is not relieved. But we've just told you that most pain can be relieved, so what's going on here? A few things.

- Many people think that dying is supposed to be painful, or that their pain is a kind that can't be relieved—or they may even believe that their pain or discomfort is something that's too embarrassing to talk about—and so they don't complain about how they feel. They just put up with it. But they shouldn't put up with it. They should demand good pain control, which is part of the good medical care that every patient is entitled to. As for being embarrassed, try to remember that health care workers have seen pretty well everything there is to see and they're not there to pass judgment or to make people feel ashamed of their bodies.
- Nurses may be instructed by doctors' orders only to give medication to relieve pain when a patient asks for it—so a patient should not assume that her pain will be treated automatically. The patient and family must be sure to ask for medication if there is pain, and to keep asking until the pain is properly relieved. If there is continuous pain, pain medication should be given at regularly scheduled times rather than on request. Pain needs to be assessed on an ongoing basis, and treatment or medication needs to be adjusted if the amount of pain changes.
- Doctors, including specialists such as oncologists, do not always view pain control as a priority. If the doctor or nurse in charge doesn't seem very interested in pain control, or says that the pain will lessen as treatment

progresses and not to worry about it now, then the patient and family should insist that a pain specialist or palliative care specialist be called in.

• Most doctors have little or no training in pain relief—they don't know what the best drugs are to relieve certain kinds of pain or discomfort. This is why you may need to ask for a pain specialist rather than simply assuming that the specialist treating the disease is doing everything possible to treat the pain as well.

• Some people have a higher risk of not receiving proper pain relief. These may include patients in nursing homes who are very elderly, who have dementia (such as Alzheimer's), or who are taking a lot of other medications. They may also include children, especially very young children who cannot explain how much they hurt. Treating children for pain can still be rather difficult because a child's metabolism (the rate at which the body processes a drug) is different from an adult's and because less research has been done on relief of children's pain.

• Many patients and their families are afraid of strong opioid pain relievers like morphine, and so they refuse them. They think that such drugs are a "last resort" only given to those who are going to die very soon, or that they are very addictive. In fact, morphine is not particularly addictive when given for pain relief, and it's a safe and effective drug that's not just reserved for those who only have days or hours to live.

• Many people may refuse strong pain relievers like morphine because they're concerned about the side-effects, which can include drowsiness, confusion, nausea and constipation. However, these side-effects can usually be easily managed by adjusting dosage or adding another drug.

Emotional Pain

There is a link between the emotions and pain. Emotional pain—fear and anxiety—can also cause physical symptoms such as intestinal pain, aching in the back or neck or head, inability to sleep, dizziness or shortness of breath, or just a general sense of feeling unwell. If a person is frightened or upset, the pain that he is feeling may be made worse.

People who are dying are afraid of physical pain but they are also afraid of being abandoned by the people they love or feel close to or simply need at this time. This is not an irrational fear. When someone they love is dying, many people start to withdraw. Family and friends may simply find it too painful to watch a loved one die, or they may feel that there's no point in being with the dying person because there's nothing they can do to help. They may stop visiting the dying person, or visit only by phone or letter, or come only occasionally and not stay long, or spend time with the dying person but act distant and avoid touching her. This withdrawal from a dying person is natural, but it has terrible consequences. The person who is dying will feel very lonely, deserted and unloved. And the person who survives may feel guilt and self-hatred and may have more trouble coping with the death when it comes.

WHAT CAN BE DONE TO RELIEVE PAIN?

We've already told you a couple of important things that can be done to control physical pain:

- Be sure to *ask* for pain relief.
- Insist on seeing a pain specialist if the doctors you're dealing with seem unable to provide pain relief.

There are many other ways of helping to bring relief to a person in pain if drugs have not been completely effective. For example:

- Tranquillizers can partially relieve pain and other symptoms caused by fear and tension.
- Sometimes people who are in a lot of pain while they are in the hospital get immediate relief simply by coming back home.
- If a person who is in pain has other things to think about, the pain may be lessened. Conversation, interesting books, funny videos, a pet to talk to and cuddle—all of these things can help.
- Listening to favourite music can, according to recent studies, reduce pain significantly.
- Alcohol can be an effective pain reliever and tranquillizer (no, you don't have to drink a whole bottle of whisky like in the cowboy movies before someone uses a Bowie knife to dig a slug out of the hero—a glass or two of wine a day is enough). Always ask the doctor about alcohol and its possible effects with prescribed medication.
- It's possible to lessen to some extent the physical pain of a person who is frightened and upset by staying with him, holding his hand, listening to him if he wants to talk, showing interest in him and affection for him.
- Massage, physiotherapy, acupuncture or hypnosis can help.
- Fluid in the lungs or bowels that is building up painful pressure can be drained, and oxygen therapy can ease breathing problems.
- In difficult cases, nerve connections can be deadened: temporarily, by injecting local anesthetic directly into the nerve connection; or permanently, by injecting certain chemicals.

- In rare cases, pain centres can be deadened by brain surgery or spinal surgery.

What about the very small percentage of people whose pain cannot be relieved—people who suffer what is called "intractable pain"? Statistics for the general population of dying patients suggest that as many as five of every 100 dying people have intractable pain—although if you talk to a pain specialist, she will probably cite a much lower figure than that. In cases where pain really cannot be effectively treated, something known as "terminal sedation" can be used in the last few days of life. In effect, the dying person is put into a deep sleep. But intractable pain can go on for weeks or months before terminal sedation is an option.

An elderly man who was dying of cancer suffered severe pain that his pain specialist was unable to ease, despite his best efforts. The doctor was so distressed by his patient's pain that he began to think that legalizing euthanasia might not be such a terrible idea. But despite his unrelieved pain, which lasted for nearly 18 months before he died, this man never once suggested that he would like to die in order to end the pain. In fact, he clung fiercely to life.

What about Illegal Drugs?

If the drugs that are legally available are used properly, there doesn't usually need to be any question of using drugs like heroin and marijuana. The problem is that many doctors do not know how to make the best use of the drugs that are available. However, in a few cases, patients think that only an illegal drug can make them feel better.

Although heroin is regularly used for pain relief in many countries, in Canada and the United States it is not. It's not completely outlawed in Canada; it can be legally prescribed in a hospital setting, but it almost never is. Morphine is the drug that is used. Heroin and morphine are closely related. They are both derived from opium, and they provide very similar pain relief. The main difference between the two is that heroin is stronger, and a smaller dose is required to relieve the same amount of pain. This, and the fact that it dissolves more easily than morphine, make it better for injection. There is also another drug available in Canada called hydromorphone. It is very potent and very soluble. Morphine and hydromorphone, if properly used, do just as good a job of relieving pain as heroin. Don't even think of buying heroin on the street—you have no way of knowing whether it's very pure (and therefore very powerful) and likely to kill you within a short time of injecting it.

Marijuana is a slightly different story. Although it is illegal, it is generally considered a fairly harmless drug, and some people believe that it controls nausea and vomiting associated with chemotherapy, and helps symptoms associated with AIDS, such as nausea, loss of appetite and anxiety. However, there are legal prescription drugs available that are effective in most cases for these problems. A number of studies about marijuana as a medicine have been done. It has a known sedative effect; but apart from that, some studies say that marijuana hasn't been scientifically shown to be medically effective; others say that it is effective in some cases to control pain and nausea. Pharmaceutical companies are investigating marijuana and creating drugs based on its chemical components. A drug derived from tetrahydrocannabinol, the active ingredient in marijuana, is already available to treat nausea and vomiting.

There are some people who have tried everything else and only seem to get relief when they take marijuana, and so they grow it or buy it illegally. If you are caught in possession of marijuana for medicinal purposes, you can be charged with possession of a controlled drug.

Jim, who had been suffering from AIDS for nine years, found that smoking marijuana once or twice a day reduced his feelings of anxiety, and relieved the nausea and loss of appetite caused by the massive drug doses he took every day. Tired of feeling like a criminal, he started a court action to be given a constitutional exemption from the operation of the **Controlled Drugs and Substances Act,** which makes possession of marijuana a criminal offence. He argued in court that the law against possessing marijuana violated his right under the **Canadian Charter of Rights and Freedoms** to "life, liberty and security of the person" and that it therefore should not apply to people who use marijuana to treat symptoms of a disease. The judge dismissed Jim's case on the ground that Jim had not first formally applied to the federal minister of health for an exemption from the law— but, the judge added, if it turned out that there was no process for formal exemption, he would have no hesitation in granting Jim's request. At around the same time, Terry, who had epilepsy, was tried for possession of marijuana under the same law. He had been using marijuana for relief of symptoms for 20 years, and he was regularly arrested and charged and tried and convicted. At the end of this particular trial, the judge ruled that Terry had the right to grow marijuana for his own personal use. The Crown immediately appealed the decision.

PALLIATIVE CARE AND HOSPICE

Palliative care and hospice are the same thing. Although a hospice can be a place (such as St. Christopher's Hospice in London, England, where the hospice movement began in 1948; or Casey House in Toronto), in Canada the term hospice is used to describe a program where palliative care is provided to the dying by health care professionals and specially trained volunteers working as a team. Palliative care emphasizes the patient's comfort and pays close attention to all the needs and expectations of both patient and family—whether these are physical, psychological, social or spiritual. This of course includes pain relief. Palliative care is available in many parts of Canada in hospitals (although not usually in Intensive Care units) and through home care.

A MATTER
OF LIFE
AND DEATH

Not everybody is content to let death come in its own time. Some people want death to come sooner, while others want to delay it as long as possible. Some of these people are the dying; some are family of the dying; some are doctors and nurses. Delaying death doesn't usually cause problems, except when it is done without the dying person's consent or the consent of the family. However, hastening death can sometimes create major problems.

REFUSING TREATMENT

It is perfectly legal for a mentally competent dying person (or any mentally competent patient) to refuse treatment—any kind of treatment, including treatment that will keep her alive or keep her alive longer. (See Chapter 7, at p. 82, for more about refusing treatment.) A patient's decision to refuse treatment doesn't have to be medically reasonable, although an unreasonable decision might be taken as evidence that the patient is not mentally competent. A patient who is not competent may have left instructions in a living will about refusing treatment, or may have expressed wishes about refusing treatment, that a substitute decision maker has to respect. Dying after refusing life-prolonging or even life-saving treatment is considered natural death in law.

Nancy was 22 years old when she became completely paralyzed from Guillain-Barre syndrome, an incurable neurological disease. She needed a respirator to breathe: with it she would live a long time; without it she would die quickly. She was confined to a hospital bed and was completely dependent on others for her care. Her mind was not affected by the disease and her condition caused her great mental (although not physical) suffering, and she decided that she wanted to be taken off the respirator. The hospital and medical staff, concerned that they would be committing a crime if they took away the respirator that kept Nancy alive, refused, so she asked a court to help her make the hospital and her doctor do as she wished. The judge listened to Nancy's family and to doctors and nurses who looked after Nancy, visited Nancy herself in hospital, and reviewed the law of consent to treatment. Nancy lived in Québec, and the law there is the same as in the rest of Canada—Québec's CIVIL CODE states that "No person may be made to undergo care of any nature…except with his consent." The judge therefore made an order permitting Nancy's doctor to stop the treatment if Nancy wanted. Shortly after the judge made his order, Nancy was disconnected from the respirator, and she died the same day.

SUICIDE

It's perfectly legal in Canada to refuse treatment that will save your life, and it's also perfectly legal in Canada to commit suicide, as long as you can do the job all by yourself. There is a book called *Final Exit* by Derek Humphry which is aimed at people with a terminal illness or an incurable illness that causes great suffering and which explains how to commit suicide with as little unpleasantness as possible. You can find a copy in bookstores and libraries.

Some people who are determined to end their suffering have very few options available to them because of their physical condition. And yet they too have the right to end their lives without interference if they can do so without assistance.

Robert was an active, athletic man. At the age of 34 he was completely paralyzed from the neck down in an accident. Finding life as a quadriplegic unbearable, he stopped eating in order to die. The extended care facility where he lived asked the court to decide whether the facility could legally allow Robert to fast to death. The court said that Robert was mentally competent and that only he could judge the quality of his life, and that the facility had to honour his "balanced and clear-minded" decision to end his life. The judge also said that the facility was committing no crime by respecting Robert's decision and that allowing Robert to die did not constitute either euthanasia or mercy killing.

However, the fact that someone says she wants to die may not mean that she wants an opportunity to commit suicide. It more likely means that she is very unhappy, or wants to be reassured that she is not a burden to the people who are looking after her. If a dying person talks about wanting to die sooner rather than later, instead of handing her a copy of *Final Exit*, you should talk. Find out if "I want to die" really means, "I'm lonely," or "I'm frightened you'll leave me," or "I'm giving you too much trouble." If you are able to reassure the dying person, you may not hear any more talk about suicide.

> Mac was 26 when a motorcycle accident left him a quadriplegic who needed a respirator to stay alive. After four years he reached the decision that he did not want to go on living, and applied to a court to require the facility he lived in to remove his respirator. The court agreed that he had the right to be taken off the respirator. However, the publicity over this ruling brought Mac to the attention of a number of individuals and organizations with resources for people with severe disabilities. When Mac was offered help to make his life more bearable, including a voice-activated computer, he changed his mind about being taken off the respirator.

ASSISTED SUICIDE

Although suicide is legal in Canada, helping another person to commit suicide is not. The person who helps another to commit suicide is, legally, committing a form of homicide—and can be charged with the crime of **aiding suicide**.

> A doctor who specialized in treating patients with AIDS gave prescriptions for a lethal dose of sleeping pills to two different patients. The patients were HIV-infected, but they were not seriously ill; they were deeply depressed. Both men took the prescribed pills—one died and the other recovered. The doctor was convicted of aiding suicide, the first doctor in North America to be convicted of this crime, and sentenced to a jail term of two years less a day.

There has been a lot of discussion in Canada recently about assisted suicide, much of it because of the Sue Rodriguez case.

> Sue Rodriguez had amyotrophic lateral sclerosis (ALS) or Lou Gehrig's disease, a degenerative disease of the nervous system that gradually paralyzes a patient

over a period of years. Eventually the paralysis spreads to the respiratory system and the patient dies of suffocation. Sue was terrified of facing a slow death that would, at the end, leave her completely unable to move or speak. She did not want to die while she could still move because she valued her life; she wanted to die when she could no longer move—and that meant she would need help. Knowing that it is a criminal offence to assist another person to commit suicide, Sue asked a court for a ruling that a doctor could help her when she wanted to die. She argued that if she had a right to commit suicide while she was physically capable of doing so, it was discrimination to take away that right because she was physically disabled. Discrimination against disabled people is forbidden by the **Canadian Charter of Rights and Freedoms**. She also argued that she was being subjected to "cruel and unusual treatment" (also forbidden by the Charter of Rights) by being forced to stay alive in a completely paralyzed state when she wanted to die, and that her right to "security of the person" (guaranteed by the **Charter of Rights and Freedoms**) was being taken away because she was being denied the right to make her own decision about her body. The court refused to rule that a doctor could help her to commit suicide. She appealed the decision to the Court of Appeal (of British Columbia) and lost. Then she appealed to the Supreme Court of Canada—and again she lost. A panel of nine judges of the Supreme Court, in a 5 to 4 decision, said that it was morally and legally wrong for one person to participate in the death of another, that the state was not subjecting Sue to cruel and unusual treatment because it was not doing anything to control her, and that even if she was being discriminated against, it was reasonable discrimination in a free and democratic society. Shortly after the Supreme Court decision, Sue died—with the help of a doctor. The identity of the doctor has never been discovered.

Assisted suicide is permitted by law in the state of Oregon, and also in the Netherlands. The Oregon *Death With Dignity Act*, approved by Oregon voters in 1994, allows an adult resident of the state who is suffering from a terminal disease to make a written request for medication to end his or her life. The person's doctor may write a prescription for the medication in 15 days, after following certain steps that include referring the patient to another doctor to confirm that the disease is terminal and that the patient is mentally capable and acting voluntarily, and not suffering from depression. Very few people have resorted to this Act as yet. Assisted suicide and euthanasia are technically crimes in the Netherlands, but they have been practised there openly since 1970 and were given legal acceptance in 1993. Physicians there who assist suicide or euthanize patients will not be criminally charged if they follow certain guidelines, which include determining that the patient is mentally competent, is suffering unbearable pain (not necessarily physical pain) that cannot be relieved by accepted medical treatment, and has repeatedly asked to die. The physician, before acting, must consult fully with the patient, the patient's family, and at least one other doctor; after acting, she must notify the coroner of her actions. It has been estimated that as many as 5 to 10 per cent of all deaths in the Netherlands now involve doctor-assisted suicide or euthanasia.

Polls in Canada suggest that a substantial majority (about 75 per cent) of citizens in general would like to see assisted suicide made legal, and that a majority of Canadian physicians opposes making assisted suicide legal. Most people probably have no trouble imagining a situation in which they would want to end their life quickly and quietly because a medical condition made it unbearable. But some of the examples above suggest that in certain cases suicide and assisted suicide may offer cheap, easy answers to difficult problems. Although there may be a place for suicide and assisted suicide in Canadian society, that place should be made as small as possible through efforts such as making sure that everyone has the best pain relief possible, that everyone has someone to care for and take an interest in him when he is incapacitated by illness, and that everyone who is capable of leading a life—however short—that is productive and meaningful has the chance to do so.

MEDICAL DECISIONS THAT HASTEN DEATH

A doctor is not legally or ethically required to treat a patient if that treatment has no reasonable hope of giving the patient any benefit. If a patient is very, very ill and is not getting better as time passes, or is in fact getting worse, a doctor may recommend that treatment be stopped or that no new treatment be started. A doctor might suggest, for example,

- putting a "Do Not Resuscitate" order (see Chapter 7 at p. 82) on the chart of a patient who is expected to die shortly, if it would be useless to attempt resuscitation or if resuscitation might work but would be cruel because the patient would be alive (for a while) but in very bad shape
- not giving a patient who is about to die of one disease or condition antibiotics to combat a second disease (often pneumonia)
- disconnecting the respirator of a patient who cannot breathe without it, if the patient is about to die of another disease or condition, or
- removing feeding tubes that provide the only source of nourishment for a patient who is about to die of a disease or condition

Doctors, in consultation with the family, quite routinely stop life-prolonging treatment if the patient is in a **persistent vegetative state** (she has no conscious awareness but has sleep/wake cycles, and her eyes are open while she is in a wake cycle) or in an **irreversible coma** (he has no conscious awareness and his eyes are always closed).

Canadian courts have not expressed concern about doctors withdrawing treatment from or failing to treat patients for whom treatment would do no good, even when it meant that the patient died or would not live as long.

A three-month-old baby was brought into a Manitoba hospital suffering from severe brain damage, possibly caused by being shaken. Although his brain was badly damaged, there was still some activity in his brainstem so that his heart and lungs functioned. He lived in a persistent vegetative state for several months, suffering from one illness after another. His doctors believed that he would soon contract some very serious illness that would require them to use "intrusive heroic measures" to save him; but saving him would only mean bringing him back to the persistent vegetative state he was in. Against the parents' wishes, child welfare officials (who had taken him into custody after he was injured) got an order from the Provincial Court to have a "Do Not Resuscitate" order put on his chart. When the baby's father appealed the order, the Court of Appeal said the order was unnecessary—the doctors did not need permission from the baby's parents, the child welfare officials, or even from the courts to decide how to act in the baby's best interests. One of the judges said, "The wishes of the patient's family or guardians should be taken into account, but neither their consent nor the approval of a court is required. [I]t is in no one's interest to artificially maintain the life of a terminally ill patient who is in an irreversible vegetative state." The Manitoba College of Physicians and Surgeons noted that this court decision did not give doctors any new legal or ethical power.

Doctors are not doing anything legally wrong, either, if they shorten the life of a person who is near death by giving large doses of morphine to relieve severe pain. The effect of such large doses is to depress the respiratory system and therefore to bring on death more quickly. As long as a doctor's intention is to relieve pain and not end the dying patient's life, and the doctor prescribes the painkiller in a dose appropriate to ease suffering, he will be protected from any criminal blame when death occurs.

MERCY KILLING OR EUTHANASIA

Any person, including a doctor or nurse, can be charged with murder for giving drugs to a patient with the intention of ending the patient's life, if the patient dies—even if the doctor or nurse is only doing it in the belief that it is necessary to end the suffering of a patient who is going to die soon anyway.

Mary was 68. She had cancer of the lungs, mouth and cheeks, and was dying. She needed a respirator to stay alive. She asked her doctor to remove her respirator to hasten her death. Her doctor did so and gave her morphine so she wouldn't suffer, but he then immediately also gave her potassium chloride, which directly caused her death. (Potassium chloride is not a pain reliever or a respiratory drug. In high doses it simply stops the heart.) The doctor was charged with second-degree murder. Mary's family did not condemn the doctor in any way, and publicly said that he had given Mary a peaceful, dignified and humane death. The doctor was allowed to plead guilty to the much lesser offence of administering a noxious thing and received a three-year suspended sentence. The College of Physicians and Surgeons of Ontario, which has the power to discipline doctors, gave the doctor the choice between being suspended from practice for 90 days or developing a protocol on withdrawal of life support from terminally ill patients.

A similar case involving a nurse rather than a doctor had a somewhat different outcome.

Joseph was 78 and dying from kidney, liver and lung failure. He was in a coma. After consulting with Joseph's family, Joseph's doctor had the ventilator that was keeping him alive disconnected and gave him an injection of morphine and valium in high doses intended to prevent him from feeling in any way the suffocation that would follow. Death was expected to occur within the hour. The doctor left Joseph with a nurse, and the doctor gave the nurse orders to repeat the morphine and valium in 30 minutes if necessary. The nurse, in fact, had to repeat the dose because Joseph, once disconnected from the ventilator, began to convulse, cough and throw up mucus. However, Joseph's heart was still strong and he continued to live. The nurse, unwilling to stand by and watch this, gave Joseph an injection of potassium chloride. Minutes later, Joseph's heart stopped beating. The nurse did not hide what he had done, and was arrested and charged with first-degree murder. However, the Crown accepted a guilty plea to the offence of administering a noxious thing, and the nurse was sentenced to three years' probation and ordered to give up his Certificate of Competence to the College of Nurses so that he could not practise nursing. When Joseph's family heard the sentence, they thanked the judge for not imprisoning the nurse. Following a discipline hearing at the College of Nurses of Ontario, the nurse's registration was cancelled so that he could no longer work as a nurse.

Is it common for doctors and nurses to help a suffering patient to die, even though it is illegal? If you ask a doctor or a nurse, or officials at the governing bodies that oversee doctors and nurses, you will probably be told that it is very uncommon. After all, it is against the law—it is homicide. However, in a survey (reported in the *New England Journal of Medicine* in 1998) of nearly 2000 physicians practising in the United States in specialties that made it likely that they would receive requests for assisted suicide or euthanasia, about 30 per cent of the physicians said they had received such requests and about 7 per cent said they had complied with such requests at least once. Over half of them said they would be willing to hasten a patient's death if requested to do so by prescribing medication or giving a lethal injection—if it were legal. Further, in a survey (reported in the *New England Journal of Medicine* in 1996) of about 850 critical care nurses in the United States, 17 per cent said they had received requests from patients or their families for assisted suicide or euthanasia, and 16 per cent said they had complied with such requests (most commonly by administering a high dose of painkiller). Another 4 per cent said they had helped to hasten death by only pretending to provide life-prolonging treatment that a physician had ordered.

THE END
OF LIFE

The leading causes of death in Canada, in order, are cancer (with lung, colorectal, breast and prostate being the most common), heart disease, cerebrovascular disease (mostly stroke), accident, suicide and AIDS. Cancer and heart disease are almost neck-and-neck as causes of death and, if added together, cause more than half of all deaths in Canada. Strokes account for less than 10 per cent of all deaths. AIDS accounts for about 1 per cent of all deaths. Children and young people under the age of 25 are most likely to die in an accident, people in middle age are more likely to die of cancer, and the elderly are more likely to die of heart disease and stroke. In elderly people, the cause of death is often really old age—their bodies are worn out, and one thing or another is going to carry them off. The number of deaths per year is increasing in Canada, but that's because the total population is growing and the population of elderly people is also growing.

Can you ever really be ready for someone's death? Maybe as many as one-quarter of people die suddenly, unexpectedly, within a few hours of the first symptoms of the disease (usually a heart attack) that kills them, or in an accident. There's little you can do to prepare for such a tragedy. But if your family member is dying gradually, you should talk to her doctor or other knowledgeable people, or read about the disease, so that you will have some familiarity with the stages of the disease. You probably don't want to know—but your not knowing is not going to lengthen the dying person's life, and knowing may prepare you better to cope when the death process begins. It may even help you to protect your family member from suffering or to ease her dying.

The dying person and the family should also discuss with the doctor what values are important to them—do they want to lengthen life as much as possible regardless of the dying person's condition, do they want to shorten life if the dying person's condition is very unpleasant, or do they want neither to lengthen nor shorten life but to make dying as easy as possible? These options are discussed later in this chapter.

Finally, beware of Dr. Elizabeth Kübler-Ross's model of the five stages of dying (denial, anger, bargaining, depression and acceptance). Kübler-Ross has been so influential that many people believe that it's a requirement of dying to go through the five stages. It's not. Do not try to make a dying person go through the stages if he doesn't want to—you'll do more harm than good. Some people reach denial and stop right there, and a great many people never accept the fact that they are going to die, right up to the moment they do.

AS DEATH APPROACHES

As a dying person gets very near to death, you will probably see physical changes and changes in behaviour. Most of them are caused by changes in the dying person's metabolism (the rate at which the body processes food and drugs) and by decreased oxygen reaching the brain—that means there's a real physical reason for the changes. Here are some signs that a person who has been dying gradually is now ready to complete the process. These signs will not all be present at once, and some of them may never be present. The dying person may

- start to withdraw from the everyday world. She will lose concentration, and lose interest in activities like visiting and talking, or watching television or reading. She will spend more and more time sleeping until she is sleeping almost all the time. When this happens, it doesn't mean that family members should leave the dying person alone. Instead, they should try to be with her when she is most likely to be awake, and should sit quietly with her, talk softly to her, even if she doesn't respond, and hold her hand.

- lose his appetite, and may also not be thirsty and may not want to drink. If forced to eat or drink, he will only be made uncomfortable. If hospital staff want to use nasogastric feeding tubes or intravenous fluids, discuss with them whether it will ease discomfort or cause discomfort, and whether it will make life longer or will just make dying take longer. It may make the dying person feel more comfortable if his lips are kept moist.

- be confused about where she is and who is with her. She may mistake one person for someone else, or may speak to people who are not there or who have died or even to God, or may see places that are not visible to anyone else. Don't argue with the dying person about what she is seeing or hearing, because it is a real experience to her.

- be restless, for example, pulling at the sheets or at his clothing. To soothe him, speak quietly or read to him or play pleasant music or rub his forehead lightly. Sometimes the dying person is anxious about some unfinished matter, and may become calm if you can find out what that is and reassure him about it.

- start to lose her physical senses, particularly eyesight. Hearing fails last, and even when the person is unresponsive you should assume that she can hear.

- need less painkiller because there is now less pain

- lose control of bladder and bowels because his muscles have started to relax.

- have a lower body temperature as circulation slows. Skin may become cool to the touch in the hands and arms, feet and legs, may feel clammy or damp, and may become bluish, or blotchy or darker where the person is resting on it.

- experience increasing paralysis

- look increasingly worse—paler, thinner, more hollow-eyed. Or if there is a new infection such as pneumonia, the dying person may actually look better because the skin becomes flushed with fever.

- have congestion in the chest that causes gurgling sounds. (This may upset the family more than it upsets the dying person.) Difficulty in breathing is common because the person can no longer cough up mucous secretions in the lungs. These secretions can be suctioned out, but this often causes a lot of discomfort and can even increase the secretions. If hospital staff suggest suctioning, discuss whether it will help (and how much and for how long) and whether it will cause the dying person pain. It may also be possible to dry up the secretions with medication.

- experience changes in her breathing pattern. A common change is to **Cheyne-Stokes breathing**. She will breathe shallowly and irregularly, then not breathe at all for as long as a minute, and then will pant or gasp for breath. Just before death occurs, breathing will become more infrequent, and then finally it will stop.

- if he is awake, say something to indicate that he knows that death is coming shortly

GIVING PERMISSION TO DIE

Some dying people hang on to every moment of life; they may be determined to live until a certain day (such as a birthday) or until a certain event has happened (such as a wedding or the birth of a grandchild), and once the day or event has come and gone, they die. Others are ready to die but feel that they are being held back by the love, grief, quarrelling or even the business affairs of their family. If the family will settle affairs, or stop quarrelling, or even simply loosen their hold, the dying person can die. Sometimes a dying person doesn't want to upset the family members who are keeping vigil in her room —and will slip off into death when they leave the room for a few minutes. When your family member is ready to die, don't make her go on living for you.

DYING IN A HOSPITAL

Nobody would want to see the end of life-saving treatment, but it's not always the right treatment when someone is dying. If life-saving measures do nothing to cure the underlying condition of which the patient is really dying, it means that life is only being saved temporarily and is perhaps being saved at a high cost to the patient in discomfort and distress. So you need to know what the dying person's chances of living are both with and without life-saving treatment, what the quality of life will be if life is in fact saved, and what the different life-saving treatments involve. Then you will be able to make an informed decision about requesting or refusing treatment.

Some of the life-saving, or "death-stopping," treatments available include:

- **Cardiopulmonary resuscitation** (CPR), which is used to try to restart heartbeat and breathing when they have stopped. Trained staff press on the chest and apply shocks to the heart to restart it; and they insert a tube past the vocal cords into the windpipe (**intubate**) and connect it to a **ventilator** to supply air. When CPR is necessary, the patient will die without it; if CPR is successful, the person will probably be unconscious and in intensive care for several days and may well die anyway, depending on why the heart stopped beating and how seriously ill the person was before it stopped beating. CPR restarts the heart in about 40 people out of 100 on whom it is used, but only about 14 of those 40 people live to be discharged from the hospital.

- A ventilator may be used on its own to breathe for a patient or to help a patient breathe for herself. If the person's lungs have been damaged beyond repair by disease or injury, she can never be taken off the ventilator or else she will die. A ventilator tube is uncomfortable, and in many hospitals a patient on a ventilator is kept lightly sedated so that she won't notice the discomfort as much.

- **Drugs**, which may include **inotropic** drugs to help the heart pump harder if blood pressure has fallen (as it does if the patient's heart has stopped beating and been restarted), and antibiotics, which are used to treat infections (such as pneumonia). The patient may die within hours or days without these drugs. However, drugs can have side-effects. For example, antibiotics can cause nausea and vomiting.

- **Surgery**, which could cover many different procedures—for example, surgery to stop internal bleeding or to repair a perforated intestine. Without surgery, the person may die within hours or days. In some cases, the person may die during or shortly after surgery.

- **Blood transfusion**, which involves inserting a needle into the person's vein and allowing blood to flow into the vein. A person who is bleeding heavily will die within hours without a transfusion.

- **Dialysis**, which involves using a machine to clean the blood when the person's kidneys (which normally remove waste from the blood) stop functioning. If a person's kidneys stop working, he will die within one to two weeks. As long as the kidneys are not working, the person will require dialysis to stay alive. Dialysis usually has to be performed three days a week, takes two to four hours each time, and can have unpleasant side-effects such as weakness, dizziness and nausea (caused by a sudden drop in blood pressure), muscle cramps, stomach gas and anxiety.

- **Tube feeding**, which involves putting a nasogastric tube into the person's stomach through the nose and throat, or putting a tube through a hole in the abdomen, and giving nourishment in liquid form through the tube. Without tube feeding, a person who cannot or does not wish to eat will die within a few days to a couple of months, depending on how weak she is from illness or injury.

In all of these cases, whether the person lives or dies after receiving the treatment will depend on the nature of his underlying illness or injuries. If it's up to you, how do you decide what treatment your family member should have? A palliative care doctor has suggested asking the following questions in the following order: Will this treatment cure? If not, will it prolong life—and how pleasant will that life be? Finally, if treatment will not prolong life, will it improve quality of life? If the answer to all of these questions is no, then perhaps treatment should be refused.

Some families insist on doing everything possible even when there is no likelihood that the patient will live—sometimes because no one has taken the time to explain the dying person's situation to them in non-technical language and make them understand the reality. Some hospitals automatically use life-saving measures like CPR when anyone dies, even if the person is dying at the end of a terminal illness. (More and more hospitals are taking a second look at these practices, and forgoing them if instead of prolonging life they are really prolonging the dying process.) Find out what the policy about life-saving measures is in the hospital where your family member is. Talk to the doctors in charge about your family member and get as much information as you can about his chances of living and the quality of his life if he does live. Try to find out what is really best for him. If he has been dying for some time, and death was more or less expected, is there any point in reviving him so that he can die again a few minutes, hours or days later?

At the same time, remember that doctors are people too. They have their own values—and their values may influence their treatment decisions. One doctor may feel that it's always best not to use aggressive treatment on a very elderly person, another that if a person has a terminal illness it doesn't make much difference if she dies now or two weeks from now. Let the doctors you're dealing with know what your family member's values and yours are, so that you don't misunderstand each other. For example, if what your family member wants (or would ask for if she could) is to be made as comfortable as possible but be allowed to die as soon as the time comes, make sure that the doctor and hospital staff are informed of that and that any automatic procedure to resuscitate your family member won't be carried out.

Comfort Care

"Comfort care" or "compassionate care" involves giving morphine in a high enough dose that the dying person does not suffer (from pain or from experiencing suffocation if the respiratory system has broken down) while completing the dying process. It is most appropriate if active measures are not or are no longer being taken to keep the patient alive. Giving comfort care is not always automatic, and sometimes the doctor might not order it even though the patient needs it. In a situation like that, the family should speak up right away and ask for it—don't just assume that your family member's suffering *can't* be relieved, or that there's some particular medical reason for not providing relief.

DYING AT HOME

It is becoming more and more common for family members to look after a dying person at home. Hospitals send terminally ill patients home and terminally ill patients choose to go home to die because it is usually a more pleasant way to spend the last months or weeks of life. If you are caring for a dying person, it is very important to be able to tell when death is close and to know what the actual process of death will look like.

Most people still die in hospital, even if they were receiving care at home until 24 to 48 hours before they die. That's because family caregivers find it hard to cope when the final stage of dying begins. The dying person may need an oxygen tube, or a catheter to drain the bladder, or painkiller by injection even though he could receive it orally before. To provide this care, a nurse may have to be constantly available. Even families with good home care resources and who are committed to caring for the dying person at home may panic when breathing problems (such as Cheyne-Stokes breathing) develop. Although these breathing problems are normal in the dying process, they can be frightening—and so family members call 911. There's probably nothing worse you can do if you want your family member to die as peacefully as possible. Calling 911 will summon an ambulance AND the fire department AND the police—and the medics who burst through your front door have a legal duty to try to resuscitate anyone who is dying. If the dying person is lucky, she will be completely dead before the troops arrive to perform vigorous cardiopulmonary resuscitation; if she is unlucky, she will be revived briefly by the CPR and other interventions, and will have to die all over again later.

> **TIP:** Don't call 911 if you are expecting the death!

THE MOMENT OF DEATH

The great majority of people are in a coma or drugged into a sleep when they die, and the actual moment of death is very quiet and apparently painless. (People who are conscious as they die sometimes indicate that the experience is pleasant or even joyful. For example, Thomas Edison is reported to have said, "It's very beautiful over there," and the poet Gerard Manley Hopkins to have said, "I'm so happy, so happy.") If the person is in a hospital, monitoring equipment may be the first to notice that death has occurred. If the person is awake, he may just close his eyes and be gone. After a person dies, an observer without sophisticated medical equipment can see that

- there is no breathing
- there is no heartbeat
- the eyes are fixed and motionless and do not blink, and the pupils are enlarged, do not react to changes in light, and look dull ("the light goes out of the eyes")

- the mouth is slightly open, the jaw relaxed
- because the muscles have relaxed completely, the bladder and bowels may release urine and feces

There is no legal requirement for a person to be "pronounced" dead. It is traditional for a doctor to pronounce a patient dead, and it is just sensible practice for an expert (a doctor or a nurse) to make sure that the person actually *is* dead before a funeral home collects the body. However, there is a legal requirement for a doctor who has knowledge of the person's final illness to fill out a medical certificate of death (see Chapter 13 at p. 140). If the person dies in a hospital or extended care facility, staff there will arrange for a doctor to complete the certificate. If the person dies at home, contact your family doctor—but not in the middle of the night. This is not an emergency. Wait until morning. And remember there is no need to call 911 or the police if the death was expected. If the police are summoned, they may imagine they have a duty to investigate the death, and you may find yourself sitting in a squad car answering questions while the neighbours peer out from behind their curtains and rehearse what they'll say to the media ("We had no idea! They seemed like such a nice family.").

PART V

AFTER DEATH

13 POST-MORTEM MATTERS

Your family member is dead now. But that doesn't mean that the rest of the world goes away. Even before the funeral takes place, you may have quite a number of things to do and think about. These may include organ donation, an autopsy, contacting people who should be informed of the death, arranging for time off work or a plane ticket to attend the funeral and perhaps even an investigation into the death.

ORGAN DONATION

Human organs are practically treasure in Canada. The heart or lungs or liver or kidneys from a dead person can save the life of a dying person, or the cornea can restore sight to a person who is going blind. The majority of people are aware of this, but only a small minority of people consent to donate their own organs or to donate the organs of a family member who has just died. A 1998 report comparing a number of western nations showed that Canada has just about the lowest organ donation rate of all. Canada's organ donation rate is low partly because seat belts and air bags and helmets for motorcyclists and cyclists have greatly reduced the number of people who die in traffic accidents—the major source of organ donors. But the donation rate is also low because most people don't volunteer while they're alive to be organ donors after death, and their families don't volunteer on their behalf after they're dead, and hospital staff feel very uncomfortable asking grieving families to agree to organ donation. So nobody wants to think about it or talk about it, and the result is that other people die whose lives could have been saved. Meanwhile, scientists are exploring new options to save lives—for example, using organs from animals, such as pigs, that have been genetically modified to be more like humans, growing new organs from human cells, and creating organs from synthetic materials.

Who Has the Right to Authorize Organ Donation?

The original law (the **common law**) governing a dead person's control over his body said that a person has no right to control what is done with his body after death. That meant that a person could agree to be an organ donor, but after he died, his consent had no meaning because only the executor or the family had the right to decide what was done with the body. So each province passed a law that if a living adult consents to be an organ donor, that consent remains valid after the person dies. (For more on consenting in advance to organ donation, see Chapter 2, at p. 23.) In practice, however, a hospital will not accept an organ donation if the person consented but family members object after the person has died.

If the person who died did not indicate that she wanted to be an organ donor (or if the person was a child and therefore could not give consent while alive), then the family can consent to an organ donation. In most provinces, the family members who have the right to consent are ranked, so that the person who has to be asked for consent first is the spouse of the person who died; and if there is no spouse, then an adult child of the person who died; if there is no adult child, then a parent of the person, and so on. The complete list runs like this: spouse (in some provinces a "spouse" has to be a person of the opposite sex, but in most provinces marriage is not necessary), adult child, parent, adult brother or sister, any adult next of kin (the next nearest relative, which could be an aunt, uncle, nephew, niece, grandparent, and so on). If the person highest on the list says no, then no one further down the list can be asked. Usually if the person highest on the list says yes but someone close to the dead person and further down refuses, then the hospital will not accept an organ donation.

In a very few provinces, the doctor who last attends the person who died is required by law to decide whether the person is a suitable organ donor, and then to ask the family to consent to donation if the person didn't leave any directions about donating organs. However, the doctor doesn't have to bring the subject up if, for example, he thinks it would offend the religious beliefs of the person who died or would upset the family. In the United States, nearly every state has a law that requires the doctor to ask the family about organ donation. In most states, however, the law has not had much effect on the rate of donation—probably because doctors don't like to add to the distress of a family in shock and grief. In Spain, there is a similar law and the rate of organ donation has increased substantially, probably because they have specially trained people to talk to the family. In some Canadian hospitals, a person who did not consent to be an organ donor but who appears to be a suitable donor may be kept on a heart-lung machine for two or three days so that the family has time to adjust to the shock before the hospital staff ask whether they'll consent to an organ donation. In Québec, it is not necessary to have a direction from the person who died or permission from the family for an organ donation if two doctors state in writing that there is serious hope of saving the life of the person who would receive the organ, that the operation is urgent for the recipient, and that it is impossible to get the family's consent in time. In a couple of other provinces, it may not be necessary to get permission for an organ donation in order to remove the corneas for transplant.

Before an Organ Donation Can Take Place

Organ donation cannot take place until the donor is dead. But in the world of organ donation, death may not look exactly the way you expect.

The Legal Definition of Death

To most of us, someone who is breathing and whose heart is beating is probably alive, and someone who is not breathing and has no heartbeat is probably dead. But this is not necessarily how doctors see things, and it's not necessarily the way the law sees things.

Doctors used to consider a person dead if the heart and lungs had stopped functioning and could not be made to start functioning again ("irreversible cessation of cardio-pulmonary functioning"). In theory, that is still the test for death that the law applies in almost every province. However, doctors have moved on to a new test, which is "total brain death." (In fact, it normally only takes a few minutes of irreversible cessation of heart and lung function before total brain death occurs too because the brain starves from lack of the oxygen that is brought to it in circulating blood.) A patient who is permanently unconscious has not suffered total brain death, only "cerebral brain death." That means that all the higher functions of the brain have stopped (thinking, seeing, hearing), but the brainstem is still alive. The brainstem controls basic functions of the body such as respiration and blood circulation. Once total brain death occurs, the brainstem stops functioning too, and there is no independent respiration or blood circulation. Before a body can be used for organ donation, there has to be total brain death. However, that does not necessarily mean that heartbeat and breathing have stopped. Because most internal organs will be damaged if blood circulation stops, an organ donor who is brain dead will be put on equipment that keeps the heart beating and the lungs working, until the organs can be removed.

Safeguards for Organ Donors

To make sure that there is no conflict of interest when a potential donor is declared brain dead, there are certain rules in all the provincial statutes that govern organ donation. They include:

- two doctors who have no conflict of interest in determining whether the potential donor is dead must certify that the potential donor is brain dead—in particular, no doctor can play a role in determining whether the potential donor is dead if he has had an association, that might influence his judgment, with the person who will receive the organs.
- no doctor who played a role in determining whether the potential donor was dead can participate in any way in the transplanting of the organs

THE DEATH CERTIFICATE

A dead person is not dead for official, bureaucratic purposes until the death has been registered with the province's registrar of vital statistics, who also issues the death certificate. In fact, the body cannot be buried or cremated until the death has been registered and the registrar has issued a burial or cremation permit. To register a death, the registrar must have a medical certificate of death and a statement of personal information about the person who died. A doctor who is familiar with the person's final illness (or in some cases, a coroner—see below at p. 143) must fill out the medical certificate of death. The certificate asks for the person's name, date and place of death, the cause of death, information about whether an autopsy was held, certain details if the death was the result of accident or violence, and the doctor's certification that the person died in the place and of the cause stated. The funeral director often completes the statement of personal information, but it must be based on information obtained from a relative or other person who has some knowledge about the person who died. That means that the funeral director will have to ask a family member questions about the person who died such as the place and date of death, the person's usual residence, her marital status, occupation, birthdate and birthplace, the names of the person's father and mother, and also for information (name, address and so on) about the family member providing this information. When the death certificate is issued, it will contain the following information: the name, age, sex and marital status of the person who died, the date and place of death, and the date of registration and registration number.

PEOPLE YOU SHOULD CONTACT IMMEDIATELY FOLLOWING THE DEATH

At this time you may not feel like talking to anyone, but certain people should be notified right away that death has occurred. If you don't feel up to doing it yourself, ask a friend or a family member who is not closely affected by the death to help you, or write a letter and fax or email it to the people who need to be informed. You should contact:

- the executor of the will, if there is a will and if you know who the executor is; the lawyer of the person who died if you're not sure whether there's a will or if you don't know who was named as executor. It is the duty of the executor, if there is one, to make the funeral arrangements. If there's no executor, the closest family members make the arrangements

- the funeral home or transfer service, if you're the one who has to make arrangements, to have the body picked up and, if there was no pre-planning, to plan the funeral and disposal of the remains

- your religious advisor, if there is to be a religious ceremony—and also if you need some comfort

- other family members and friends of the person who died

- the employer of the person who died, if he was employed at the time of death

See if someone is willing to answer the phone for you for a few days following the announcement of the death. When no one is available, you may prefer to leave the phone on voice mail, or simply turn the ringer down and not answer at all.

AUTOPSIES AND INQUESTS

It's very common for surviving family to ask, Why did this person have to die? They often mean it in a very broad sense—was it fair or just that this person was taken, or that she was taken and not someone else? However, there may be people you've never met before who take a very concrete interest in why this person died, and they may want to examine the body and inquire closely into the cause of the death. We're talking about a doctor who may want to perform an autopsy, or a coroner who may be required to perform an investigation and perhaps hold an inquest.

Autopsy

An autopsy is an examination of the body after death, to find out the cause of death. The body is opened up and the internal organs (brain, heart, lungs, liver and so on) are examined for signs of disease or damage. Bits of the organs may be taken away for more detailed examination (for example, under a microscope) or for testing (for example, an analysis of blood or urine). The autopsy takes a couple of hours, and once it's finished, the surgical incisions are sewn up. It is usually possible to have an open casket at the funeral after an autopsy, if the body was not disfigured before the autopsy.

When Can an Autopsy Be Requested or Ordered?

Doctors may ask the family for permission to perform an autopsy on a person who died if the person died a natural but unexpected death, or if she died of a rare disease or of a disease in which there is a lot of research interest. A doctor cannot perform an autopsy without the family's permission in these circumstances. Autopsies used to be performed in hospitals much more frequently than they are now (now there's an autopsy in only about 10 per cent of deaths). They are performed less often partly to cut costs, and partly because there used to be more questions about how or why people died than there are now. These days, most people die of diseases that have been diagnosed before death and have already been thoroughly studied, and there may be less medical knowledge to be gained from an autopsy. However, doctors misdiagnose diseases and conditions in as many as 20 per cent of patients who die—so autopsies are not a waste of time.

Each province has officials, either **coroners** or **medical examiners**, who investigate unexplained, accidental or violent deaths. These deaths are called **coroner's cases**. (Most deaths that occur in the emergency department of a hospital are considered coroner's cases because they're unexpected; in some provinces, all deaths that occur in a nursing home are coroner's cases.) If the coroner considers an autopsy necessary to the investigation, he will order one. The coroner does not need the permission of the family or anyone else to perform an autopsy. A coroner can even get government permission to have a body exhumed (dug up after it's been buried, to put it bluntly) for an autopsy.

Coroner's Investigation

A death is considered a coroner's case and, by law, must be investigated by the coroner if the person died

- as a result of violence (including suicide or homicide), an accident, or poisoning, or negligence or malpractice
- during or immediately after an operation
- suddenly or unexpectedly
- from a disease that was not being treated by a legally qualified physician
- as a result of pregnancy
- in a nursing home or home for the aged or a psychiatric hospital
- of a disease or injury related to his employment

(This list may vary in each province, but the lists all look similar.)

In Ontario, for example, the coroner's office investigates about 40 per cent of the deaths that occur every year. Generally speaking, any person, not just a health care worker or the police, has a duty to inform the coroner or medical examiner, or the police, if she has reason to believe that a person died in any of the circumstances listed above. If you wonder whether a death should be reported, contact your provincial coroner's or medical examiner's office for more information.

The coroner's investigation is held to determine whether an inquest is necessary. The coroner or medical examiner takes possession of the body and decides whether an autopsy should be held. In addition to holding an autopsy, in most provinces the coroner or medical examiner can ask family members, health care workers, or any witnesses questions about the death and the person who died, ask to see and take away documents such as medical records, or other items such as clothing and personal effects, and visit places where the person was before or at the time of death. In some provinces, there is a special investigator from the coroner's office appointed to do these things; in others, the police do them.

If at the end of the investigation the coroner or medical examiner is satisfied that the death was from natural causes, he will sign the death certificate. If, however, the coroner or medical examiner is not sure about

- who the person who died was, or
- when the person came to her death, or
- where the person came to her death, or
- how or by what means the person came to her death

or if the coroner or medical examiner believes that an inquest will prevent similar deaths in the future, then he may order an inquest. (In provinces with a medical examiner, the examiner recommends an inquest and the board or government body that supervises the examiner orders the inquest.) Sometimes the family's desire to have an inquest or not to have one influences the coroner's decision or medical examiner's recommendation or board's decision, and pressure brought to bear by the government or the press or special interest groups can also influence the coroner or board to hold an inquest.

Only a small percentage of investigations end in an inquest. Often the investigation itself will give the family enough information about the death to satisfy their concerns, and the coroner or medical examiner enough information to make recommendations, designed to prevent similar problems in the future, to any institution or official involved in the death. This means that everyone can avoid a lot of public interest. If the family wants an inquest but the coroner refuses to order one, the family may be able to make a request in writing to a regional coroner or to the chief coroner of the province, asking for a review of the coroner's decision; or, if that fails, the family may apply to a court for an order that an inquest be held. Sometimes an inquest is ordered to quiet public speculation and gossip about a death by uncovering the truth.

The family can use evidence from the coroner's investigation in a civil lawsuit if they decide to sue someone over the death. (See below at p. 146 for wrongful death lawsuits.) If there is already a criminal investigation into the death going on, or if the coroner's investigation reveals evidence of a criminal offence, the coroner's investigation will not proceed until the criminal investigation and any court proceedings arising out of that investigation have been completed.

Coroner's Inquest

An inquest is a formal court proceeding intended to find out the "who, when, where and how" of a person's death. It is not intended to lay blame for the death, and, in fact, it has no legal authority to lay blame. Its purpose, once the facts about the death have been found out, is to make recommendations that will prevent similar deaths. For example, inquests have made recommendations such as:

- A hospital should strictly enforce its policy that patients admitted to the emergency department are to be seen by a physician within four hours (in this case, a patient died after being in the hospital's emergency department for eight hours without being examined by a doctor).

- A nursing home should closely supervise violent or aggressive residents, and should have early access to medical records of incoming patients to help it determine which patients are violent (in this case, a nursing home resident died after being attacked by another resident).

- A nursing home should regularly have its mechanical lifting equipment inspected and should have a minimum number of staff members present when equipment is used to lift residents (in this case, a resident died after falling from the broken sling of a lifting device).

In provinces where there is a coroner, the coroner presides over the inquest, while in provinces where there is a medical examiner, a judge presides. In some provinces, a coroner's jury listens to the evidence and makes the recommendations. The coroner or judge can issue subpoenas to force witnesses to attend and give evidence. The witnesses are questioned by a Crown Attorney (a government lawyer); the family of the person who died may have the right to ask questions of witnesses and make statements to the presiding coroner or judge. If family members have this right, they can usually have a lawyer ask the questions and make the statements for them. In some circumstances, witnesses are allowed to have a lawyer attend the hearing with them. Because family members sometimes want to use the evidence that comes out at an inquest for a lawsuit they are contemplating, inquest proceedings may get rough as lawyers cross-examine certain witnesses and try to get them to admit that they acted in a manner that was wrong or careless.

If someone does not like the conclusion that the inquest reached, it is very difficult to get it changed once it has been made. In fact, it is very rare for a higher court even to hear an appeal of the inquest verdict. One of the few circumstances that would persuade a court to set aside an inquest verdict would be the inquest's failure to question a person who had important information about the death.

Public Inquiry

A public inquiry is a special procedure that can be set up by the federal government (for deaths that directly concern its legal jurisdiction; for example, the actions of a federal agency such as the Canadian Red Cross) or by a provincial government to investigate a death or deaths within the province (for example, the deaths of a number of babies at a children's hospital; or the deaths of several miners in an explosion). A public inquiry is much less common than an inquest, but it too is intended to investigate the circumstances of a death rather than to lay blame. It may cover a wider area than an inquest. A public inquiry starts with the appointment of a commissioner or commissioners to conduct the inquiry. A commissioner has more or less the same powers as a coroner or judge holding an inquest.

WRONGFUL DEATH

If you believe that your family member's death was the result of someone's carelessness (for example, a car accident or a wrong medical diagnosis or treatment), you may have grounds to start a lawsuit. A lawsuit will not bring back the person who died, but if you are successful it will provide financial compensation. You may also be able to file a complaint with an organization that has authority over an individual whose carelessness caused the death (the provincial College of Physicians and Surgeons if it's a doctor, the provincial College or Association of Nurses if it's a nurse; the provincial police commission if it was a police officer, and so on). A complaint will not bring back the person who died either, but it may call to account someone who was responsible for the death.

Civil Lawsuit

When someone dies as the result of another's carelessness, the family may be able to sue the person who was responsible for the death and get money damages to compensate for such things as lost income for the dependants of the person who died, loss of the care, guidance and companionship of the person who died, the cost of caring for the person before her death, and funeral expenses. If you are contemplating a wrongful death lawsuit, you should see a lawyer as soon as possible. You may think there's something very distasteful about rushing from your family member's bedside to a lawyer's office, and perhaps you're right. However, there are legal rules about starting a lawsuit, including how quickly it must be started, and you need to know about these rules as soon as possible. If you wait to see a lawyer until you're over the shock and grief, you may have waited too long to start a lawsuit. In every province there are **limitation periods** that prevent a person from bringing a legal action after a certain period of time has passed. The time period varies from situation to situation (as well as from province to province). While in one situation you might have as long as six years from the date of injury causing death to start a lawsuit, in another you might have only a few days! Only a litigation lawyer will be able to tell you how long the limitation period is in your particular case.

When you meet with your lawyer, she will probably advise you to do a number of things to prepare for a lawsuit. Most of them have to do with collecting the evidence you will be required to present at trial to prove first, that the person being sued (the **defendant**) caused the death, and second, that the defendant ought to pay money in compensation. Your lawyer will suggest that you and other family members

- keep all documents relating to the illness or injury and death (for example, a copy of a police report, any documents provided by a doctor or hospital or nursing home)
- write a history of what happened, including conversations you had with people involved in the injury or illness and death
- make notes of all conversations you have in the future with people involved in the death
- keep receipts for everything—gas or mileage to the hospital where your family member died, parking, drug prescriptions or medical supplies purchased, restaurant meals, accommodation near the hospital, funeral, cemetery plot, and so on. The defendant, if found liable, may have to reimburse you for all these expenses
- keep a diary of or tape-record your personal health and feelings—your reaction to the death may be something the defendant has to pay compensation for
- not sign any documents (for example, from an insurance company or from the hospital) until you have had a lawyer review them
- avoid speaking to representatives of the person you believe is responsible for the death (his lawyer, spokesperson, insurance adjuster)—refer them to your lawyer

DEATH AWAY FROM HOME

To compound the nightmare of a family member dying, she may die while working or vacationing in another city or another country. If this happens, contact a funeral home—either one in your home city or one in the city where the person died. If you are in a foreign country and don't know how to find a funeral home in either place, contact the Canadian embassy or consulate for assistance. The funeral home, once found, can make necessary arrangements to return the body to the country and city of residence.

Shipping a body is expensive; it might cost $2000 or $3000 to ship a body across Canada, and from remote parts of the world it might cost as much as $25,000 to ship a body home to Canada. If the person who died had life insurance, contact the insurance company to find out whether it will cover the cost of shipping. If the person had traveller's insurance, it may cover the cost of shipping. If the person's funeral was pre-planned and pre-paid, the contract may include a clause that the body will be returned to the chosen funeral home at no extra cost if death occurred more than a specified distance from home (for example, 100 miles/160 kilometres).

If it seems as though it will be too expensive to ship a body home, or if religious rules dictate that the body must be buried immediately, you can bury the body in the place where death occurred, or you can have the body cremated there and ship the ashes home.

 **14**

FUNERAL ARRANGE- MENTS

For most people, funeral arrangements mean holding a ceremony of some kind and then burying or cremating the body. It's perfectly possible to bury or cremate a person without holding a ceremony, however. It's also possible to hold a ceremony after the person has been buried or cremated—in that case it's called a memorial service rather than a funeral service. You can set up a funeral or memorial service through your church, synagogue or mosque and have it held on their premises, or through a funeral home and have it held in the funeral home's chapel. You can arrange for burial or cremation through a funeral home. If you don't intend to have a visitation (an opportunity for family, friends and acquaintances to come and speak to the immediate family with the body present, in an open or closed casket) or a funeral service, you may prefer to make burial or cremation arrangements through a **transfer service** rather than a funeral home. A transfer service will take the body from the place of death to the cemetery or crematorium and will arrange for a casket or container, and for a cemetery plot and burial, or for cremation. You can also deal directly with the cemetery or crematorium, if you wish.

WHO DECIDES ABOUT FUNERAL ARRANGEMENTS?

Some people pre-arrange their own funeral and burial or cremation down to the last detail. Others tell their family or friends exactly what arrangements they would like (or what arrangements they would hate) in conversation, in a letter or in their will. Other people never let on a word about what they want or don't want, either because they don't want to think or talk about it, or because death comes suddenly and they had no opportunity to plan or discuss arrangements.

Strange as it may seem, from a legal point of view, all of these people are in the same position when it comes to funeral and burial arrangements. In almost every province, the directions that a person gives about how his body is to be disposed of after death are not legally binding on any of the living, even if the directions appear in a will. Under Canadian law, if the person who died made a will and appointed an executor under the will, the executor is responsible for making funeral and burial or cremation arrangements that are suited to the dead person's position in life (while he was alive, that is) but that are not unduly expensive. The executor does not have to do what the person who died wanted, nor does the executor have to do what the person's husband, wife, child, parent or lover wants—although in practice most executors respect any wishes that the person who died expressed or the wishes of the immediate family.

If there is no executor (either because the person who died did not make a will or because the named executor is unable or unwilling to act), then a member of the family has the right and the legal responsibility to make funeral and burial arrangements. The law would first look to the person's husband or wife; if there is none, then the next of kin—the closest living relative (child, parent, brother or sister, nephew or niece, etc.)—would be expected to look after arrangements. A partner who was not legally married to the person who died would not have the rights of a husband or wife in most provinces, so matters can become unpleasant if the partner and the closest blood relative don't see eye to eye about disposing of the remains.

THE FUNERAL HOME AND THE FUNERAL SERVICE

The family of the person who died may decide to make the funeral arrangements through a funeral home. The funeral industry doesn't have a very good reputation. It's sometimes seen as taking advantage of people who are upset and confused, playing on their love or guilt, overcharging them and forcing them to buy goods and services that they don't really want or need. In fact, most funeral homes provide their services in a professional manner and help grieving people through a difficult time.

It's true that funerals can be expensive. By one estimate, a funeral is the third most expensive purchase consumers ever make—coming behind a house and a car. The average funeral costs about $5000 in Canada. But there are a couple of things people should think about before they condemn the entire funeral industry. First, would anyone make any other major purchase in a state of shock and grief? Second, even though it's legal for family members to make all the arrangements themselves, how many people would actually want to? A funeral home carries out quite a lot of duties that family members don't know how to perform and wouldn't feel like performing even if they did. Among other things, the funeral home removes the body from the place of death (home, facility or hospital); fills out the statement of personal information that is required to get the death certificate; prepares the body for burial (embalming if desired, dressing, putting on cosmetics—or even performing restorative surgery—if the family wants an open casket); provides visitation rooms; provides the coffin; makes arrangements for the funeral (religious service, flowers, music, pallbearers, printing of the order of service) and the burial or cremation; organizes the hearse and limousines; and may even provide grief counselling and help the family apply for insurance and death benefits. They're in business, so they charge to do all these things; and they usually charge by the hour for visitation rooms and for the funeral service. So it can all add up if you're not watching your pocketbook.

In many provinces, funeral directors and transfer service operators are required by law to have complete and current price lists of all their goods and services and to make them available to the public at no charge and with no obligation to buy anything. That means if you're pre-planning or do not have to hold the funeral within a day, you can do some comparison shopping (we know—shopping for a funeral home is not exactly like shopping for shoes). We've listed above some of the things that a funeral home can do for you; now let's look at the various things they might *charge* you for. The bill from the funeral home might include some or many of the following:

- meeting to discuss arrangements
- planning the funeral and burial or cremation
- transferring the body from the place of death to the funeral home's facilities
- keeping the body in the funeral home's refrigerated storage facilities
- delivering, receiving and preparing documents and legal permits that are required under provincial laws
- providing death certificates for estate purposes

- making arrangements with the coroner if the body is to be cremated
- helping with obituary notices
- embalming
- dressing the body
- providing a casket or other container
- placing the body in the casket or container
- rental of space for visitation
- rental of a chapel for the funeral or memorial service
- providing a visitors/mourners book
- directing the funeral service
- providing flowers
- providing an organist or other music
- providing a rosary or crucifix
- printing orders of service
- printing prayer cards
- providing ushers to guide family and friends to the visitation or service (and an additional charge for this service if activities take place away from the funeral home)
- providing professional casket bearers
- catering at the visitation or gathering
- transferring the body from the funeral home to the cemetery or crematorium
- providing a transfer vehicle for the body—or, as an upgrade, a funeral coach or hearse for the body (if you don't go for the upgrade, you'll probably get some kind of truck)
- providing sedan service or limousine service for mourners going to the cemetery
- providing a vehicle for administration of the funeral procession
- transferring the body or driving mourners outside a specified geographic area
- identifying the dead person before cremation takes place
- witnessing the cremation process, or attending a memorial service outside the funeral home or a graveside service or the interment of cremated remains
- providing a vehicle to pick up and deliver flower arrangements, documents, cremated remains, etc.
- shipping cremated remains
- providing acknowledgment cards and stationery

- keeping records (records are usually required by law and include such things as the name of the person who died, the date and place of burial or cremation, and the name and address of the person who authorized the funeral services)

plus disbursements (amounts paid to a third party that have to be paid by you) such as

- any applicable provincial fees for documents or permits
- honorarium for the clergy or the musicians at the funeral
- police escort for the funeral procession

and amounts paid to the cemetery or crematorium, if the funeral home makes those arrangements on your behalf, such as

- cost of a cemetery plot
- cost of interment (burial or entombment)
- late charges payable to the cemetery for holding the committal outside the usual hours (if applicable)
- cost of cremation
- cost of an urn

And don't forget

- sales tax (GST of 7% or HST of 15% on all goods and services supplied, provincial sales tax on goods supplied)

Whew!

You don't have to buy all these goods and services in order to hold a funeral—many of them are completely optional. However, some funeral homes offer various packages rather than an à la carte (so to speak) selection, and you may find that to get five things you want, you'll have to take (and pay for) another two that you don't want—it's rather like buying a new car.

Family members are usually happier with the funeral arrangements and cost if they pre-plan when they can think rationally about the options. People who can't or don't pre-plan for a dying family member and make the arrangements after death should at least take someone with them. That someone should not be another grieving family member, but someone with a little distance and business sense.

EMBALMING

One of the most frequently asked questions is whether embalming is necessary. Embalming is a practice that developed in the United States during the

Civil War (1862–65), when bodies were being shipped home long distances. The process involves draining the blood and replacing it with embalming fluid (such as formaldehyde). The fluid keeps the body from decomposing for some time. Embalming does not preserve a body for very long—it stops decay for a few months and possibly as much as several years, depending on the quality of the preservation method, how air-tight the casket is, and the local climate (temperature and humidity). Bodies are kept in refrigerated facilities at a funeral home, so there isn't likely to be much decay in two or three days whether a body is embalmed or not.

Embalming is not required by law in most situations, although some provinces, states in the United States, and foreign countries have laws requiring bodies to be embalmed if they are to be shipped by a public carrier (including airlines, railways, shipping lines, and most trucking firms). Your funeral director will be able to tell you if embalming is required for shipping to a particular destination. Some funeral homes require a body to be embalmed if it's going to be kept at the funeral home for more than a certain period of time. Other than these things, embalming is a matter of choice. You might opt for embalming if the funeral is to be delayed for several days and the body is to be put in an open casket.

If you don't want the body embalmed, say so as soon as possible to the funeral director—when you are pre-arranging, or before the body is taken to the funeral home. If you say nothing, the funeral home may assume that you want embalming, and do it and charge you for it.

THE CONTRACT WITH THE FUNERAL HOME

The dying person or family members can make funeral arrangements in advance, or the executor or family can make the arrangements after death. Pre-planning just means choosing what you want (the casket, the service, and so on) and signing a contract to that effect with the funeral home or transfer service. The contract tells the funeral home or transfer service exactly what to do when the time comes. If a funeral is merely pre-planned and not pre-paid, the price may not be guaranteed (ask the funeral director whether the price is guaranteed and for how long). If you want a guaranteed price, you can pre-pay as well as pre-plan. Pre-payment can be made by paying the full amount at once, or by installments, or by purchasing a life insurance policy. When you pre-pay with cash, some or all (depending on the province) of the money has to be held in trust and not used by the funeral home until the services are performed.

When you make the arrangements and pay or pre-pay, make sure that

• there is a contract in writing, signed by both you and the funeral director

- the contract describes exactly what you're buying, the total amount charged, the amount you have paid, and when the goods or services are to be provided (before, on or after death)

- you are given a contract that has your and the funeral director's original signature on it (that is, you don't want a photocopy of the original contract; you want an original contract)

In some provinces, a pre-paid contract is not valid unless most or all (depending on the province) of these conditions are met. But whether or not the law requires all of these things, it's just good business sense to have them.

If the contract involves pre-payment, it should also set out your rights to cancel, and state how much money will be refunded on cancellation. Most provinces have consumer protection legislation that requires the funeral home to refund all the money, less a stated administrative fee, on cancellation. The allowable administrative fee varies from province to province, but in some it is as much as 12 per cent of the amount paid. Whether any interest that has accrued on the amount paid will be returned also varies from province to province. Several provinces have a "cooling-off" period of a few days to a few months. If you change your mind and want to get out of the contract within the cooling-off period, you can get all the money back. If you do change your mind after you've pre-paid (for example, if you move out of the area or if the person for whom you've made the arrangements miraculously recovers), ask in writing for your money back.

If you want more information about funeral contracts in your province, contact the provincial board of funeral directors (which oversees funeral homes). They are:

Alberta: Alberta Funeral Service Regulatory Board (Edmonton)

British Columbia: Ministry of the Attorney General, Cemeteries and Funeral Service Board (Victoria)

Manitoba: Manitoba Board of Administration Under the Embalmers & Funeral Directors Act (Winnipeg)

New Brunswick: New Brunswick Board for Registration of Embalmers & Funeral Directors (Hampton)

Newfoundland: Newfoundland Board of Registration for Embalmers & Funeral Directors (St. John's)

Nova Scotia: The Nova Scotia Board of Registration of Embalmers & Funeral Directors (Kentville)

Ontario: Board of Funeral Services (Toronto)

Prince Edward Island: Prince Edward Island Funeral Directors & Embalmers Association (Kensington)

Québec: Corporation des Thanatologues du Québec (Sainte-Foy)

Saskatchewan: Saskatchewan Funeral Service Association (Regina)

If any money is left over after a pre-paid funeral, it should be returned to you or to the estate of the person who died if she did her own pre-arranging. After the funeral, make sure that you get an itemized bill showing all the services performed and their cost, as well as a statement showing how much money, including interest, was held by the funeral home for the funeral.

CHOOSING A FUNERAL HOME

Losing a family member is a bad experience to begin with, so don't make it worse by dealing with a funeral home that won't provide the service you want at the price you want. To avoid problems, choose the funeral home carefully. You need to do an investigation—before the death if possible. That means (if circumstances allow) not waiting until your family member is dead and you're extremely upset and under pressure before you go looking for a funeral home. In many communities, you have some choice or even lots of choice about which funeral home you use. To narrow that choice:

- Ask others—family members, friends, co-workers or business associates— for recommendations (or warnings about where not to go). Ask what they liked and what they didn't like about the funeral home they used. Your family may have used a particular funeral home for many years, but don't automatically assume that it's the best place now. However, if it's important to you to have a funeral for this family member that is very similar to funerals held in the past for other family members, the funeral home that your family has used before will have all the information on record about previous funerals.

- Call the funeral homes that have been recommended and speak to a representative. Have a general conversation about the kind of funeral you want (for example, short visitation, service in their chapel, burial in a family plot outside of town) and ask for a rough estimate of the cost. Ask about the price range of coffins. Ask what funeral service associations the home belongs to. If you don't like the treatment or answers you receive or if the representative makes you feel uncomfortable, call the next home on your list. If you are pleased with both treatment and answers, make an appointment to meet the funeral director.

- Meet personally with the funeral director. Take someone with you who won't get upset but will be able to ask questions about what the funeral home can provide and the price. Ask for current price lists for services and caskets. Look at their casket selection, and ask for pictures and information about models in your price range if they are not on display. Ask if you can purchase a coffin elsewhere and if the funeral home will charge for using it (for more about this, see below at p. 158). Ask to see their standard contract and for an explanation of anything in the contract you don't understand. If you are pre-planning, ask about your right to cancel before any services are provided. Again, if you don't like your treatment or the director's answers, cross the funeral home off your list.

• Study the information from each funeral home. See whether the various packages will provide you with the funeral arrangements that you want or whether you will have to pay extra for some or many things. Compare prices and services provided. You may want other family members or a friend with experience to look over the materials as well.

• When you've made an informed decision, go back to the funeral home you've chosen and actually make the arrangements.

BURIAL OR CREMATION?

Actually, there are three options, not two. A body can be

• buried

• cremated, or

• donated to science

   Either a transfer service or funeral home can remove the body from the place of death and fill out the necessary documents for burial or cremation. And it's not actually necessary in most provinces to have a transfer service or funeral home make the arrangements for transportation of the body or burial or cremation. The family of the person who died can do it themselves as long as they follow the requirements of provincial law, which normally means getting a burial or cremation permit from the provincial authorities (and in the case of cremation, a coroner's certificate).

BURIAL

Burial involves two major expenses, leaving aside the funeral service and other arrangements: the casket, and the cemetery.

Casket

A casket can be very expensive—but it doesn't have to be. And in fact you don't even have to have a casket. All that's required by law is an enclosed rigid container. Funeral homes and transfer services have these available as well as caskets, and you can buy one for as little as $100—but it's *really* basic (it's cardboard). You can get fancier containers for a few hundred dollars, or you can get a basic casket for about $500. Or you can go all out and get a deluxe

casket for several thousand dollars. There are models at almost every price.
Or you can rent a casket for the visitation or funeral (but that could cost as
much as $1000) and then bury the body in a basic cardboard container.

In a few provinces, a funeral home that has caskets on display is required
by law to include its least expensive casket model, and also to make available
a brochure showing its entire line of caskets. If your funeral home doesn't
have all its models on display, ask to see a complete brochure whether or not
one is required by law in your province. What you probably want to look at
is not the cheapest casket or the most expensive, but a range of mid-priced
models.

In almost all provinces you can buy a coffin from a discount coffin out-
let and ask the funeral home to use it, instead of buying direct from the
funeral home. Discount outlets are less expensive because their mark-up on
the coffin is considerably lower. In some provinces, a funeral home is allowed
to charge a handling fee for using a coffin bought elsewhere—this can be as
much as $200. Don't be surprised if the funeral home gets a bit huffy when
you say you want to buy a coffin elsewhere.

Cemetery

Cemetery fees can run into the thousands of dollars. The major expenses are

- a plot or tomb
- interment (burial or entombment), and
- a monument

A plot (known in the industry as "interment rights") can run up to about
$5000, depending on the size of the plot and the location and fashionable-
ness of the cemetery. A "single" adult grave or plot can actually hold two
coffins, stacked one over the other. A lot contains more than one adult grave,
so, for example, a lot with two graves could hold four coffins. In some cemeteries you can choose burial above-ground instead of underground, in a **tomb**
(also called a **crypt**), or in a **mausoleum**, if the thought of burial in the
earth is troubling. A tomb or crypt usually holds one or two coffins or a similarly small number; a family mausoleum can hold several coffins, and a community mausoleum can hold many coffins.

The owner of the interment rights has to give permission for burial after
death occurs and before burial. If the person who died had purchased the
plot, his estate must give permission for burial there (yes, we know this
sounds nutty). If the plot was purchased by two (or more) people as joint
tenants and one of them was the person who died, then full ownership of
the plot passes to the survivor(s) on the death of one joint tenant. That means
the survivor must give permission. If two or more people bought the plot as

tenants in common (that is, with no automatic right of survivorship), and one of the tenants in common is the person who died, then the survivor(s) *and* the person's estate must give their permission. What all this means is that if the plot was pre-purchased, someone (the funeral home if you are using one) has to contact the cemetery immediately following the death to find out who is required to sign the form giving permission for burial in the plot.

When the coffin is buried (rather than entombed), interment involves locating boundaries of the grave, excavation of the grave, placing the coffin in it, and closing the grave. This can cost several hundred dollars.

A monument is an upright stone at the grave, and a marker is a stone or metal plaque that is set flush with the ground at the grave. Even a marker can cost several hundred dollars; with a monument you're probably looking at $1000 or more. Monuments are usually made of granite, while a marker can be made of granite or bronze. You may be able to (or may have to) arrange for a monument or marker through the cemetery, or you may have to contact a monument maker yourself. The cemetery may have by-laws about the size and shape of the monument or marker that you can put on the grave, or even whether you must put up a monument or marker or whether you are forbidden to. In some cemeteries you may be able to arrange to plant a memorial tree instead of or in addition to putting up a monument or marker.

Besides charges for the fairly obvious things discussed above, you may find the cemetery has extra charges for such things as:

• administrative fees

  – to determine ownership of the plot

  – to obtain permission for burial

  – to fill out documentation such as a provincial burial or entombment permit

  – to maintain the cemetery's files (to record such information as the name of the person and the specific location of the plot)

• holding the funeral late in the day (after about 3 or 4 p.m.) or on a weekend

• placing artificial grass and coco-matting at the grave site

• removing the excavated earth from the area of the grave site during the committal

• levelling, tamping down, re-grading and sodding the grave site

• levelling and resodding the gravesite after the earth has settled

• interring at the deeper level so that a second coffin can be added later

• providing a concrete or steel outer container. These are not required by provincial law but some cemeteries require them. They prevent the earth from falling in as the casket decays and they cost about $200. Placement of the container in the grave can add another $100 or more to the cost of using a container.

- use of a tent during the committal service

And again, don't forget that there's GST or HST on goods and services, and provincial sales tax on goods.

Just as with the funeral arrangements through the funeral home, you will have a contract with the cemetery. You should get an original signed contract to take away with you. The contract should

- be in writing and be signed by both you and the authorized representative of the cemetery

- describe exactly what you're buying and the price charged, and when the goods or services are to be provided (before, on or after death)

- if you're pre-paying, set out your rights to cancel the contract, and how much money you will get back if you cancel

- have attached to it the by-laws of the cemetery. A cemetery's by-laws set out rules such as the cemetery's hours and whether pets can enter the cemetery; what planting or trimming is charged as extra work; what articles, such as flower vases and wreaths, can be left at a gravesite; the liability of the cemetery for any damage or injury that occurs within the cemetery—and many other matters that may be important to you.

In some provinces, a pre-paid contract is not valid if all or most of the conditions set out above are not met.

You'll have to pay at the time you make the arrangements, either in a lump sum or in installments, unlike pre-arranging a funeral.

In many provinces, the owner of "interment rights" cannot sell them to anyone else. However, the owner can require the cemetery to buy the rights back before they are used (that is, before someone is buried there), although a small fee for the buy-back may be chargeable. Make sure that your contract or the cemetery's by-laws state any rights you have to require the cemetery to buy back the plot before it has been used.

Continuing or "Perpetual" Care

In almost all provinces, the law requires commercial (privately owned) cemeteries to set aside a specified amount of the money received from the holders of interment rights for continuing care of the cemetery—cutting the grass, planting trees, providing a water supply, roads and snow removal, and re-grading of the earth.

Municipal cemeteries and cemeteries operated by religious organizations have not been required to set aside money for continuing care because law-makers assumed that municipalities and religious organizations would not go out of business or run off with the cemetery funds. However, some munici-pal cemeteries are now penniless and their municipalities have no money to bail them out. Some religious organizations are in financial trouble too. If you're concerned about what the cemetery will look like in a few years' time, ask questions about the financial health of the municipality or organization that is running it.

You may be able to make special arrangements with your cemetery to get extra care for your family member's plot, such as extra watering, trim-ming of the grass, planting and caring for flowers or shrubs, either through a renewable contract or through an **endowment**. With an endowment, you pay a lump sum of money, and the lump sum and interest earned on it fund the special care for a period of time into the future.

Burial outside a Cemetery

In some provinces (notably Alberta, British Columbia, Ontario and Saskat-chewan), legislation specifically says that a human body cannot be buried outside a cemetery. In the other provinces, it's usually not a matter that provincial legislation addresses one way or another. However, this doesn't mean that in those provinces you can go ahead and bury Great-Auntie under the rosebushes that she loved so much. Even if you own the land yourself and you can get the provincial burial permit that is required for all burials, you may have trouble with

- the municipality, which zones different areas for different uses and doesn't allow property owners to do whatever they like with their own land (unless the municipality likes it too)
- the public health authorities. In almost all provinces, it is illegal to bury something that could endanger the health of others—and a body under the rosebushes might fall into that category
- the neighbours
- any future purchaser of the property

Burial at Sea

If the idea of burial at sea seems appealing, there are some obstacles in the way. The federal government has jurisdiction over the oceans around Canada, and Environment Canada (Marine Conservation and Protection Branch) has discouraging rules about burial at sea:

- A permit is required, and in order to get one
  - a notice of intent to bury a body at sea must be published in a local newspaper
  - a certificate that the body is free from infection must be obtained from the doctor of the person who died
  - an application fee of $2500 must be paid (it's a blanket fee and might be reduced if more than one burial at sea took place through the same funeral home or funeral association in the year) and at least eight weeks are needed to process the application
- The body cannot be embalmed (don't forget that embalming is required in many provinces before a body can be transported by air, rail, boat or truck).
- The body must be contained in a coffin, preferably solid soft wood, that is weighted to keep it on the bottom and is designed not to release the body.
- The site for burial should be chosen to avoid trawling grounds, dredging activity and currents that will move the coffin.
- The site for burial should be located at least three nautical miles from land, and in at least 200 metres of water.

Even if you're prepared to meet all these conditions, you may have trouble finding a funeral home that is willing to arrange a burial at sea for you. Many funeral homes are concerned about their liability if the coffin is later trawled up by a fishing vessel.

Not surprisingly, no one has gone through with getting a permit for burial at sea in Canada for the past few years. Environment Canada recommends that the family have the body cremated and scatter the ashes at sea instead. No permission and no fee are required to scatter ashes at sea or on a lake (unless it's privately owned) or on a river.

CREMATION

More and more people are choosing cremation over burial these days, partly because it is seen as less expensive than burial. When a body is cremated, it is placed (inside a container or casket) in a cremation chamber—a small furnace—and the temperature in the chamber is raised to about 1000°C. The body is not removed at any time from the container it arrives in at the crematorium, and the container is not normally opened before being put into the cremation chamber except for someone to identify the body before it is placed in the chamber. (It is possible for family members to witness the container being placed in the chamber, or to appoint witnesses to do this.) If there are metal handles on the casket, they will be taken off, but that's really the only modification that happens before the body and container are put into the cremation chamber. Since the container is cremated along with the body, whether it's cardboard or mahogany, you may not want to buy the fanciest, most expensive casket. (In some U.S. states, it's illegal to transport a body for cremation in a casket. This is to prevent funeral homes from persuading people to buy a casket for cremation instead of a cheaper container.) Only one body is cremated at a time. After about an hour and a half, the soft tissues of the body (the flesh and organs), and the container or casket, will have been consumed and all that is left are bone fragments. The fragments are then pulverized to fine ash. (If they aren't pulverized, they'll rattle around in the container they're returned in.) What's left after cremation and pulverization is probably heavier than you're expecting because we usually associate "ashes" with wood ashes which are very light—the container will weigh from about 2 to 4 kilograms.

All medical devices, such as pacemakers and other implants, and prosthetics, must be removed before cremation; otherwise they may explode and damage the crematorium equipment. Funeral homes often remove pacemakers without any charge. It is also necessary to get a coroner's certificate, because if any question later arises about the death, there will be no body to examine. That means that the coroner must be satisfied before cremation about the cause of death. There is usually a 48-hour waiting period before a cremation certificate will be issued. Of course, if the coroner refuses to issue a certificate, cremation cannot take place. It will have to be burial instead. All provinces require a permit to be obtained before cremation, just as they require a permit before burial. The funeral home, transfer service, or crematorium will take care of getting the coroner's certificate and the cremation permit.

Cremation itself costs a few hundred dollars, but, as with burial, there are additional charges that will increase the total cost. For example, the crematorium may charge extra for

- meeting and discussion
- documentation (coroner's certificate, cremation permit)
- administration fees
- transfer to the crematorium (from the place of death or from the funeral home)
- mileage charges for transfer of the body from outside a specified geographical area
- placing the body in the chosen container (if the body is not coming from a funeral home)

- witnessing the cremation process (if requested to do so)
- an urn (the temporary one you get the remains back in)
- shipment of cremated remains

The Ashes

After the cremation, you can do whatever you like with the ashes —keep them in an urn or scatter them. You can purchase an urn through a funeral home or cemetery (if you're going to bury the ashes). An urn can cost whatever you want to spend—you can pay as little as $50 or as much as $1000 or more. You don't have to buy an urn specifically designed to hold cremated remains—you can buy any container you like, such as a beautiful vase or a finely carved wooden box.

Once the remains are in the urn, you can either keep the urn or have it buried in a cemetery. You can bury it in a casket burial plot you have purchased, or you can buy interment rights in a cremation burial plot. Such a plot can cost several hundred dollars. You may also be able to purchase a niche in a wall in a **columbarium** (an arrangement of niches for cremated remains). A niche is more expensive than a cremation burial plot and may cost $1000 or more. In either case, you can normally have a marker or monument put up.

If you choose to scatter the ashes, you can scatter them on private property if you have the owner's permission; on Crown land (owned by the provincial or federal government); or at sea or over a lake or river without permission. If you want to scatter the ashes in a cemetery, you will probably have to pay for the privilege—you may be charged $100 or more (check with the cemetery).

Sometimes people choose cremation over burial because they assume it is much less expensive—but as you can see, cremation costs can add up too. Although a cremation can cost less than a burial, it can still cost a significant amount of money.

DONATING THE BODY TO SCIENCE

Some medical schools and research institutions accept donations of bodies for training students in anatomy and for research purposes. But don't just assume that the school or institution of your choice (or any school or institution for that matter) will accept the body. It's best to check it out in advance. Some schools have more bodies than they need already, and they'll refuse this one; or a research institution may have special criteria for accepting a body. Others may accept the body but ask that transportation to the school be paid by the estate or family.

After the body has served its purpose (this may take up to two years), it will be buried or cremated at the school's or institution's expense. Ask what the institution of your choice will do with the body. In a few provinces, the institution must fulfill the expressed wishes of the person who died about disposal of the remains.

HOW ARE YOU GOING TO PAY FOR THE FUNERAL?

Now you know that funerals are expensive, and you have an idea why. Not everyone—in fact, very few people—have set aside several thousand dollars for a funeral, either their own or a family member's. So is there anywhere the person who has to arrange the funeral (the executor or the next of kin) can get financial help? Yes, there are several possibilities to look into.

• The estate has the primary responsibility to cover the cost of funeral expenses—not the executor or the family. You may be able to arrange for payment of immediate expenses out of the estate. You will have to contact the bank of the person who died in order to get access to estate funds. Usually there will be no problem; the bank will agree to pay a reasonable funeral bill. But this isn't much use if the person who died had very little money saved or was a child.

• If the person who died had a life insurance policy, the insurance company can make funds available. Contact the insurance company.

• Look through the person's documents to find out whether she pre-planned and pre-paid for the funeral and burial or cremation.

• If the person who died was, or a spouse or close surviving relative is, a member of a union, a club or fraternal organization, it may have a fund for funeral expenses. Contact the organization.

• The employment benefits package of the person who died or of a surviving spouse may provide an allowance for funerals. Contact the employer.

• If the death was due to a work-related disease or injury, workers' compensation may make a contribution to burial expenses. Contact the provincial workers' compensation board.

• If the person who died was receiving social assistance, the authorities may arrange for a simple burial if there are no funds in the estate.

• If the death was the result of a motor vehicle accident, contact the insurance company of the person who died. Some provinces have no-fault insurance, and money may be forthcoming to help with funeral expenses. If the driver who caused the accident had no insurance, the provincial accident claims fund or uninsured motorist fund may provide money for expenses.

- If the person who died was a veteran, the Last Post fund will provide an honourable burial if there isn't enough money from other sources. Contact the federal Department of Veterans' Affairs.

- Some funeral homes are willing to discount funeral services, especially if survivors make their own pre-arrangements at the same time. You may also be able to pay on an installment plan. Speak to the funeral director.

- Some cemeteries allow you to pay for the plot on an installment plan.

GETTING TIME OFF WORK— BEREAVEMENT LEAVE

Whether you are responsible for coordinating the funeral arrangements or are simply a mourner attending the funeral and comforting others, you will probably need to take time off work. If you work for yourself, you will probably just have to absorb the loss of income, and explain to your customers or clients that you have to take time off because of a death in the family. Almost everyone will understand and try to be accommodating.

If you are an employee, you will have to find out whether you are entitled to take time off work and whether you will be paid for that time off.

- If your workplace is unionized, the right to bereavement leave is addressed in your collective agreement. Contact your union representative for more information.

- If your employment is governed by federal or provincial employment standards legislation, check what right you have to take time off work. The employment standards legislation of some provinces does not include bereavement leave at all. The bereavement provisions are different in every province, and provincial legislation is different from federal legislation. One thing they have in common, though, is that the person who has died must be a close relative (immediate family) before an employee is entitled to bereavement leave—generally it must be a spouse, child, parent, brother or sister, mother-in-law or father-in-law, and it may be as distant as a grandparent or grandchild, or a brother- or sister-in-law, but it usually can't be a relative any more distant than that unless he lived with the employee. Alberta, Ontario and Prince Edward Island have no bereavement leave; the federal government, British Columbia, New Brunswick, Newfoundland, Nova Scotia, and the Northwest Territories offer up to three days' leave (in some cases with pay); Québec has up to four days' leave; Saskatchewan, five days; and the Yukon, one week.

- If you are an employee but do not come under either a collective agreement or employment standards legislation, speak to your employer as soon as possible. You may have a written contract with your employer that covers bereavement leave, or the business you work for may have a policy about bereavement leave. If not, most employers are understanding, at least in the short term. Your employer may allow you unofficial unpaid bereavement leave, or may allow you to use paid sick days or paid vacation days. Failing that, you'll have to take a day or two off and lose the pay.

For students, getting time off school is as important as getting time off work is for employees. Time off is usually only a problem if the death and funeral occur during an examination or testing period (assignment deadlines can usually be extended informally unless the term is ending). The student (or student's parent) will have to speak to the school, college or university authorities about missing exams. The school may want proof of the death and proof that the person who died is a close relative. If the school is satisfied, it will usually permit the student to write the examination(s) at a later time, or in some cases may allow the student's final mark to be calculated on the basis of all evaluations excluding the examination.

GETTING TO THE FUNERAL— BEREAVEMENT FARES

If you've ever tried to book a plane ticket on the spur of the moment, you know how expensive air fares can be. And if you get a sudden call that a family member has died, you don't have any choice—you have to travel immediately. Fortunately, almost all airlines offer bereavement or compassionate fares.

Bereavement fares can be half the cost, or even less, of full-fare economy-class fares. Ask a travel agent for help, or contact the airline directly for information about cost and documentation required. For bereavement fares on flights within Canada and the United States, the airline may only require information about the funeral home and the funeral date. For international travel, the airline will probably require a copy of the death certificate before the flight. This will be impossible in most cases because government offices of vital statistics don't move at the speed of light; so there is usually an alternative, which is to pay the full fare and then apply for a refund after the trip is over. When you apply for a refund, you will need the death certificate (see Chapter 13 at p. 143), and you will probably also be required to fill out a special form (usually available through the airline's ticket offices) and present your original tickets and boarding passes. There will be a deadline on the length of time after the death that you have to apply for the refund (for example, 90 days), so check what it is either before or immediately after you fly. There will also be restrictions on the people whose death makes a survivor eligible for compassionate fares—it must usually be immediate family. Check with the airline to find out whether this particular death makes you eligible for a compassionate fare, and what you have to show to prove your relationship with the person who died.

LOOKING AFTER THE LIVING

*To every thing there is a season
and a time to every purpose under heaven...
A time to weep, and a time to laugh;
a time to mourn, and a time to dance;
A time to cast away stones,
and a time to gather stones together....*

Almost everyone knows this beautiful passage from Ecclesiastes in the Old Testament and understands its wisdom. In this chapter, we'll talk about mourning, but we'll also talk about dealing with the practical problems that may follow a death.

PAYING THE BILLS

Sometimes the time to mourn and the time to plant, and gather stones together come at the same time. Even though a family member has died, those left behind have to eat and pay the rent or mortgage. If the person who died left behind family members who depended on her financially, the survivors may have to take immediate steps to find new sources of money for living expenses. If the person who died made a will, the executor of the estate is responsible for tracking down any money owing to the survivors or the estate (see Chapter 18 at p. 202). However, many people die without a will, and the survivors may not be able to wait until the court appoints an administrator to look after the estate. Or one of the survivors may *be* the executor. In either case, it will be up to a family member to do something about financial affairs.

There are a number of possible sources of money for a surviving partner and family, but in most cases getting the money will take a little time and a little effort. If the person who died had enough money to carry the family through this period, with luck or good planning he had the foresight to open a joint bank account so that surviving family members can continue to draw funds without any trouble. But if all the person's money, investments and property were in his own name, they now belong to his estate and surviving family members do not have an automatic right to get money out of the estate. The executor or administrator has to take up her duties and go through the necessary steps to get access to the property of the estate, and this may take some time. So surviving family may have to find money for living expenses elsewhere in the short term.

Apart from the money and property that the person owned at the time of death, the survivors or the estate may be entitled to money from other sources. The estate or a named survivor may be entitled to payments associated with:

- life insurance policies—if you're not sure whether the person who died had any life insurance, look for individual life insurance policies among her personal papers, and also contact her employer or past employer(s) as well as any union, professional or fraternal organizations to which she belonged to find out if she was insured under a group life insurance policy. If you find any information about a life insurance policy, write to the insurance company for information about the policy, including the amount payable under the policy and whether an individual was named as **beneficiary** (and can therefore receive the money directly and soon, instead of waiting until the estate has been settled). Also ask what you have to do (what form you have to fill out, what documents you have to provide) before the insurance company will make the payment. If the person owned or co-owned property on which there is a mortgage, check among her papers or with the mortgage lender to find out if she had **mortgage life insurance.** This insurance will pay off the mortgage.

- pension plans—if the person who died was contributing to a pension plan, a **death benefit** may be payable to a named individual or to the estate. Contact the person's employer or past employer(s) and any union, professional or fraternal organizations to find out whether the person was contributing to a pension plan. Write to the pension plan to find out if any benefits are payable and the amount, and who is entitled to receive them. If the person who died was a veteran and was receiving or was eligible to receive DVA (Department of Veterans' Affairs) benefits, write to the local Veterans' Affairs office to find out if surviving family members are entitled to receive any benefits.

- the Canada Pension Plan—if the person who died was employed and made contributions to the Canada Pension Plan, several different benefits may be payable to the estate and/or family members. The estate may be entitled to receive a one-time death benefit; the person's spouse may be entitled to receive a monthly survivor's benefit, and children under the age of 18 (or under the age of 25 and in full-time attendance at school) may be entitled to receive a monthly orphan's benefit. Write to Health Canada to find out what benefits are payable and to whom.

- employment termination pay—if the person who died was employed at the time of death, contact his employer to find out if his estate is entitled to receive any form of termination pay.

- Old Age Security benefits—if the person who died or her spouse was receiving Old Age Security, contact Health Canada, Income Security Program, to find out if increased benefits are available for the survivor. If neither the person nor the surviving spouse was receiving benefits at the time of death but the surviving spouse is between 60 and 65, the survivor may be eligible for benefits anyway.

- other death benefits—if the person who died belonged or the surviving spouse belongs to any organization or social club or lodge, contact that organization to find out if it provides a death benefit to the estate or to surviving family.

Any money that belongs to the estate of the person who died, of course, is not immediately available to the survivors.

If surviving family members are in great financial need and there seem to be no sources of income, relatives and friends might pitch in with help if they understood the situation. This may not be the time to stand on pride and carry on as if there's no problem. If there is no help from that direction, though, a surviving spouse or child can approach the social assistance authorities to apply for benefits. It will probably take a few weeks to start receiving regular benefits, but there may be an emergency fund that can provide a small amount of urgently needed money quickly.

Sometimes it turns out that the person who died left a will that failed to provide for someone (for example, a spouse or a child) who was financially dependent on the person who died. The surviving dependant can apply to the court to override the will and be given enough money to live on (depending, of course, on how much money is in the estate). This is a job for a litigation lawyer.

WHEN YOU CAN'T PAY THE BILLS

Sometimes people live very close to the financial edge. They can pay the bills from month to month as long as nothing unexpected and expensive—such as a death in the family—happens. Or the death may be the end of a long illness, and long illnesses can use up the family funds and put the family into debt. So once family members start trying to put their lives back together after the death, they may realize that they owe money that they can't pay. It may be possible to persuade some **creditors**, the people or organizations to whom the survivors owe money, to give some extra time for payment. Contact them and explain the situation.

If the financial situation is very serious and survivors owe more money than they are likely to have in the near future, they may have to go **bankrupt**. Many people are confused about the difference between **bankruptcy** and **insolvency**. A person is insolvent if she owes an amount of money that is greater than the value of what she owns, or if she cannot pay her debts as they come due. A person is not bankrupt until a court declares her bankrupt, and a court cannot declare a person bankrupt unless she is insolvent and has debts of at least $1000. A court can declare a person bankrupt at the request of the person or a creditor. You may wonder why anyone would ask to be declared bankrupt. After all, if a person goes bankrupt, she loses most of her property. Under federal bankruptcy law, she can technically only keep furniture worth $2000 and personal effects (such as clothing, books and jewellery) worth $1000. (If the debtor owns a house, there is probably a mortgage on it by this time. The mortgage lender acts independently of any bankruptcy proceedings to take possession of the house and sell it to get back the unpaid amount of the mortgage loan. If the house is not mortgaged, in most provinces it too will have to be sold in the bankruptcy.) Everything else is sold by a court-appointed **trustee in bankruptcy** to pay the creditors. But if this is the person's first bankruptcy, it doesn't last very long. She will be automatically **discharged** from bankruptcy after nine months, and being discharged means that all debts (with very few exceptions) are wiped out. The creditors have to take a hike and leave her alone forever. Then the debtor can safely start to rebuild her financial life.

A debtor may be able to avoid going bankrupt by making a **consumer proposal** to creditors. Under a proposal, the debtor can offer to repay the money over time, or to repay at a reduced rate (for example, at the rate of 75 cents on the dollar). However, the creditors may not agree to the proposal, especially if it's for repayment at a very low rate or over a very long period, or if the debtor doesn't seem to have a decent source of income, and they may instead ask the court to declare the debtor bankrupt.

If your finances are in very bad shape after the death, you should contact a trustee in bankruptcy (you can find the names of trustees in the Yellow Pages). The trustee will give you advice about what to do, and help you write a consumer proposal; if that doesn't work out and you choose to or are forced to go bankrupt, the trustee will sell your belongings and deal with the creditors on your behalf. If the debts were owed directly by the person who died, then they should be paid by the estate, not by the surviving family members. (See Chapter 19.)

ARRANGEMENTS FOR CHILDREN OR OTHER DEPENDANTS

If the person who died was caring for children or other family members, it may be necessary to find someone to look after them for a little while. Even if there is a surviving parent or other caregiver, he may be too overwhelmed to look after anyone else properly. Relatives, friends or neighbours may be willing to come into the home to help or to take children or an elderly parent or grandparent into their own home—although they may have difficulty handling several children or someone who needs a lot of care, and may want to share the responsibility with others. If the person who died was receiving provincially funded home care before she died, it may be possible to get respite care. A visiting homemaker might come in to care for children several hours a day, or a care facility might accept, for a few days or weeks, an adult who needs care. If an adult dependant was not receiving subsidized home care before, he may be eligible to receive it now if family caregivers cannot cope (see Chapter 4 at p. 36). If it does not appear possible to find anyone else to look after children, contact the provincial Children's Aid authorities. They may be able to provide assistance, or they may take the children into care temporarily (find space for them in a group home or with foster parents).

If the person who died was a divorced or separated parent and had custody of a child, in almost all cases the surviving parent has both the right and the duty to look after the child. If other relatives are concerned that the surviving parent will not look after the child well, they can apply to the court for custody. To do this, they will need the help of a family law lawyer. If the person who died was the last surviving parent, she should have made a will naming a **guardian** for her child or children or naming someone to have **custody** of the child or children. If there is a named guardian, he may look after the child or children. In some provinces, the named guardian must apply to court within a short time to be formally given custody or appointed guardian. If the person had made no will, or if the named guardian is unable or unwilling to care for the children, other relatives or friends can take the children in and apply to court for custody. If all else fails, orphaned children will be taken into care by the provincial Children's Aid authority and put up for adoption.

ARRANGEMENTS FOR PETS

What should you do with a pet that belonged to the person who died, if arrangements were not made by the pet's owner for the pet to go to a new home? If you can't look after it yourself, try to find some competent person who will look after the pet, at least until you decide what to do. If you don't know of anyone, and you can't afford to board the pet at a privately run kennel, you can ask your local Humane Society to take the pet until better arrangements can be worked out. They may keep it in their own facilities, or send it out to foster care with volunteers. In cases of sudden death of a person living alone, the police or neighbours usually contact the Humane Society to take an animal into its care until the family can be notified.

The best plan in the long run is to find the pet a new home with people who will take good care of it. Animals usually adapt quite well to a new home and new family, so don't get the idea that Fido or Frisky can never be happy again without its owner who is now dead. If the person who died thought this and wanted to have the animal put down after his death (or even wrote into his will that the pet should be euthanized), think twice before you carry out this wish. You can find a new home for the animal with the help of the Humane Society, by spreading the word among your friends and acquaintances, or by contacting local veterinary offices and perhaps posting notices there, or by advertising in a local newspaper. Be very careful about giving the animal to people you know nothing about. Ask them lots of questions about how they will look after the animal, ask to visit their home, ask for references from a veterinarian. Have them agree to take the animal for a trial period during which you can visit them and see how the animal is getting along. Take the animal back if it is being mistreated or seems very unhappy.

GRIEF

Trying to sort out funeral arrangements and financial arrangements and care arrangements for children or elderly relatives or pets is enough of a struggle all by itself, but the struggle will be compounded by the grief that you're experiencing at the loss of your family member.

Everyone's grief is different. It may be influenced by such things as the grieving person's relationship with the person who died, how the person died, the grieving person's social and cultural and religious background, and the people and activities that surround the grieving person. However, there are some general, recognizable stages of grieving that most people go through.

- If the death was expected for some time before it occurred, many survivors go through a stage of mourning in advance called **anticipatory grief**. In some ways, feeling the pain of loss but still having the person you've "lost" with you can help the transition from life to death; but it can also lead to the survivor putting distance between herself and the dying person. This can be painful for the dying person, and it can also lead to feelings of guilt for the survivor, both before and after the death actually happens.

- When the death happens, whether it happens expectedly or unexpectedly, the survivors often feel numb and in a state of shock for several days. During this time, the mind is also occupied with necessary work (the funeral, the finances), and this helps to delay full realization of the death.

- After the numbness wears off, pain and despair set in. This stage of grief lasts about a year for most people (although it can last much longer than that for some), and during that time the grieving person may experience many other unpleasant feelings as well, from bewilderment and purposelessness to wondering if he is going mad or is going to die himself, to pain so acute that only suicide seems to provide any hope of release. In this stage of grief, holidays and anniversaries of events can be especially painful and stressful.

- Eventually, a person in grief accepts the death and becomes resigned to it. Terrible despair becomes sadness that may never go away completely—but sadness may be the price of remembering, and when you lose someone you love, you would probably rather remember and be sad than forget and be peaceful.

What to Do about Grief

Everyone has to grieve; you can't get rid of this burden yourself or take it away from another person. But there are things to do to help yourself cope so that the grief does not become an illness or an obsession.

- Express your emotions, whatever they turn out to be. Some of the things you're feeling may include
  - overwhelming sadness, much deeper than you would have expected
  - relief—that the person is not suffering any more, or, if you were the caregiver, that the responsibility is over
  - guilt, if the relationship was difficult and you feel there are things you still want to say, or things you said and now wish you hadn't, or things you wish you had done with that person (spent more time with him, called more often, shown more affection)
  - anger, because a loving relationship has been ended; or, in some cases, unresolved anger because the relationship was unpleasant or abusive and the death brings up old painful feelings

  Cry if you feel like it; it's perfectly natural and it's also healthy. Keeping a tight rein on your feelings can be bad for both your mental and physical health. Find someone who will listen if you want to talk, preferably someone who has been through a death and has some understanding of what you're feeling. If you have no friends or family you feel you can talk to the way you'd like to be able to talk, consider joining a bereavement group—a group of people who have recently lost someone and who meet regularly to talk and give each other understanding and support. Your family doctor, or priest, minister, rabbi or other religious advisor, or the funeral home should be able to direct you to one.

• Find interesting things to do or think about, and to look forward to. Redecorate a room, get a dog or cat, take up a hobby, sign up for classes in a new subject, go on a trip, do your garden over, join a club. (One of the authors has told her husband that if he dies before her, she'll cope with her grief by throwing out all the junk he wouldn't let her throw out in his lifetime.) For some people, it may be especially necessary to find new interests and new friends: while many times a death will bring out a mourner's support network in force, at other times the mourner will find herself suddenly abandoned. This often happens to a woman who has been widowed if her network consisted of couples who were friends of the husband and wife as a couple. In a network of couples, there is no place for a single woman (newly single men are tolerated quite well, though), and a widow may discover this in unpleasant ways. When this happens, there's very little to do except forget these "friends."

• Find *amusing* things to do and think about too—don't shy away from seeing a funny movie or reading a funny book; don't forbid yourself to laugh.

• Remember the person who died. Share stories about him with your family or friends. Put together an album of photographs, letters and cards, and other reminders. Visit his favourite places. Make a memorial—a tree or garden in his memory, or get involved in a project that would have meant something special to him or that reminds you of him in a special way.

• Think about your spiritual beliefs: this might be a time when you want to reflect on what gives meaning to your life. If you were brought up following a religion, it has something to say to you about the nature of death. Many people have been comforted by listening to the age-old teachings of their faith. Or if you've never paid much attention to matters of faith before, this might be a time you want to start.

• If you find that you need to keep yourself occupied, go back to work (it's not as interesting as taking a trip to the South Pacific but it doesn't cost as much either).

• Avoid making important decisions (like selling a house, changing your job, getting married or getting divorced) during the pain-and-despair stage of grief, because your judgment may not be very good at this time.

- Try not to lean on alcohol and drugs to get you through the rough spots.
- If you feel that you can't cope on your own, get bereavement counselling. Speak to your family doctor, rabbi, minister or other religious advisor, a chaplain or social worker at the hospital, the funeral director; or find out if your employee benefits include counselling.

Helping Others Who Are in Grief

You may not be the only person mourning this death. If your thoughts are turning to others besides yourself, here are some things to think about.

If there are children in the family, don't forget that they are grieving too. Include them in the mourning so that they don't feel alone in their grief or isolated from the older members of the family. Allow them to help plan the funeral; allow them but don't force them to attend the funeral. Talk about the death with them in words they can understand, and be honest and open with them. And don't just talk to them—listen to them as well. They may need to be reassured that there's nothing wrong with being sad and crying, or with being angry or feeling guilty; that they will not feel the pain of this death forever; and that they will be taken care of whatever happens (children may react to a death by worrying what will happen to them if a parent dies). They may ask the same questions over and over again, but try not to become impatient because the repetition of questions and answers helps them adjust to the death.

If one of your parents has died, don't assume that you know what your surviving parent is feeling simply because you have both lost the same person. The death of a husband or wife means something different from the death of a father or mother. If you have brothers and sisters, the death of a parent may lead to family quarrels over things like the funeral and the will (some sibling rivalry never ends—it just hides and waits for an excuse to resurface), which will make everyone feel even worse. However, a death can knit surviving family members closer together, so look for opportunities to comfort and help each other rather than opportunities to fight.

If there has been a death in the family of a friend or acquaintance, don't avoid the friend because you find the situation distressing and uncomfortable. Instead, keep in touch with your friend (attend the funeral, write a note, call every now and then, make short visits), listen to him if he wants to talk, offer your help with errands and chores that need to be done and are beyond your friend's energy and coping ability at the moment (answering the phone immediately after the death, making a meal, doing the laundry or picking up the dry cleaning, vacuuming the house, looking after the children). Don't try to change the subject if your friend wants to talk about the person who has died, don't try to find something positive to say about the death ("At least she's out of his pain," etc.), and don't say things that will feed any concern your friend may have that he did not get adequate care for the person who died ("If I were you, I'd sue that doctor!"; "Why did you let them/not let them carry out that procedure?" etc.). Don't tell your friend that you know how he feels unless you've been through this exact same thing yourself (because if you haven't, you don't). And don't tell your friend how he should feel or when ("You're taking this awfully hard"; "Isn't it time you stopped moping and got on with your life?"). Remember that anniversaries and holidays will be especially hard on your friend.

Suicide Prevention

If someone in grief is extremely upset and distraught, take it seriously. Don't let that person be alone, even if she wants to be. A friend or relative, a religious advisor or a social worker should stay by the person's side, perhaps for some time. For some survivors, suicide is a real possibility. In a 1967 study, researchers found that recent widows and widowers (especially if they were under 30) had a much higher suicide rate than the general population.

Debbie and Dean married when they were 20, and were still inseparable 15 years later when he died unexpectedly of a heart attack. Debbie tried to kill herself that night, but she failed and was admitted to hospital. After four weeks she was released. Two weeks later a friend who had gone to her house to check on her, as she had done regularly since Debbie got out of the hospital, found a note telling her not to come upstairs but to call the police. This time Debbie had succeeded. "At the very least I will no longer be in so much pain," the note said. "At the very best I will be with Dean again." At a memorial service for Debbie, a friend said, "It was almost like Debbie had a terminal illness for six weeks, and although we kept hoping that the doctors or medicine or our love or a peaceful place would help make it better, it couldn't."

The Physical Consequences of Grief

Studies have shown that suffering the loss of someone close to you can cause or worsen an illness, and this seems to be especially true for people who have lost a wife or husband. Physical health can be weakened and recovery from illness delayed by severe emotional pain, even to the point where the survivor dies within a year or two of the loss. The 1967 study of widows and widowers that we mentioned above showed that they were two to three times more likely than others their age to die within the 18-month period following the death of their spouse, often of illnesses such as heart disease, stroke, alcoholism, and cancer. (There's no medical evidence that you can die of a "broken heart," though.) Another study showed that people suffering from acute grief are six times more likely to be hospitalized than the general population. Extreme grief can affect almost every system in the body and may cause physiological changes that make a mourner more vulnerable to diseases. Psychological changes (including depression) may lead to personal neglect, which in turn can result in not noticing physical problems and not getting early help for them, or in not paying attention to the management of a chronic disease like diabetes. Depression may also lead to drinking, which can cause health problems of its own or worsen existing problems.

The physical side-effects of grief may include

- sleeplessness
- loss of appetite and weight loss, or increased appetite and weight gain
- fatigue, loss of energy, and inability to concentrate
- anxiety and restlessness
- headaches
- indigestion, nausea or constipation
- dizziness or fainting spells
- asthma attacks
- tightness or pains in the chest and palpitations
- changes in menstrual patterns
- prostate problems
- sexual difficulties

A person who is grieving should try to

- get enough rest (this may mean discussing sleeping medications with the doctor)
- eat regular meals and follow a well-balanced diet
- get a reasonable amount of exercise
- avoid unnecessary stress (you don't have to keep yourself as busy as possible)
- get social support from loving people
- have medical check-ups more frequently

PART VI

THE ESTATE

16 AN OVERVIEW OF ESTATE ADMINISTRATION

When someone dies, all the property she owned in life and which now belongs to her **estate** must be identified and rounded up, and used to pay any debts she left and to pay taxes. The property that remains must be given away according to the instructions in the person's will if there is a will. If the person who died made no will, she is said to have died **intestate**. Each province has a statute setting out the rules for giving property of the estate to the intestate person's family.

AN ESTATE GLOSSARY

The law of estates positively crawls with legalese and jargon, so it may take a while before you feel comfortable thinking about estate matters. To get you started on the right path, here is a brief list of some of the terms you will encounter. You may want to bookmark this page!

administrator the person appointed by a court to look after the estate if there is no executor

beneficiary a person named in a will, or in an insurance policy, pension plan or retirement savings plan, to receive property or money after the death of the maker of the will, or owner of the policy or plan

distribute assets of the estate   give property of the estate away to the beneficiaries named in the will or, if there is no will, to relatives named in the provincial statute on intestate succession

estate   the property of the person who died; the **assets** of the estate are the individual pieces of property in the estate; **administering** an estate means looking after the estate and finally giving away the assets of the estate according to legal rules

executor   the person named in the will to look after the estate

intestate   not having made a will; the law of **intestate succession** is provincial statute law about who inherits from a person who died without a will

personal representative   the general term for a person who looks after an estate, including both an executor and an administrator

testator   the person who makes a will

trust   an arrangement where someone holds and deals with property for the benefit of others (the beneficiaries of the trust)

trustee   the person who has the duty to hold and deal with the trust property

WHAT IS THE PROPERTY OF THE ESTATE?

When a person dies, all of his property must be given away. However, not all of his property is considered to be part of his estate, and property outside the estate is not given away according to the will or the provincial statute on intestate succession. This property is given away according to different rules. Whether property is part of the estate depends on how it was owned by the person who died.

Property (such as a house or money in a bank account or certificates of deposit or mutual funds or other investments) can be owned by one person alone or by two or more people together. When property is owned by two or more people, in almost all provinces there are two kinds of ownership: **joint tenancy** and **tenancy-in-common**. (In Québec, there is no joint tenancy, only tenancy-in-common.) The most important feature of joint tenancy is the **right of survivorship**, which means that if one owner dies, that owner's interest in the property automatically passes to the surviving owner or owners, no matter what the dead owner's will says. The property does not become part of the estate of the person who died. (You should be aware, though, that if the joint tenancy was created for convenience—for example, to allow one child to help a sick parent with banking matters—the jointly held property may well end up in the estate.) If the person owned tenancy-in-common, her share of the property does not go automatically to the other owners. The share is part of her estate and can be given away by will.

The person who died may also have had a life insurance policy or pension plan that required him to name a beneficiary to receive the proceeds of the policy or plan on his death. If the person who died named a specific person or organization (such as a charity) as beneficiary, the proceeds will be paid automatically to the beneficiary and do not form part of the estate. If the person named his estate as beneficiary or didn't name a beneficiary at all, then the proceeds form part of the estate and can be given away by will. A registered retirement savings plan usually works the same way, but if there aren't enough assets in the estate, the money in the plan may have to be used to pay the debts of the estate even though there is a named beneficiary.

THE PERSONAL REPRESENTATIVE

The personal representative of the estate has the job of locating the property that belongs to the estate, paying the debts and taxes of the person who died, and giving away what's left of the estate to the beneficiaries. If there is a will, the personal representative is named in the will and is called an **executor** (a **liquidator** in Québec and an **estate trustee with a will** in Ontario). If there was no will, the personal representative must be appointed by the courts and is called an **administrator** (a **court-appointed liquidator** in Québec and an **estate trustee without a will** in Ontario). In Chapter 17 we talk about the rules to decide who should be the administrator of an estate.

The personal representative must give away the property of the estate in accordance with the will, if there is one, or in accordance with the provincial statute on intestate succession if there isn't. She must also make sure that jointly owned property passes to the surviving joint owner (if it wasn't just joint ownership for convenience) and that life insurance proceeds and pension and registered retirement savings plans are paid out to the beneficiaries named in the policy or plan.

WHAT ARE THE DUTIES OF THE PERSONAL REPRESENTATIVE?

The duties of a personal representative are the same whether he is an executor or an administrator. The next five chapters discuss these duties in detail, but we'll start off slowly, with an overview of what the personal representative must do:

- Make funeral arrangements—The personal representative has the legal responsibility to make the funeral arrangements and has the final say on what those arrangements should be. But you should check to see if the person who died left any instructions, and also consult with the family. See Chapter 13 for a discussion about funeral arrangements and ways of finding money to pay for the funeral. If there is no will and therefore no executor, it is highly unlikely that an administrator will be appointed in time to handle the funeral—the closest relatives will have to make the arrangements.

- Get information about the estate—The personal representative must find out as much as possible about the property of the person who died and about his debts, including the approximate value of both. The personal representative will need this information to formalize her appointment as personal representative, to locate and collect the estate property, and to pay debts and taxes. See Chapter 18 at p. 202 for a discussion about gathering information about the estate.

- Apply for **letters probate** (if necessary) or **letters of administration**—To administer the estate, the personal representative must be able to prove that he has the legal authority to administer the estate. If there was no will, someone (usually a relative) will have to apply to court to be formally appointed as administrator and to receive letters of administration (known in Ontario as a **certificate of appointment of estate trustee without a will.**) If there was a will, the executor may or may not have to apply for letters probate (known in Ontario as a **certificate of appointment of estate trustee with a will**) depending on the size and complexity of the estate. See Chapter 17 for a discussion about applying for letters of administration and letters probate.

- Protect the property of the estate—The personal representative must take steps to safeguard any valuables such as cash, jewellery or artwork, and must make sure that the estate assets are properly insured. If the person who died left an ongoing business or investments that need active attention, the personal representative must manage them personally or hire someone to manage them. See Chapter 18 at p. 209 for a discussion about protecting the property of the estate. If the person who died was a tenant, the executor has to arrange to terminate the lease.

- Gather in the assets of the estate, make an inventory of them, and value them—The personal representative has to track down all the property of the person who died and have some of it (such as a house, car, investments, bank account) legally registered in the estate's name. The personal representative must keep a list of all the assets and find out what each asset is worth. It is also the personal representative's responsibility to track down any insurance, pension or survivors' benefits that may be payable to surviving family members. See Chapter 18.

• Keep the assets of the estate in proper investments until the debts and taxes are paid and what's left has been distributed to the beneficiaries. See Chapter 18.

• Pay debts and taxes—The personal representative must find out who was owed money by the person who died and then pay all legitimate debts and also pay income taxes. See Chapter 19 for a discussion of debts and Chapter 20 for taxes.

• Distribute the estate to the beneficiaries—Once the personal representative has gathered in all of the assets and paid all of the taxes and other debts, she must give away the remaining assets to the beneficiaries. If there was a will, she must follow the instructions set out in the will. If there was no will, each province has a statute setting out how the estate of a person who dies intestate is to be distributed. See Chapter 21 for a discussion about distribution of the estate.

   Some wills create **trusts**, usually where children under the age of majority or a spouse are involved. In such a case, the executor is the **trustee**, and will be required to keep and manage the property of the estate on behalf of the beneficiaries of the trust, in accordance with the instructions in the will. This may involve, for example, making regular payments to a spouse or child, or investing money so that the capital grows. When the trust ends—often on the death of the spouse or when the children have all reached the age of majority—the executor/trustee distributes the assets of the estate. See Chapter 21 at p. 248 for a discussion of ongoing trusts.

• Account to the beneficiaries—The personal representative will have to give a statement to the beneficiaries that sets out all money and property received into the estate and paid out or given away to beneficiaries. See Chapter 21 at p. 247 for a discussion of accounting.

WHAT KIND OF TROUBLE CAN A PERSONAL REPRESENTATIVE GET INTO?

A personal representative owes a duty to the beneficiaries of the estate to act with the highest level of trust, loyalty and honesty. He is required to handle the estate's money in the way a reasonably prudent business person would handle his own affairs. A beneficiary may be able to sue a personal representative for any losses she suffers if the personal representative behaves dishonestly. The personal representative may also be held legally responsible to the beneficiaries if he doesn't do something he was supposed to do as a personal representative. For example, if the personal representative fails to pay a debt and then distributes all the assets of the estate to the beneficiaries, the personal representative may have to pay the debt personally. In addition, the personal representative may be held responsible for losses suffered by the estate if he is not careful in carrying out his work. For example, if the estate loses money because the personal representative puts the estate's money in unsound investments, he may have to pay back the loss to the estate.

A beneficiary can apply to the court to have the personal representative removed if the beneficiary believes that the personal representative is not handling the estate properly. A court will usually not agree to remove a personal representative who is carrying out her duties competently and honestly. If there is more than one executor and they cannot agree (executors are required to act unanimously), one executor can apply to court to have the other removed.

DO YOU HAVE TO ACT AS THE PERSONAL REPRESENTATIVE?

Now that you have some idea how much work there is to do as personal representative, and that you have to do it right or you could be in trouble, the next thing you want to know is, Do you have to be a personal representative? Before naming you as the executor in his will, the testator should have asked if you would agree to be executor. If you weren't asked, you don't have to accept the position. In fact, even if you agreed at the time, you can still change your mind. In either case, you will have to sign a document in which you **renounce** (give up) your right to be the executor. So—who's going to do it if you don't? If the will named joint executors, the remaining executor(s) can act. If the will named an alternate executor and that person is willing to act, that person may apply to court to be appointed as the executor. If no one was named in the will, or if no one named agrees to act, someone (usually a beneficiary or a family member of the person who died) will have to apply to the court to be appointed as administrator.

If there was no will, you cannot be made an administrator against your wishes. To be appointed administrator, you have to apply to court for the job. If you don't want the job, simply don't apply.

Once you have been formally appointed by the court as the executor or the administrator, it is harder to step down. You will have to apply to court to be released from the position, and you'll have to give an accounting (see Chapter 21 at p. 247).

A PERSONAL REPRESENTATIVE HAS THE RIGHT TO BE PAID

If you've read to this point and decided you'll give personal representative-hood a pass, here's one additional fact you should know. A personal representative is not only legally entitled to be paid back by the estate if he spends any of his own money to administer the estate, but is also legally entitled to be paid a fee out of the estate for his work. Depending on the province, the fee is usually 3 to 5 per cent of the value of the estate (more if a will says so), although the actual amount will depend on how complicated the estate is and how much work has been involved. If you have a lawyer or accountant do work you could have done yourself, such as making funeral arrangements or gathering information about the assets of the estate, you will be entitled to a smaller amount of compensation. You should keep careful records about the amount of time you spend doing estate work and about the nature of the work, and of expenses you pay out of your own pocket, in case someone (for example a beneficiary) challenges the amount you're claiming for compensation.

You don't have to accept compensation if you do not want to. If the beneficiaries are family members or close friends and the estate is small and the work is not too time-consuming, you may decide not to ask for your fee.

A PERSONAL REPRESENTATIVE CAN GET LEGAL AND OTHER PROFESSIONAL HELP

You don't have to do this alone—you can and should get professional help if you need it. We'll tell you in the following chapters when we recommend that you get help. Most personal representatives hire a lawyer. You may want the lawyer to handle most of the administration of the estate, or you may just want help in getting letters probate or letters of administration and some advice from time to time. Many personal representatives also need the help of an accountant, especially if the estate is at all complicated. You may also require the services of other professionals such as evaluators, real estate agents and stockbrokers. The estate pays for necessary professional services, but you must make sure that the fees are reasonable.

17 LETTERS PROBATE AND LETTERS OF ADMINISTRATION

In carrying out your duties as personal representative, you will have to deal with different individuals, businesses and government institutions. But before any of them will be willing to deal with you, they will want proof of two things: first, that the person who died is in fact dead, and second, that you have the legal authority to represent the person's estate. Letters probate provide that proof for an executor and letters of administration provide that proof for an administrator. We encourage you to hire a lawyer to do the legal paperwork to get letters probate or letters of administration. It's not very expensive (as legal fees go) and it may save money and trouble in the future. Anyway, you may not be at your best at this time to master the ins and outs of probate practice.

LETTERS PROBATE

When an executor **probates**, or proves, a will, she is asking the court to make findings that

- the testator is dead
- the will naming the executor is valid and is the most recent will made by the person who died

- the person claiming to be executor is the person authorized in the will to act as executor

If the court makes these findings, it will issue a formal document. Depending on the province the document may be called **probate, letters probate, letters of probate, grant of probate, letters testamentary,** or **certificate of appointment of estate trustee with a will.** For simplicity, we'll use the term letters probate. Once the executor has letters probate, he can offer them as proof of legal authority to carry out any business relating to the estate.

Are Letters Probate Always Necessary?

If the person who died left a will and you were named as executor, one of your first decisions will be whether to apply to court for probate of the will. To put it as simply as possible, letters probate are necessary if anyone you are dealing with insists on seeing letters probate. Most large financial institutions will not transfer assets from the name of the person who died to the name of the estate unless they are shown letters probate. Corporations usually also insist on letters probate before they will transfer shares registered in the name of the person who died to the estate. In addition, the laws of most provinces require an executor to have letters probate before the executor can deal with any real estate interests that belonged to the person who died, or before the executor can start a lawsuit on behalf of the estate.

In other words, an executor does *not* need letters probate if

- the individuals and businesses the executor is dealing with will accept other evidence of her authority to act as executor
- the executor does not have to deal with any real estate, and
- the executor does not want to start a lawsuit on behalf of the estate

By law an executor does not require letters probate in Québec if the will was prepared by a notary. And in Manitoba and Saskatchewan an executor does not need letters probate for an estate worth less than $5000—instead, the executor can get a court order giving power to deal with the estate.

Most people and organizations you deal with as executor will start off by asking for letters probate. But you may be able to persuade them to accept other evidence of your authority as executor, such as a copy of the will and a death certificate, and perhaps a sworn statement by you that the will is valid. They are more likely to accept this kind of evidence if the asset involved is small and you are a close relative of the person who died and are also the beneficiary named in the will to receive the asset.

The Application for Letters Probate

To get letters probate the executor must apply to the appropriate court. Depending on the province you live in, the court may be called Probate Court, Surrogate Court, Wills and Estates Court, Queen's Bench, Superior Court or the Supreme Court. The application must be made in the court in the county or district where the person who died normally lived at the time of death. The application does not usually involve an appearance in court, just filling out documents and taking them to the court office.

The executor must provide a number of documents to the court office. While the documents differ from province to province, the court will always require

- the signed original will (not just a photocopy)
- an **affidavit** (a written, sworn statement) that the will was properly signed by the person who died
- a statement of the total value of the assets (and sometimes of the debts) of the estate, and in some provinces an inventory of the assets and debts
- the executor's affidavit that
  - the will is the last (most recently made) will of the person who died
  - the statement of the value of assets or the inventory is accurate
  - he will properly administer the estate
- an application in the form required by the court

The court may or may not require a death certificate. We have more to say about each of these documents below.

The executor has to give notice of the application for letters probate to any beneficiary named in the will. If the executor lives outside the province where probate is being sought, she may be required to post security with the court—as a guarantee that she will administer the estate properly—by purchasing a bond from an insurance, guarantee or commercial bonding company. The court office or a lawyer will know of an appropriate company.

If you decide not to take our advice to hire a lawyer to handle the probate application for you, you can contact the court office to find out what documents are required in your province. The court office staff should tell you what forms you need, and where you can get them (usually from a legal stationer, not the court office itself). They may even help you fill in the forms and tell you what steps you must take. (In Saskatchewan, the court will type the documents for you if the estate is worth less than $10,000.) Or they may get testy with you because they're not there to run an educational service. If you need additional help, you may be able to find a do-it-yourself book on probating a will or to get information from your provincial Law Society or

Public Legal Education Society. If you prepare the forms yourself, you will still have to have any necessary affidavits sworn in the presence of a notary public or a commissioner for taking oaths. The court office may have someone on staff who can officially witness the swearing of the affidavits. If not, you'll probably have to go to a lawyer to swear the affidavits—and the lawyer may quote a lower fee for doing the entire application himself than for helping you to figure out the details.

Probate records are public. Anyone who wants to can look through the court file for the estate and see the will, the inventory of the estate, and the affidavits.

Original Will

If you are lucky, the testator gave you a copy of the will when it was signed and told you where the original will was. If you weren't told where to find the original will, you can:

- check among the person's documents and papers at home or at her office
- look in any safety deposit box the person rented at a bank or trust company, or
- contact her lawyer

Here's a catch-22 about wills and safety deposit boxes. It may be tricky getting access to the person's safety deposit box to search for a will because banks and trust companies usually only give access to the safety deposit box to someone who can prove legal authority to represent the estate. They'll want to see letters probate. And of course you can't get letters probate until you have the will. (This is why lawyers always advise their clients not to leave the original will in a safety deposit box.) However, most banks and trust companies will grant supervised access to the safety deposit box for the specific purpose of looking for a will, if you are an immediate family member or you have a member of the family with you, and you show them a copy of the will naming you as executor, and a death certificate.

If the lawyer of the person who died has the will and you don't ask him to handle the probate application, the lawyer may charge an administrative fee to find the will and send it to you.

Affidavit of Execution of the Will

The court will require evidence that the will was properly **executed** (signed and witnessed). The best evidence is an affidavit from one of the witnesses to the will. Many lawyers have the witnesses complete this kind of affidavit at the time the will is signed, and they keep the affidavits together with the original will. If a lawyer has the will, she almost certainly also has the affidavits. If you've found an original will among the person's papers but no affidavit, contact the lawyer who prepared the will to find out if she has the affidavit. If no affidavit can be found, you will have to track down at least one of the witnesses and get an affidavit from him. If you do not know the witnesses personally, the lawyer who prepared the will may know them—lawyers often have clerks or secretaries from their office act as the witnesses. If you can't find the witnesses or they have died, check with the court to see what other form of evidence is legally acceptable.

If the will was a **holograph will** (one totally written in his own handwriting by the person who died), there may be no witnesses. In that case, you will need an affidavit from someone familiar with the person's signature and handwriting, stating that the whole will, including the signature, is in the person's handwriting.

Value of the Assets

You will have to provide a statement of the value of the assets of the estate and, in some provinces, the value of the debts of the estate. In certain provinces you must make an inventory of the assets and debts and provide a list of them as well. In most provinces you only have to value and/or list the assets that are part of the estate, and so you do not include

- jointly owned property
- life insurance proceeds, or
- pension benefits payable directly to a named beneficiary

In some provinces, however, you must list and/or value *all* property.

Whatever the requirements of your province, you will have to make a preliminary list of the assets and debts of the estate so that you can start to do your work as executor. If the person who died was very organized, she may have given you a list of all the assets and debts. Otherwise, you will have to do some investigating. Here are some tips:

- Ask the person's lawyer, accountant, stockbroker what assets they are aware of.
- Go through the person's personal papers at home and at the office for any information on bank accounts, investment accounts, insurance policies or other investments; then contact the bank, insurance company, investment dealer, etc. for details of investments and to ask if they know of any other investments.
- Look at the last few years' income tax returns for information about bank accounts, stocks, bonds and other sources of income; then contact the bank,

investment dealer, etc. for details of investments and to ask if they know of any other investments.

• Contact any bank or trust company you think the person may have dealt with and ask for information about any accounts, guaranteed investment certificates, registered retirement savings plans or safety deposit box.

Depending on the assets involved, you may have to get the help of various professionals to put a value on the property of the estate. For example, you might have to contact a real estate appraiser to find out the value of a house or cottage, or a stockbroker to find out the market value of shares.

Application Form and Affidavit of the Executor

Depending on the province, the application form may be called an **application, a petition** or a **praecipe** (that's Latin—to avoid embarrassing yourself, pronounce it to rhyme with recipe). The affidavit of the executor may be part of the application form or may be a separate document. Other court forms may be required as well.

Death Certificate

We discussed the process of making an official death certificate in Chapter 13. You can get the death certificate for a small fee from the vital statistics department of the province where the person died. You can also get a (less official) funeral director's death certificate from the funeral home that handled the funeral, which is often included in the cost of the funeral. The court office may accept this certificate.

Probate Fees

Probate fees are, in theory, administrative fees for the court's work in issuing letters probate. The fees are fixed by the province, but in almost all provinces they have been based on the value of the assets in the estate rather than on the court's time and effort. The higher the value of the assets, the higher the fee, even though the court's work is just about the same for every estate. Furthermore, in calculating the fees, in most provinces debts (other than mortgages on real estate) are not deducted in order to arrive at the value. However, assets that are not part of the estate (jointly owned property, and RRSPs, pension plans and life insurance proceeds payable directly to a beneficiary) do not have to be included in the value. Probate fees can amount to thousands of dollars. In 1998, only Québec charged a probate fee that actually reflected the work involved for the court office. Probate fees have been a handy source of revenue for the provinces. Many personal representatives have got annoyed about paying high probate fees, and finally one of them did something about it.

When Donald Eurig died he left an estate worth $414,000. Under Ontario probate regulations, his executor (who was his widow) was required to pay $5710 in fees to probate his will. Mrs. Eurig applied to court for a declaration that the regulation setting the payment was unlawful and for an order that she be given probate without having to pay the fee. Her application in the Ontario Court (General Division) in 1994 and her appeal to the Ontario Court of Appeal in 1997 were both dismissed. She kept going—to the Supreme Court of Canada, which took a different view. In a 1998 decision, the Supreme Court said that the probate fee was really a tax, not an administrative fee, because there was no relationship between the amount of the fee and the cost of granting letters probate, and because fees paid were used not simply to cover the court costs of granting probate but to run the court administration generally. The provinces have the constitutional right to impose taxes, but they have to do so through legislation. They can't do it by having the cabinet or government bureaucrats set fees behind the scenes, which is exactly how all the provinces set their probate fees. The Supreme Court therefore held that the probate fee was unconstitutional and could not be charged, but they gave Ontario six months to come up with a solution.

This decision affected *all* the provinces that tied probate fees to the value of the estate rather than to the work done. They all had to pass proper laws about probate fees—and many of them began facing lawsuits from people who had paid probate "taxes" in the past. It will probably take a while to sort out the whole question of probate fees across Canada.

After the Application Is Filed

In most cases, the court will review the documents and issue the letters probate, usually within a few weeks, without anyone having to appear in court. If a beneficiary who thinks he should have been given a larger share of the estate by the testator, or someone who would have liked to be a beneficiary but wasn't named in the will, or any other interested party, contests the will, a formal hearing in court may be required to prove the validity of the will. A will can be contested on a number of grounds including that

- the testator was not mentally capable of making a will
- the testator made certain gifts in the will as a result of threats or because she had been unduly influenced by another person

• the will was not signed and witnessed as required by provincial law

If someone opposes your application for letters probate, you should talk to your lawyer.

Once you receive the letters probate from the court, have several **notarial copies** made. These are copies certified by a lawyer or notary public to be exact copies. When you deal with a person or business that asks for proof of your status as executor, provide a notarial copy of the letters probate. Keep the original letters probate.

LETTERS OF ADMINISTRATION

In some circumstances, someone will have to be selected and appointed by the court to act as the estate's personal representative. The personal representative in this case is known as the administrator rather than the executor. Usually an administrator has to be appointed because the person who died did not make a will, but there can be other reasons too—including that the executor named in the will died before the testator did or that the executor named in the will cannot or does not want to accept the position. The court issues letters of administration naming the administrator of the estate. (If there was a will, the document will be called letters of administration with a will, or with will annexed.) The letters of administration are proof of legal authority to administer the estate, and no one has authority to administer the estate until the formal appointment is made.

Who Can Be the Administrator?

Any person who will receive a share of the estate has the right to apply to be the administrator. If more than one person applies, the provincial statute that sets out who has the right to act as administrator comes into play. Usually, the closest relative of the testator who applies will be appointed, with the surviving spouse (in some provinces, this includes a spouse who was not legally married) having the greatest right. It is also possible to have joint administrators. What if no one applies? The beneficiaries who are entitled to receive the biggest share of property may agree to the appointment of someone else as administrator if none of them wants to take on the job. If the person who died had no relatives and the beneficiaries don't agree to appoint someone, then a government official administers the estate.

The Application for Letters of Administration

As with letters probate, the application for letters of administration must be made to the court in the county or district where the person who died ordinarily resided at the time of death. The documents required are similar to those for an application for letters probate. They include

- an application form
- a statement of the value of the assets
- the affidavit of the applicant (the person who wants to be administrator) stating
  - that no will could be found (or that the named executor died before the testator, etc.)
  - his relationship with the dead person that gives him the right to act as administrator
  - (if there is no will) the names of all persons entitled to share in the estate under the provincial statute that states how an estate is to be distributed in an intestacy
  - that he will properly administer the estate
- written consent to the applicant's appointment as administrator from all other relatives with an equal right to be administrator (and in some provinces a written statement from each of them that they do not wish to act)

A death certificate may or may not be required in your province.

The applicant will have to give notice of the application for letters of administration to any person who is entitled to receive a share of the estate. Unless more than one person applies to be administrator, the application will be processed within several weeks and a court hearing will not usually be required. If appointed, the applicant will probably have to post security with the court in the form of a bond, although a bond may not be necessary if all of the beneficiaries and creditors of the estate agree in writing that it is not necessary. Probate fees are payable as with an application for letters probate.

When you receive the letters of administration, have a number of notarial copies made. When you deal with a person or business that asks for proof of your status as administrator, provide a notarial copy of the letters of administration. Keep the original letters of administration.

CHECKLIST

FOR PERSONAL REPRESENTATIVES WHO WANT TO DO IT ALL THEMSELVES

If you decide to apply for probate or letters of administration without the help of a lawyer, here's a list of questions to ask the court office so you don't have to call them 16 separate times.

• What forms does the court office require to apply for letters probate/letters of administration?

• Where can you get blank copies of the forms?

• Can the court office give you samples of completed forms?

• Is a death certificate required? If so, is the funeral director's death certificate acceptable?

• Must you value assets and debts, or just assets?

• Must you list assets (and debts) in addition to valuing them?

• Will you need to post a bond? If so, where can you go to get one? How much does this cost?

• Does the court office have someone on staff before whom affidavits can be sworn?

• (For letters probate) If you can't get an affidavit of execution from a witness to the will, what other form of evidence will the court accept?

• How are probate fees calculated?

18

MANAGING THE PROPERTY OF THE ESTATE

Now you're the personal representative of the estate. You have letters probate or letters of administration, and you are ready to start the real work of administering the estate. (Sorry—everything you went through in Chapter 17 was just a warm-up.)

All of the property in the estate of the person who died becomes the property of the personal representative, **in trust** for the beneficiaries named in the will, if there is a will, or for the people named as beneficiaries by the provincial statute on intestate succession if there is no will. The personal representative cannot use the property for his own benefit, but must deal with it for the benefit of the beneficiaries.

Here's a quick review of what we told you in Chapter 16 about the work in store for you. The personal representative

- has to gather in all of the assets of the estate

- has to have certain assets such as a house, vehicles, cash or investments transferred from the name of the person who died into the name of the estate

- may have to sell assets of the estate—for example, a house or car or shares in a corporation—to turn them into cash or into investments specified by provincial law

- must keep cash safely invested until it's needed
- has to pay debts and taxes
- must distribute whatever is left of the estate to the beneficiaries after the debts and taxes have been paid

This chapter deals with gathering in the assets and having them transferred into the estate's name, and converting assets into cash or specified investments if necessary. In the three following chapters we'll take you through paying debts and paying taxes and distributing the estate. All these chapters speak generally about estate administration. Your estate may be simpler or it may be more complicated.

FIRST TASKS

The personal representative has to find the will, if there is one, and make a preliminary list of the assets and debts of the estate. You've probably done that by now in order to get letters probate or letters of administration. The personal representative should also

- speak to the beneficiaries—contact all the people who are entitled to receive a share of the property of the person who died to tell them about their share, and to find out (if you don't already know) whether immediate family members of the person who died have any pressing financial needs
- go through safety deposit boxes—if you know that the person had a safety deposit box and you haven't already been through it to look for a will, make an appointment with the manager of the bank or trust company to examine the contents of the box and to empty it. The bank or trust company may ask to see letters probate or letters of administration.
- protect the assets of the estate:
  - pets—make sure that pets are properly cared for by you or by friends or relatives of the person who died; if no one can care for the pet, contact your local Humane Society (see Chapter 15 at p. 174)
  - jewellery, stocks, bonds and other valuables—make arrangements with a bank or trust company for a safety deposit box in the name of the estate for storing valuable property
  - other personal property—go through the person's belongings and make sure that all perishable items such as food are disposed of and that other property is stored in a safe place; if there's a car, notify the insurance company immediately if it's being driven by someone else, or not being driven at all

- real estate—notify the home insurance company of the death immediately, and secure the property and contents against damage if no one is living there (see below at p. 211)

- active businesses—see that any ongoing business is being properly managed by senior employees or else hire someone to manage it

- cancel credit cards—notify all of the credit card companies to cancel the cards and send their final bills to the estate (arrange to have joint credit cards transferred to the name of the spouse)

- cancel utilities, telephone, cable TV, magazine and newspaper subscriptions, and any services—ask for a refund for any prepaid portion of a subscription or service, and for a final bill to be sent to the estate; or arrange to have these utilities, services and subscriptions transferred to the name of other family members living in the house

- deal with outstanding cheques:

  - cheques written by the person who died—these cheques are no longer valid and will not be honoured by the bank. If you know of any outstanding cheques, contact the payees and ask for the cheques to be returned to you, and replaced (if appropriate) by cheques from the estate; ask the bank to notify you of cheques as they come into the bank, so that you can contact the payees to let them know that they will be paid out of the estate (if the debt is legitimate—see Chapter 19).

  - cheques made out to the person who died and not yet cashed—these cheques can usually be cashed by the estate or deposited in the estate bank account. If there's a problem, return the cheque to the payor and ask to have it reissued in the name of the estate.

- open a bank account in the name of the estate—you will need a bank account to deposit money you receive on behalf of the estate and to pay the estate's debts and expenses. It's a good idea to choose a chequing account that gives monthly statements and returns cancelled cheques.

GET ORGANIZED

The personal representative will have a lot of documents to deal with as he administers the estate, and he is required to provide the beneficiaries with a full and complete accounting of all money received and paid out. So it is important to keep full and complete records of everything and to be very organized right from the start.

Get a package of legal-sized file folders and create:

- a master file—to keep track of everything you do as personal representative, including finding and collecting assets and finding and paying debts.

Create a checklist to help you do this (a sample checklist is found at the end of this chapter). Clip this checklist to the inside front cover of your master file. Keep copies of all the letters you write asking for information about the assets and debts of the person who died, and keep all the replies.

- a probate file—to keep the original and extra notarial copies of the letters probate or letters of administration, and the original and notarial copies of the death certificate

- asset files—to keep information about each separate asset of importance (for example, the house, the cottage, the car, the investments). Label a separate file folder for each asset that you know about.

- debt files—to keep information about each separate debt (for example, mortgage, car payments, credit cards). Label a separate file folder for each debt that you know about.

- an accounting and inventory file—to keep a record of all money you receive and spend on behalf of the estate. You can use ledger sheets, a columnar pad or an accounting notebook. Note the date, amount and source of any money you receive, as well as the date, amount and reason for any payment. For the inventory, list all the assets. As you collect assets, add each to the list and make a note of its value as of the date of death.

Get a legal-sized accordian file folder to hold all these files.

FIND AND TAKE POSSESSION OF THE ASSETS

It is the personal representative's responsibility to find and take into possession all the property that is part of the estate. Some property, such as cash, jewellery, clothing and furniture, you may simply take physical control of by keeping them in a safe place; while for other property, such as real estate, cars or investments, you will have to have title to the property legally transferred from the name of the person who died into the name of the estate.

You may already know about some assets but will have to find out about others. The personal representative is responsible for contacting anyone who has or might have, or knows or might know of, money or other property belonging to the person who died, or who owes or might owe the person or the estate money. These might include banks, stockbrokers, corporations, customers, etc. You should advise each person or organization of the death and of your appointment as executor or administrator, ask for information about any assets, and find out what you must do to take possession of the assets and/or have them transferred into the name of the estate. Besides wanting proof of the death and of your authority to handle the estate, many of these organizations will want special documents filled out. Once you know each one's requirements, send the requested documents together with a letter asking for the assets to be delivered to you and/or transferred into the name of the estate.

Money and Securities

The person who died may have had money on deposit in a bank, trust company or credit union, and may have owned stocks, bonds, debentures or other securities. You can find out by looking through personal papers for bank books, bank statements, investment statements, trade slips, and share certificates; by looking at recent income tax returns to see if they show interest income or capital gains; by asking family members and the person's employer for information. If you find evidence of money or investments:

• Write to the branch of a bank, trust company, etc. where you know or think that the person had money on deposit and ask about accounts, guaranteed investment certificates, RRSPs or safety deposit boxes, request account numbers and balances, and ask for the financial institution's requirements for transferring the accounts, etc. into the name of the estate.

• Write to the stockbroker, commodity broker, mutual fund company or other investment house where the person may have had a fund, RRSP or an account; ask whether the person had dealings with the organization, and, if so, request account numbers, balances and particulars of the specific investments in the account, and ask for the organization's requirements for transferring the fund or account into the name of the estate.

• Write to the corporation that issued the shares or debentures for particulars and for the corporation's requirements for transferring the securities into the name of the estate.

• Write to the Bank of Canada with Canada Savings Bonds certificate numbers and ask for the value of the bonds, including accumulated interest, as of the date of death, and for the forms required to transfer the bonds into the name of the estate.

Some people are "hiders." The person who died may have concealed valuable property (cash, bonds, securities, jewellery) around her home. You may have to turn into Sherlock Holmes before you can start your work as personal representative. Check these places:

• top shelves of cupboards and cabinets

• the freezer

• behind and under drawers

• inside curtain hems

• under the carpet, including stair carpet

• inside teapots and cookie jars

If you find something hidden in one location, you should assume that things are hidden other places as well. Make a thorough search.

Insurance and Pensions

The estate or a named beneficiary may be entitled to:

- Proceeds from life insurance policies—Look for individual life insurance policies among the papers of the person who died, and contact his employer or past employer(s) and any union, professional or fraternal organizations to which he belonged to see whether he had group life insurance. If you find any information about a life insurance policy, write to the insurance company to ask for particulars of the policy, including the amount payable under the policy and whether there was a named beneficiary. Also ask about the insurance company's requirements for payment of the proceeds.

- Pension plan benefits—Contact the person's employer, past employer(s), and any union, professional or fraternal organizations to see whether she was contributing to a pension plan. If so, there may be a death benefit payable to a named beneficiary or to the estate. Write to the pension plan to find out the amount of any benefits and who is entitled to receive them. If the person was a veteran, write to the local Veterans' Affairs office to find out if there is a veteran's pension.

- Canada Pension Plan—If the person was employed at any time during his life and made contributions to the Canada Pension Plan, several different benefits may be payable to the estate and/or family members. The estate may be entitled to receive a one-time death benefit; the person's spouse may be entitled to receive a monthly survivor's benefit, and children under the age of 18 (or under the age of 25 and in full-time attendance at school) may be entitled to receive a monthly orphan's benefit. Contact Health Canada to find out what benefits are payable and to whom.

If a beneficiary is named in the policy or plan to receive the proceeds, the proceeds are not part of the estate. However, the personal representative and the beneficiary should agree who will be responsible for collecting the proceeds.

Personal Property

The person who died will have owned clothing, furniture and other personal effects and may have owned a car, a boat or other vehicles. She may have left artwork, jewellery, antiques or collections of some value. You must sort through all of this property, place a value on the items (with the help of a dealer or appraiser) and make sure that everything is in a safe place. You will have to arrange for vehicles to be transferred into the name of the estate—contact your provincial department of motor vehicles.

Real Estate

The person who died may have owned a home or other real estate, or may have had other interests in land. If the person owned

- a home or cottage—find out whether the property was owned by the person alone, or with others (as a joint tenant or as a tenant-in-common; see Chapter 16 at p. 184), and whether there are any mortgages on it. You may find title and mortgage documents among the person's papers. Otherwise you will have to check the title documents at the local land registry office (you can hire a lawyer to do this for you). If the property was owned in joint tenancy, full ownership will usually pass automatically to the surviving owner, and you, as personal representative, don't have any responsibility for the property because it does not form part of the estate. (If the jointly owned property was subject to a mortgage, the mortgage will have to be paid by the surviving owner.) If the person owned the property alone or as a tenant-in-common, then the person's interest in the property forms part of the estate, and will either have to be transferred to the beneficiary named in the will to receive the property, or sold if no beneficiary is named or if there is no will. You will have to hire a lawyer to deal with the transfer of title.

- rental or commercial real estate—you must find out how the property was owned—by the person alone, as a joint tenant, or as a tenant-in-common. You will have to hire a lawyer to have the property transferred to a beneficiary or sold. If the property is rented out to tenants, you will have to notify the tenants of the death and request that all future rent cheques be made payable to the estate and sent to you.

- mortgage investments—if the person who died had money invested in mortgages, you will have to contact the mortgagors (the borrowers) to advise them of the death and to request that all future mortgage payments be made payable to the estate and sent to you.

VALUING THE ASSETS

As you locate and take possession of each asset, you must find out how much it was worth on the date of death. You need this information for tax purposes (see Chapter 20) and you may need it to calculate the fee to get letters probate or letters of administration. So whenever you write for information about assets, remember to ask about their value as of the date of death.

Money and Securities

Banks, trust companies and credit unions will tell you the balance of any accounts, guaranteed investment certificates, or RRSPs on the date of death, and the Bank of Canada will tell you the value of any Canada Savings Bonds, including accumulated interest. Stockbrokers, commodity brokers, mutual fund companies and other investment houses should also be able to give you the value of the person's accounts on the date of death. You can find out the value of shares in publicly traded corporations by asking a stockbroker or by checking the stock listings in the newspaper on the date of death. You may have to hire a business valuator to find out the value of shares in a private corporation because a private corporation's shares are not sold to the general public and are not listed on stock exchanges. The only way to find out the value of these shares is to determine the value of the entire corporation and then divide it by the number of shares issued to shareholders. This can be an expensive procedure.

Insurance and Pensions

Find out from the insurance company or pension plan the value of any proceeds from life insurance policies or pension plan benefits that are payable to the estate (rather than payable directly to a named beneficiary).

Personal Property

You will have to get a valuation of valuable items such as vehicles, jewellery, art, antiques, or collections from dealers or professional appraisers.

Real Estate

You can hire a land appraiser or a local real estate agent to tell you the value of real estate on the date of death. Make sure that you tell the appraiser or real estate agent that you need the valuation for estate purposes. If the appraiser or agent thinks you are having it appraised for the purpose of a sale, you are likely to end up with a higher value because they are used to giving optimistic values for sale purposes.

MANAGING THE ASSETS

Once the personal representative takes possession of the assets of the estate, she has to manage them until the estate can be distributed to the beneficiaries. How the personal representative goes about managing the assets depends on whether there was a will and on the kinds of assets in the estate.

If There Is a Will

If there is a will, the personal representative's powers and duties are defined by the will. We will tell you about the powers and duties that are commonly found in wills. But you must carefully read the will that named you executor to see exactly what *you* can or must do.

Executors are not usually required to turn the assets of the estate into cash unless it's necessary to pay debts and taxes of the estate and to pay gifts of cash to beneficiaries who are named in the will to receive cash. In fact, most wills direct the executor to give beneficiaries certain identified assets just as they are—for example, a will may leave specified pieces of jewellery to one beneficiary and a piano to another. In addition, many wills allow the executor to distribute some or all of the estate among the beneficiaries **in specie**, which means that the executor can give beneficiaries assets of the estate in their current form, rather than selling the assets and giving cash to the beneficiaries. For example, if the will says to divide the estate equally between two beneficiaries and it allows distribution in specie, you don't have to convert the entire estate into cash and then divide the money in half. You just have to divide up the existing assets (house, vehicles, furniture, investments, etc.) so that each beneficiary gets property of the same value from the estate.

Most wills give the executor at least some power to choose how the assets of the estate should be invested until the estate is distributed to the beneficiaries. Often the choice of investment is left completely up to the executor. If that is the case, you can keep the investments that the testator had or replace them with other investments of your choice, as long as you handle the estate's money the way a reasonably prudent business person would handle his own money.

If There Is No Will

If there is no will, the personal representative's powers and duties are defined by provincial law. An administrator must convert the assets of the estate into cash and/or investments that are permitted by provincial law as soon as possible (the person who died may have left permitted investments, and they won't need to be changed but simply transferred into the name of the estate), use the cash to pay the debts and taxes of the estate, and then distribute the remaining cash and investments to the beneficiaries named in the provincial statute on intestate succession. The administrator has no authority to give beneficiaries specific items that are part of the estate unless all of the beneficiaries agree to this.

The investments permitted by law are ones that are generally considered to be very safe. Each province has a statute that sets out what investments are allowed, and they usually include:

- government securities of Canada, a province of Canada, the United States of America or the United Kingdom
- deposits or guaranteed investment certificates in a Canadian bank, trust company or credit union
- first mortgages on land in Canada, as long as the mortgage is not for more than 75 per cent of the value of the land (a mortgage for more than 75 per cent is allowed if it is insured by the Canada Mortgage and Housing Corporation)

Some provincial statutes allow a certain portion of the estate's money (usually no more than about one-third) to be invested in slightly riskier investments such as certain types of corporate bonds and shares.

Managing Specific Assets

Different kinds of assets require different treatment.

Money and Securities

The personal representative should close the bank accounts of the person who died and deposit the money into the estate bank account or place the money in permitted investments. Remember that a joint account usually belongs to the surviving owner and is not part of the estate (unless it was set up for convenience alone—see Chapter 16 at p. 184).

If there is a will and the will permits it, the personal representative may keep investment funds, bonds or other securities in their current form, but must keep track of the investments and securities, and convert them into other investments if they start to lose money. If the will leaves a specific investment to a named beneficiary, the personal representative should not convert the investment to cash unless it is necessary to pay the debts or taxes of the estate.

> **TIP:** If the person who died had an RRSP and the beneficiary was the estate or there was no beneficiary named, do not cash in the RRSP without getting income tax advice from an accountant (see Chapter 20 at p. 230).

Insurance and Pensions

If there are proceeds from an insurance policy or pension plan and the beneficiary was the estate or no beneficiary was named, the personal representative should collect the proceeds and deposit the money into the estate bank account or put it into permitted investments.

Personal Property

Even if there is a will, the personal representative may have to sell some or all of the personal property to pay debts or to give gifts of cash to beneficiaries named in the will to receive cash. If the will says to divide personal belongings among certain beneficiaries, the personal representative should not sell anything before finding out the wishes of the beneficiaries (see Chapter 21). If there is no will, the personal representative will have to sell the personal property unless all of the beneficiaries agree to some other arrangement, such as giving it to one or more of the beneficiaries or donating it to charity.

If the personal representative sells property of the estate, she is required to get the best price reasonably possible. So make sure that items that are worth something have been valued by dealers or appraisers, and don't sell them for much less than their value—whether to a dealer or a friend or someone who answers your newspaper advertisement. For less valuable items, there are businesses that conduct sales of household contents, and businesses that buy used clothing or sell it on consignment. You can donate clothing and unsold household effects to charity.

Real Estate

If real estate forms part of the estate, the personal representative must look after the property until it is transferred to a named beneficiary or sold. The personal representative should contact the insurance company immediately to tell them of the death. If no one is living on the property, the insurance company will probably insist that someone inspect the property regularly (maybe even daily), and they may have other requirements as well; for example, that the property be boarded up to protect it from trespassers and vandalism. The personal representative has to pay property taxes and the mortgage (out of the estate bank account) until the property is sold or transferred.

As with personal belongings, real property must be sold for the best price reasonably possible.

APPENDIX

Master Checklists

ASSETS				
Description of Asset	Information Requested	Information Received	Documentation Sent	Asset Received

Each time you discover an asset, add it to the asset list. When you write for information about how to collect the asset, note the date of your request in the second column. When you receive the information, note the date you received the information in the third column. When you send off the documents to collect the asset, note the date you did so in the fourth column. When you receive the asset, note the date you received the asset in the fifth column.

DEBTS			
Description of Debt	Information Requested	Information Received	Debt Paid

Each time you find out about a debt, add it to the debt list. When you write for information about the debt, note the date of your request in the second column. When you receive the information, note the date you received the information in the third column. When you pay the debt, note the date you did so in the fourth column.

19 PAYING THE DEBTS OF THE ESTATE

The person who died may have left a variety of unpaid debts—credit card bills and utility bills, mortgages and personal loans, medical expenses, child support payments, even debts from a business that was not incorporated. As well as the person's debts, there will also be expenses of the estate—funeral expenses, lawyer's bills, valuation fees, perhaps accounting fees. The personal representative cannot distribute the assets of the estate until the debts and other claims of the estate have been dealt with (and taxes have been paid—see the next chapter).

The personal representative must find out what debts there are, then decide whether they are legitimate, and finally pay the legitimate debts fully or persuade the creditor to accept less than full payment. If the personal representative distributes the assets of the estate without first paying or settling the debts and other claims, he may have to pay them personally if there is not enough money left in the estate after the distribution to pay them.

FINDING THE DEBTS

You may have been looking after the person who died for some time before death and you may already know exactly what debts she had, or even that she had no debts at all. If you're not familiar with the affairs of the person, though, you'll have to make a thorough investigation. Go through the person's mail and personal papers at home and at the office. Don't just look for unpaid bills, look for any correspondence that suggests an outstanding debt. Check the person's recent chequing account statements for bills that were paid by pre-authorized payments or post-dated cheques, because people often don't receive bills for payments made in that fashion. Look for outstanding loans by examining recent income tax returns to see if the person was deducting interest from any loans. Speak to the person's lawyer and accountant about outstanding debts they may know of.

If the person who died owned any real estate, find out if there were any mortgages on the property. You may find mortgage documents among the person's papers. If not, you will have to check the title records at the local land registry office (you can hire a lawyer to do this for you). Contact the local municipality to find out if there are any outstanding realty taxes, water and sewage charges or other municipal charges against the property that haven't been paid. Contact the hydro company, the gas or fuel oil company, the telephone company and the cable television company to see if there are any balances owing. If the person was a tenant, when you contact the landlord to terminate the tenancy, ask if any rent is owing. Also ask whether utilities were included in the rent, and contact any companies providing utilities or services that were not included in the rent.

If the person had health care aides or personal attendants or was renting medical equipment, find out if any balances are owing. If the person lived in a nursing home or retirement residence, contact the management to see if there are any outstanding charges. If the person died in a hospital, check whether any charges that are not covered by provincial health insurance have to be paid.

If the person who died was a partner in a business or carried on business as a sole proprietor, the estate will be responsible for the payment of any business debts as well. Go through the business records, speak to the surviving partner(s) or any knowledgeable employees of the business or contact the business's accountant for information.

ADVERTISING FOR CREDITORS

Advertising for creditors means placing an advertisement in a government publication and/or local newspaper to give anyone to whom the person who died owed money notice that they should contact the personal representative to arrange for payment. The advertisement will give the creditors a fixed period of time in which to notify the personal representative. If a personal representative distributes the assets of the estate without advertising for creditors, and a creditor later makes a claim for payment of a debt, the personal representative may have to pay the debt out of his own pocket, if not enough assets are left in the estate to pay the debt.

Whether it's really necessary to advertise for creditors depends on the province you live in and the circumstances of the estate. In some provinces, the personal representative is required by law or probate court practice to advertise for creditors only in certain cases, for example:

• if there was no will

• if the personal representative had to post a bond with the court to get letters of administration

• if the personal representative wants to or has to have accounts approved by the court

• if the personal representative wants to distribute the assets of the estate earlier than a period of time fixed by law

In other provinces, the law requires the personal representative to advertise for creditors no matter what the circumstances of the estate. The law may state how many advertisements the personal representative must place, how frequently and for how long they must run, and how much time the creditors have to reply. Speak to your lawyer or the court office about the requirements in your province.

You may wish to advertise for creditors, even if you aren't legally required to, if you do not feel confident that you have identified all of the debts of the person who died. But if the person was incapacitated and you were handling all of her affairs for a considerable period of time before death, you probably know about all the debts. You may also wish to advertise to make it clear that you have taken all reasonable steps to locate the creditors of the estate, as you are required to do as personal representative.

DECIDING WHETHER THE DEBTS ARE LEGITIMATE

The personal representative must get full details of any debt before paying it. Find out:

• what the debt is for

• the exact amount owing

• who exactly is to be paid

• the circumstances of the debt

Don't just pay anyone who claims to be owed money by the person who died. It is your duty as personal representative to pay only the person's *legitimate* debts. Before you pay any claim, you must make sure that it is rightfully owed.

While most, if not all, of the debts you discover will be properly owing, you may find some debts that you should dispute, particularly if the person who died was living alone and was elderly or frail, and may have been taken advantage of. Don't pay the claim if

- there was no contract—you do not have to carry out any promise to pay money unless there was a contract. A contract doesn't have to be in writing, but be suspicious if there's no written contract signed by the person who died. If the person who died promised to pay money or give some object and was given or promised nothing in return, this was only a promise to give a gift—it's not a contract. Even if there is a written document, in law there is no contract unless each party gives the other something of value (the legal term is **consideration**), such as money, services, goods or even a promise to do something in the future. A court would not have forced the person to give the gift, and won't force the estate to give the gift.

Don't pay the claim—you may be able to have the contract set aside—if the person who died

- was mentally incompetent (because of disability or drugs) to understand the nature of the contract when the contract was entered into

- entered into the contract because of misrepresentation—if the party now demanding payment made a false statement about an important fact related to the contract in order to persuade the person who died to enter into the contract

- was under duress when the contract was entered into—if he entered into it because of violence or threats of violence made by the other party

- entered into the contract because of undue influence by the other party—if the person now demanding payment had a very dominant relationship with the person who died (for example, was a caregiver on whom the dead person was totally dependent)

- was badly taken advantage of in the contract (even if she had all her wits)

In addition, you may not have to pay if

- the contract is contrary to provincial consumer protection legislation

- a significant period has passed since the contract was made. Even a valid contract cannot be enforced forever. A creditor has only a certain period of time to start a lawsuit to claim payment, and once that time has passed, the creditor loses the right to sue. The period of time, called a **limitation period**, varies according to the province and the type of contract.

See Chapter 5 for more about contracts.

You should contact a lawyer if you think you may have legal grounds to dispute a debt or claim.

Even if you believe that a debt is legitimate, don't think that your only options are to pay the debt in full or not to pay at all. If you think the amount being claimed is too high, you can negotiate with the creditor to pay a reduced amount in full settlement of the claim.

> Among the papers of the person who died you find a bill for $1000 from a contracting company for home repairs. You decide that the work was necessary and was carried out properly, but you believe, based on what other contractors charge for similar work, that the bill should have been for $500 to $750 at most. You might offer to pay the contractor $500, and the contractor might agree to accept $750 after negotiations.

If the person who died had a contract to make ongoing payments, you can try to negotiate a one-time payment instead, so that the estate will not be tied up until the payments are completed.

> You learn that the person who died had signed a separation agreement in which he agreed to pay $1000 each month as support to his former wife for two more years. Instead of paying $24,000 spread out over the next two years, you could negotiate with the wife to accept one payment of $18,000. She might agree because it's a benefit to her to get a lump sum now instead of waiting two years for the full amount. Or she might refuse because of the income tax consequences for her.

If you simply do not pay a debt, the creditor may start a lawsuit against the estate or file a notice of claim with the estate court. If that happens, you should see a lawyer.

WHAT MONEY DO YOU USE TO PAY THE DEBTS?

If there is no will, you have to convert the estate into permitted investments. You can cash investments to pay the debts. If there is a will, things are more complicated. Even if there is money sitting in the estate bank account, all money is not the same. Which money or which assets you use to pay the debts of the estate will depend on what the will says.

Read the Will

First see if there are any instructions about how debts are to be paid. Sometimes a will says that a named beneficiary is to be responsible for the payment of a particular debt. For example, the will may leave the cottage to a son and state that the son is to pay the mortgage registered against the cottage. Or the will may leave shares in a corporation to a daughter and state that she is to be responsible for the payment of any fees involved in transferring them into her name.

Usually, though, there are no special instructions, and if that's the case the debts are to be paid out of the **residue** of the estate. The residue is what is left after gifts of identified property or gifts of a fixed amount of money are given out. So look over the gifts in the will and set aside

• items of real and personal property that are left to named beneficiaries, and

• enough cash to pay gifts of fixed amounts of cash to named beneficiaries

Use what is left (the residue) to pay the debts and taxes.

If there is not enough cash in the residue, you will have to sell assets in the residue of the estate to get cash to pay the debts. If there are not enough assets in the residue, you'll have to use the assets of the estate that were earmarked for named beneficiaries. If you reach this point when paying debts, you should pay a visit to your lawyer, because what happens next is not simple and you don't want to make a mistake. When you pay debts with assets that have been identified to go to beneficiaries, you have to use up those assets in the following order:

1. Money set aside for **general legacies**—gifts of money to a named beneficiary that don't come from an identified fund (for example, "I give my nephew Alfred $1000").

2. Money set aside for **demonstrative legacies**—gifts of money that are to be paid out of an identified fund (for example, "I direct my executor to sell my house and pay my dear friend Sarah $15,000 out of the proceeds of the sale").

3. Personal property set aside for **specific legacies**—gifts of identified pieces of personal property to a named beneficiary (for example, "I give my gold jewellery to my niece Andrea"). The property will have to be sold and turned into cash.

4. Real property set aside for **specific devises**—gifts of identified pieces of real property to a named beneficiary (for example, "I leave my home to my grandson Jake"). The property will have to be sold and turned into cash.

If There Is Not Enough Money to Pay Debts and Taxes

If the property of the estate is not enough to cover the debts of the estate, the estate is said to be **insolvent**. In that case, the personal representative can't just pay some creditors and not others. Provincial law sets out the order in which the debts must be paid. In many provinces, certain types of debts (such as funeral expenses and taxes) are given **priority** over others and must be paid in full before other debts are paid at all. Any money left over is divided among the other creditors proportionally to the amount each was owed (for example, if there are two creditors and one is owed $7500 and the other $2500, the first creditor would take 75 per cent of whatever was available to pay the debts). In other provinces, no debts are given priority, and all of the creditors are treated equally (for example, if there is $5000 in the estate and debts of $10,000 to be paid, each creditor would get 50 cents on the dollar). If you discover that you are administering an estate that is insolvent, you should tell creditors (they may want to look over the accounts before they believe you) and make arrangements to pay them according to the requirements of provincial law. Don't expect too much help from a lawyer if the estate is insolvent unless you're going to pay his bill personally.

CLAIMS BY DEPENDANTS AND SPOUSES

Every province has laws to make sure that the **dependants** of the person who died—certain people who relied on the person for financial support—will be taken care of out of the estate. These provincial laws allow a dependant to make a claim for support from the estate if the person who died did not leave the dependant enough money in his will, or if a dependant will not receive enough money under the provincial law of intestate succession. The definition of a dependant varies from province to province—in some provinces only legally married spouses and children can be considered dependants; in others, unmarried spouses, parents, grandparents or siblings also can be dependants. Dependants are given a fixed period of time to make a claim by starting a court action, usually six months. The personal representative cannot legally distribute the assets of the estate until the time limit for these claims has passed without a claim having been made. If a claim *is* made, the personal representative must not distribute any part of the estate unless she gets a court order or unless every dependant consents to the distribution. If the personal representative distributes any of the estate without consent or a court order, she may be personally liable to pay a dependant if there's not enough money left for the dependant after distribution.

    In some provinces, the spouse of the person who died has the right to claim a share of the person's property, if the person's will or the provincial rules on intestate succession do not give the spouse enough. The spouse is given a fixed period of time in which to start a court action, usually six months. The personal representative cannot distribute the assets of the estate until the time limit for making a claim has passed and no claim has been made, or unless the spouse consents to the distribution in writing. If a claim is made, the personal representative may be personally liable to pay the spouse for the amount of any court award if she distributes any of the estate after being notified of the claim.

20

DEATH AND TAXES

Well, you've probably just been waiting for us to say it: the only sure things in life are death and taxes. So here we are at taxes.

There are no "death taxes" or "inheritance taxes" in Canada, but that doesn't mean that no taxes are payable following a death. And in order to reduce the taxes, it is important to know and understand the income tax rules that apply to the estate.

The personal representative must look after all income taxes payable by both the person who died and the estate, including taxes owing by

• the person for the last taxation year of her life

• the person for any previous taxation years

• the estate for any income earned or capital gains made since the date of death

Before distributing the estate, the personal representative should get a **clearance certificate** from Revenue Canada acknowledging that all taxes have been paid. If the personal representative distributes the estate without getting the certificate, she may be personally responsible to pay outstanding taxes.

WHERE DO YOU GO FOR HELP?

In this chapter we will try to explain what the personal representative's responsibilities are, but we want to warn you—this stuff is very complicated, and you will probably need some help. While you are reading through this chapter, take comfort in the fact that help *is* available.

Revenue Canada has published two income tax guides that you may find useful: *Preparing Returns for Deceased Persons* and the *T3 Guide and Trust Return*. You can get these guides from your local district taxation office or via the Internet. You can also get general tax information by phoning Revenue Canada's automated Tax Information Phone Service (TIPS). If you need more personal attention, you can call your local district taxation office or make an appointment to meet with someone at your local district taxation office, to help you fill in the appropriate returns. And you can always just hire an accountant, at the estate's expense. No one would blame you—especially if they've read this chapter!

AN INTRODUCTION TO INCOME TAX

Before you can understand the special income tax rules that apply to estates, it helps to understand income tax generally. You must know something about

- income and capital gains
- tax brackets
- calculation of taxable income
- calculation of taxable capital gains
- special rules for spouses

Income and Capital Gains

In Canada, individuals pay federal and provincial income tax on their **income** and on their **capital gains**. Examples of income are

- salary or wages
- commissions
- tips
- rental payments received
- interest payments received
- dividends on shares
- profits from an unincorporated business

Capital gains are profits from the sale of property such as

- shares in a corporation
- real estate (but not a taxpayer's **principal residence**, which is what a home usually is)
- valuable art or antiques

The tax treatment of income and capital gains is different. Income tax is calculated on the full amount of an individual's income. Capital gains tax is calculated on three-quarters of a capital gain.

Tax Brackets

The percentage rate of tax that an individual pays depends on his total income. As income increases, the percentage rate at which it is taxed also increases, in steps or by brackets. The combined rate of federal and provincial tax varies from province to province, but on average, taxpayers with taxable income of

- less than approximately $6500 pay no tax at all
- between approximately $6500 and approximately $29,500 pay tax at a rate of about 27 per cent
- between approximately $29,500 and approximately $59,000 pay tax at a rate of about 27 per cent on taxable income up to $29,500 and at a rate of about 42 per cent on taxable income between $29,500 and $59,000
- over approximately $59,000 pay tax at a rate of about 27 per cent on taxable income up to $29,500, at a rate of about 42 per cent on taxable income between $29,500 and $59,000, and at a rate of about 50 to 55 per cent on taxable income over $59,000

Calculation of Taxable Income

In the annual tax return, a taxpayer is required to list her income from all sources, including:

- employment income
- commissions
- pension income, including retirement pension benefits, Old Age Security and Canada or Québec Pension Plan benefits
- amounts withdrawn from RRSPs
- disability benefits
- Employment Insurance benefits
- workers' compensation benefits

- dividends, interest and other investment income
- rental income
- net income from an unincorporated business (after deduction of business expenses)
- social assistance payments
- taxable amount of capital gains (see below at p. 227)

These different types of income are added together to arrive at the taxpayer's **total income**.

Taxpayers are allowed certain **deductions** from their total income to arrive at their **taxable income**, the income on which federal and provincial income tax is calculated. Allowable deductions include:

- registered pension plan contributions
- RRSP contributions
- annual union or professional dues
- attendant care expenses that allowed the taxpayer to earn income
- certain child care expenses
- certain moving expenses

A taxpayer is allowed **tax credits** that are used to reduce the amount of tax payable on taxable income. Tax credits include:

- a basic personal amount
- an age amount if the taxpayer is 65 or older
- a spousal amount if the taxpayer has a spouse who earns little or nothing
- an amount for Canada Pension, Québec Pension or Employment Insurance premiums
- a pension income amount if the taxpayer had pension or annuity income
- a disability amount if the taxpayer had a severe mental or physical impairment
- a portion of medical expenses for any 12-month period that ends during the taxation year
- an equivalent-to-spouse amount for separated or divorced taxpayers with dependants
- an amount for infirm dependants age 18 or older
- a caregiver tax credit
- a portion of charitable donations
- an amount for tuition fees

The final tax payable is what is owing after the tax credits have been taken off the federal and provincial income tax that was calculated on the taxpayer's taxable income.

Calculation of Taxable Capital Gains

Capital property is property with a long-term value, such as land, valuable art or antiques. A taxpayer can make a capital gain by selling capital property for more than it cost, or have a capital loss by selling capital property for less than it cost. The purchase price of capital property is not the only thing that determines the cost of the property for capital gains purposes. A capital gain or loss is calculated on the basis of the property's **adjusted cost base**, which includes not only the purchase price of the property, but also other costs of acquiring the property such as legal fees, commissions, licensing fees, and the cost of borrowing money to buy it. The adjusted cost base also includes the cost of improving the property.

Likewise, the money paid to the taxpayer when he sells the property is not the only thing that determines the sale price of the property for capital gains purposes. A capital gain or loss is calculated on the basis of the property's **adjusted sale price**, which is the sale price of the property less the cost of selling it. The cost of selling can include such things as repairs, advertising, legal fees and commissions. A capital gain (or loss) is the difference between the adjusted sale price and the adjusted cost base.

A taxpayer buys shares in a company for $20,000. She pays a broker's commission of $500. Five years later she sells the shares for $35,000. At that time she pays a broker's commission of $800.

The adjusted sale price is

	sale price	$35,000
less	commission	800
adjusted sale price		$34,200

The adjusted cost base is

	purchase price	$20,000
plus	commission	500
adjusted cost base		$20,500

The capital gain is

	adjusted sale price	$34,200
minus	adjusted cost base	20,500
	capital gain	$13,700

The capital gains is $13,700, three quarters of which must be included in the taxpayer's income for tax purposes.

You may be thinking, "Dad didn't sell any capital property, so this doesn't matter. He just gave some stocks to his grandchildren a few weeks before he died, and left me the rest in his will. So I don't have to worry about this capital gains stuff." Here's some bad news—the government considers a gift to be a **disposition** of capital property that triggers a capital gain. And here's even worse news. For tax purposes, there is a **deemed disposition** of all of a taxpayer's capital property when the taxpayer dies. That is, tax law assumes that a taxpayer disposed of all his capital property at the time of death.

Whenever a taxpayer "disposes" of property other than by a sale—whether it's a real transaction like a gift, or an assumed transaction like disposition on death—the government treats the disposition as if a sale at **fair market value** (a sale in the open market at the going price on the day of disposition) had taken place. If the fair market value is higher than the price the taxpayer paid for the property, three-quarters of the increase in value must be included in the taxpayer's income—even though the taxpayer didn't in fact receive any money! If the fair market value is lower than the purchase price, the taxpayer will have a capital loss. While the taxpayer is alive, a capital loss can be used to reduce capital gains, but not to reduce income.

The calculation of the capital gain or loss is a bit more complicated if the taxpayer used the property for business purposes and has claimed **capital cost allowance** (depreciation, or a gradual loss in value) against the property. If the person who died or the estate disposed of business property, you should talk to Revenue Canada or get advice from an accountant.

Special Rules for Spouses

A taxpayer ordinarily has to pay capital gains tax, whether the property is sold or given away or "deemed" to have been disposed of, if the capital property has gone up in value. However, there is an exception when a taxpayer transfers property to his spouse. No capital gain is triggered. Instead, the spouse steps into the shoes of the taxpayer and gets the original adjusted cost base of the capital property along with the property. It is as if the spouse acquired the property at the same time and for the same price as the taxpayer did. This is called a **spousal rollover**. There is an automatic rollover any time a taxpayer transfers property to his spouse during the marriage. (However, the taxpayer can choose not to have a rollover.) When the spouse ultimately sells the property, she includes three-quarters of any capital gain, calculated using the original adjusted cost base, in her income.

A taxpayer bought a building for $100,000 in 1990. She transferred the building to her husband in 1992 when it was worth $150,000. Her husband sold the building in 1995 for $200,000. If there is a rollover, there is no disposition for tax purposes when the taxpayer transfers the building to her husband, and the taxpayer pays no capital gains tax. When the husband sells, he assumes the taxpayer's adjusted cost base of $100,000, and he has to pay tax on a capital gain of $100,000 (the difference between the sale price of $200,000 and the adjusted cost base of $100,000).

If the person who died transferred capital property to her spouse in her lifetime, contact Revenue Canada or see an accountant. For rollovers on death, see below at p. 231.

THE PERSONAL REPRESENTATIVE HAS TO FILE TAX RETURNS

The personal representative must file an income tax return and pay income taxes (out of the assets of the estate) on behalf of the person who died, for the final taxation year of his life. This final taxation year, called the **terminal year**, runs from January 1 of the year of death up to the date of death, and the income tax return is called the **terminal return**.

In some circumstances you may be able to file up to three more separate income tax returns for the terminal year (oh joy!) each for a different type of income—for income from

• a **testamentary trust**

• **rights or things**

• an **unincorporated business** that belonged to the person who died (a sole proprietorship or partnership)

These additional tax returns are discussed more fully below at p. 232.

If the person who died failed to file income tax returns for any taxation years before the year of death, the personal representative must prepare and file returns for any missed years. See below at p. 235.

Finally, the personal representative will have to file annual income tax returns on behalf of the estate for all income earned on any of the estate assets, from the date of death until the date the estate has been fully distributed to the beneficiaries and ceases to exist. If you manage to distribute the estate fully within one year of death, you will only have to file one estate tax return; otherwise you will have to file a tax return once each year until the estate has been completely distributed. The estate tax return is discussed below at p. 233.

THE TERMINAL RETURN

The terminal return that the personal representative files on behalf of the person who died is very similar to the tax return that the person would have filed herself if he hadn't died. The form used is the same T1 General Income Tax Return. In completing the terminal return, all of the regular rules for living taxpayers apply, and there are also some special rules.

Calculation of Income

As with any other tax return, you must start by listing all of the income that the person who died received before death. In addition, you must list income from

- **periodic payments**—money that was payable to the person on a regular basis and that was accumulating but was not yet due to be paid as of the date of death. For example, the person may have loaned money to a borrower who was paying interest on the loan on the first of each month. If the person died on November 15, the next interest payment would not be due until December 1. The interest that accumulated on the loan from November 1 to November 15 must be included in the person's income as a periodic payment, even though the person did not in fact receive the payment before he died. (Interest payable after the date of death belongs to the estate.)

- **rights or things**—money that was owing to the person at the time of death, but which the person had not yet collected—for example, bond coupons not yet cashed, salary, wages or commissions earned but not yet received, or vacation pay earned but not yet taken. (A living taxpayer would not have to pay tax on these things until she actually collected the money.) You can include "rights or things" as income in the terminal return, or you can file a separate return (see below at p. 232). Or you can transfer the value of a "right or thing" to a beneficiary of the estate, within one year of the date of death or within 90 days from the date of the notice of assessment regarding the year of death. If you do this, the beneficiary pays any tax owing. If "rights or things" represent a significant amount of money, you should consult an accountant to help you choose the alternative that will result in the lowest amount of tax.

Special Rules for RRSPs

When a taxpayer dies, she is **deemed** (treated by Revenue Canada as if she has) to have cashed in her RRSPs, and the full amount of the RRSPs must be added to her income in the terminal return. There's no way to get around this rule except through tax planning before death. If the person who died named her spouse as the beneficiary of the RRSP or left the spouse the RRSP in her will, and the spouse transferred the money into her own RRSP, the money in the RRSP is not considered income and no tax is payable. If the person who died had no spouse and instead named a dependent child or grandchild under the age of 18 as beneficiary of the RRSP, or left the dependent child or grandchild the RRSP in her will, no tax is payable by the estate on the RRSP. The full amount of the RRSP proceeds are taxable as income in the hands of the child or grandchild.

Calculation of Taxable Capital Gains on Death

You must include as income in the terminal return three-quarters of any capital gains. The capital gains could have come from the sale or transfer (such as a gift to a family member) of any capital property in the taxation year in which the taxpayer died, or from the deemed disposition of capital property on the taxpayer's death. There will be an automatic spousal rollover of capital property given or left by will to a spouse (unless the personal representative elects not to have a rollover). No capital gains tax is payable for the taxpayer's home (as long as it was his principal residence).

Special rules apply to capital losses in the terminal return. In the terminal return, capital losses must first be used to reduce capital gains, but if any losses are left over they can be used

- first, to reduce the taxpayer's other income

- then, to reduce the taxpayer's other income in the taxation year prior to death

If there are still unused capital losses, the personal representative might choose to use up some or all of them by electing not to have a rollover on some assets passing to the spouse of the person who died. The result will be that the spouse pays less capital gains tax when she later sells those assets.

Deductions and Tax Credits

You can claim on the terminal return all of the deductions and tax credits that a living taxpayer can claim. There are also some special rules about deductions and credits:

- RRSP contributions—If the person who died did not make the maximum contribution to an RRSP during his final year of life, you may, on his behalf, make a contribution to the surviving spouse's RRSP (as long as you do it within a 60-day time limit), and deduct the amount of that contribution from the person's income.

- Charitable donations—You can claim a tax credit not only for the charitable donations made by the person in the last year of her life, but also for any charitable donations made in the will. If the donations exceed the allowable limit and therefore cannot all be used in the terminal return, you can carry back the excess and claim as much of it as is allowable as a credit on the person's tax return for the taxation year before death.

- Medical expenses—You can claim a tax credit for medical expenses for any 24-month period that includes the date of death, rather than for the usual time (a 12-month period that ends in the taxation year.) That means that you can include medical expenses that were billed and paid after death.

Filing the Terminal Return

The terminal return must be filed by April 30 of the calendar year following the death (which is the filing date for all taxpayers) *or* by six months after the date of death, whichever is later. If you go by the six-months rule, you may find that Revenue Canada charges interest after April 30—so file by April 30 just to be safe.

ADDITIONAL TAX RETURNS

As we mentioned above, you may be able to file additional returns for

- income from rights or things (see above at p. 230)

- income from a testamentary trust set up under someone else's will—but only if the year-end of the trust is a date other than December 31

- income from a sole proprietorship or partnership of the person who died— but only if the year-end of the business is not December 31. Recent amendments to the *Income Tax Act* have forced most unincorporated businesses to have a December 31 year-end, so it is unlikely that you will be able to file this kind of return.

In each return, report only that specific type of income and nothing else.

Why Go to All This Trouble?

You should file the additional returns if you can, because you can reduce the total amount of tax that the estate must pay:

- You can claim certain personal tax credits fully on each of the additional returns—the basic personal amount, age credit, spousal credit, dependant credit, and equivalent-to-spouse credit.

- The tax on each return is calculated as if it were filed by a separate taxpayer.

If you can divide the person's income between two or more returns, the total amount of tax payable will be less than if the income were reported on one return (because the income in each return is taxed in a lower tax bracket).

Filing the Returns

The filing deadline for returns for income from a sole proprietorship or partnership is the same as for the terminal return (see above at p. 232). The filing deadline for income from a testamentary trust is 90 days after the trust year-end. The filing deadline for the "rights and things" return is later—one year from the date of death or 90 days after the tax department mails the notice of assessment for the terminal return for the year of death, whichever date is later.

OUTSTANDING TAX RETURNS

If the person who died failed to file income tax returns in any years before death, the personal representative must file those returns. The deadline for filing them is six months after the date of death.

ESTATE TAX RETURNS

The estate is considered to be a new taxpayer that comes into existence on the date of the human taxpayer's death. It is separate from the person who died. The purpose of filing an estate tax return (the T3 Trust Information and Income Tax Return) is twofold: to report income of the estate and to give Revenue Canada information about distributions of income to beneficiaries so that distributed income can be taxed in the hands of the beneficiaries. The personal representative has to file annual income tax returns on behalf of the estate, from the date of death until the date on which the last assets are distributed to the beneficiaries, declaring all income earned on any of the estate assets.

It is not necessary to file a return for the estate in some circumstances; for example, if estate income for the year is less than $500 and no beneficiary received more than $100 of that $500. Contact Revenue Canada or an accountant to find out if you have to file a T3 return.

Estates are taxed in much the same ways as individuals. Income and three-quarters of any capital gain are taxed, and personal income tax rates (as opposed to corporate tax rates) are applied. However, an estate cannot claim any personal tax credits other than the charitable donation tax credit.

Year-End of the Estate

The year-end of the estate can be any date the personal representative chooses, as long as it is not more than 12 months after the date of death. Most personal representatives choose either the anniversary date of the death or December 31. Once you choose a year-end, you cannot change it without the consent of Revenue Canada.

Income of the Estate

The estate must pay tax on any income it earns during the year. However, earned income that is paid out or due to be paid out to a beneficiary is not considered income of the estate, but rather income of the beneficiary. Therefore, in calculating the taxable income of the estate, you should deduct all payments of income you made or were required to make to beneficiaries during that year. You should also deduct any money the estate paid to maintain property that is being held for the use of a beneficiary (for example a home), because that money is also considered to be income to the beneficiary.

> The estate earned income of $15,000 in the taxation year. The will instructed the executor to pay $2500 to the testator's son and $2500 to the testator's daughter. As of the estate's year-end, the executor had paid the son, but had not yet paid the daughter. Both $2500 amounts can be deducted from the income of the estate, reducing the taxable income of the estate to $10,000. The will also instructed the executor to pay all maintenance expenses for the testator's home and to allow the testator's wife to live there. The executor paid maintenance expenses of $3000. These expenses can also be deducted from the income of the estate, further reducing the taxable income of the estate to $7000.

When you make any payment of estate income to a beneficiary, you must issue a T3 slip (available from Revenue Canada) to the beneficiary to make sure that he reports the payment as income in his tax return for the year. Send a copy of the T3 slip to Revenue Canada. If an income payment is made to a beneficiary who does not reside in Canada, the payment is subject to a **withholding tax**. You can pay only part of the total amount to the beneficiary—you have to send the rest to Revenue Canada. How much you have to withhold depends on the terms of the tax treaty with the country where the beneficiary resides—so it's time to contact Revenue Canada again. If the beneficiary files a non-resident tax return in Canada, he may be able to get some or all of the withholding tax back.

Allowable Deductions from Estate Income

Certain expenses of the estate are deductible from its income, including

• interest if the estate borrowed money to invest in income-producing property such as shares, bonds or rental property

• fees paid for management of estate investments, including fees for investment counselling

• safety deposit box rental fees

• fees for accounting services to record estate income

Capital Gains of the Estate

The estate is deemed to have acquired the property of the person who died on the day she died at fair market value. If the personal representative sells property of the estate for more than its fair market value on the date of death, the estate will make a capital gain, three-quarters of which must be added to the income of the estate. If the personal representative sells property for less than its fair market value on the date of death, the estate will have a capital loss which can be used to reduce any capital gains of the estate. (See above at p. 227 for a discussion of how capital gains and losses are calculated.) If a capital loss occurs during the first taxation year of the estate, the personal representative can choose to treat the loss as if it had been suffered by the taxpayer in her terminal taxation year (the personal representative will have to file an amended terminal return).

Tax law pretends that the person who died disposed of his property on death directly to his beneficiaries, so there is no capital gain or loss for the estate when property is transferred to a beneficiary under the will or under the law of intestate succession—unless the personal representative elects (chooses) to trigger a capital gain for the estate, or unless the beneficiary is not a resident of Canada.

Filing the Returns

The deadline for filing annual tax returns is 90 days after the year-end of the estate.

PAYMENT OF TAXES

If any taxes are payable under any of the various returns discussed above, they are due at the same time as the return is due. If the taxes are not paid on the due date, interest and penalties will be charged. However, if there is tax payable because of income from "rights and things" or because of capital gains, that tax does not have to be paid all at once. Instead, the personal representative can pay in up to 10 equal annual installments, after first filing a special document (an **election**) and providing security to Revenue Canada. The estate will be charged interest on the unpaid balance, but there will be no penalties.

CLEARANCE CERTIFICATES

A clearance certificate from Revenue Canada certifies that the person who died and the estate have paid all income tax, Canada Pension Plan contributions, Employment Insurance premiums and interest or penalties owing, or that Revenue Canada has received a satisfactory guarantee that all taxes will be paid. If the personal representative distributes any portion of the estate without first getting a clearance certificate, she will be personally responsible (up to the value of the property distributed) for the payment of any outstanding taxes if there are not enough assets remaining in the estate to pay them.

To get a clearance certificate, the personal representative must

- file a statement with Revenue Canada setting out the details of the proposed distribution and the date on which the personal representative intends to make the distribution
- prepare and file a final T3 estate income tax return calculating what the taxes would be if the distribution is made on the chosen date
- pay the taxes as calculated
- request a clearance certificate

The income tax department will issue the clearance certificate if all returns have been filed and taxes, interest and penalties have been paid. The personal representative should distribute the estate's property as soon as possible after receiving the certificate—or may end up having to file a revised tax return if additional income comes to the estate.

A personal representative who wants to be absolutely safe will pay all debts, including taxes, contributions and premiums, and get a clearance certificate before distributing any property to the beneficiaries. But many personal representatives do not want to wait until all debts and taxes are paid to distribute the estate. It is acceptable to distribute some of the estate, such as personal belongings and some gifts of cash, earlier if you are confident that enough money will be left in the estate to pay debts and taxes.

FOREIGN TAXES

If the person who died lived or owned property outside of Canada, the personal representative may have to pay income tax or inheritance taxes in another country. Contact the foreign country's embassy or consulate for information. If you need advice from an accountant in that country, ask a Canadian accountant for a recommendation.

21

WRAPPING UP THE ESTATE

You've been slogging through estate administration for months, or maybe years, by this point. You have gathered in all the assets of the estate and converted them into cash if required; you've paid the legitimate debts of the estate; you've advertised for creditors and waited until the notice period has passed; you've waited until the period for dependants to make a claim against the estate has passed; you've filed a terminal return for the person who died, a return (or annual returns) for the estate, and paid whatever taxes were due; you've requested and received a clearance certificate from Revenue Canada. After doing all of this, you're thinking that surely you must be almost finished! Sorry, but there are still some administrative hurdles for you to jump over before your job as personal representative is done. You still have to calculate the amount that's due to you in compensation for all the work you've done as personal representative (see Chapter 16 at p. 189)—and set it aside from the assets of the estate, distribute the assets of the estate to the beneficiaries, account to the beneficiaries, and take care of a few final details. And if you're an executor and the will created a trust for a beneficiary...it could be years before you can finally wrap up the estate.

DISTRIBUTING THE ESTATE

Distributing the estate means giving the beneficiaries the property that remains in the estate at this point. (You may already have distributed some personal belongings or gifts of cash, once you were sure that there would be enough left in the estate to pay any debts or other claims and taxes.) How you make the actual distribution depends on the property that is being given to the beneficiary. If the asset is

- cash, simply write a cheque on the estate account. (Don't forget to issue a T3 if any of the cash represents income earned by the estate, and don't forget to withhold part of the income if the beneficiary is not a resident of Canada—see Chapter 20 at p. 234)
- an investment fund, corporate shares or other securities to a beneficiary, follow the institution's or corporation's requirements for transferring the asset into the name of the beneficiary (such as filling in a transfer form)
- a vehicle, arrange with the provincial department of motor vehicles for a transfer of title
- other personal property, simply hand it over to the beneficiary
- real estate, have a lawyer (in British Columbia or Québec, a notary) prepare and register a deed to transfer title from the estate to the beneficiary

But before you can distribute the assets of the estate, you need to know who gets what. You have to know who the beneficiaries are and what each beneficiary is entitled to receive. If there's a will, it names the beneficiaries and says what to give to them. If there's no will, you'll have to look to the provincial statute on intestate succession, which sets out rules about how to distribute the estate of a person who dies without a will.

Whenever you give a beneficiary her share of the estate, you should have her sign a statement acknowledging receipt of the payment or property, and releasing you as personal representative from any claims arising from the estate. You may want to have a lawyer draft this document for you.

WHERE THERE'S A WILL

Following the instructions in the will sounds simple enough but, as with all things legal, it can turn out to be complicated. The property mentioned in the will may not exist any more—the testator may have disposed of it before dying, or you as personal representative may have had to use it to pay debts or taxes. Or the beneficiary may not exist any more—he may have died before the testator did, or after the testator but before you could distribute the estate. Or the beneficiary may have been a witness to the will. Any of these eventualities will make your job as executor more difficult.

Problems That Can Arise with Gifts

Between the time the testator signs the will and the time the personal representative distributes the estate, some property may no longer be there. There are special rules for dealing with this problem and, unfortunately, special legal language for talking about the rules. There's also arithmetic. You'd better find a quiet place with no distractions before you read further.

Most wills give some specifically identified property to named beneficiaries. These gifts are called **specific bequests** or **specific legacies** if they involve personal property, and **specific devises** if they involve real property. If the testator made a gift of a specific piece of property by will, but no longer owned that piece of property at the time of death, the gift fails (the legal term is **adeems**), and the beneficiary gets nothing unless the will provides for a replacement.

> If the will says, "I leave my 1995 Chevrolet automobile to my brother Larry," Larry is out of luck if, before she died, the testator sold her Chevrolet and bought a Toyota. There is no Chevrolet to give him, and the will does not instruct you to give Larry the Toyota as a replacement. On the other hand, if the will says, "I leave my 1995 Chevrolet automobile, or whatever other automobile I may own at my death, to my brother Larry," you can give Larry the Toyota. Likewise, if the will says, "I leave my car to my brother Larry," you can give Larry whatever car the testator owned when she died. If she owned no car when she died, Larry gets nothing.

If the testator left specific property (either real property or personal property) to beneficiaries but the executor had to convert it to cash and use it to pay debts, taxes or other claims, the beneficiaries get nothing if nothing is left over after payment. If cash is left over, the executor has to divide it proportionally among beneficiaries who were entitled to receive the property.

> A testator left his car to his son and his piano to his daughter. The executor had to sell those items to raise money to pay the estate's debts of $12,000. The car was sold for $10,000 and the piano for $5000. After payment of the debts, $3000 was left. The executor pays the son $2000 and the daughter $1000 (because $2000 is proportionally to $1000 as $10,000 is to $5000).

Many wills contain gifts of cash to named beneficiaries. If the will identifies a specific fund out of which the gift is to be paid, the gift is a **demonstrative**

legacy. If the fund for a demonstrative legacy does not exist when the testator dies, the gift fails and the beneficiary gets nothing.

> A will directed the executor to sell the testator's Bell Canada shares and out of the proceeds of the sale to pay the testator's niece $10,000 and the testator's nephew $5000. The testator had sold her Bell Canada shares a few months before her death to pay for nursing care. The gifts both fail.

If the specific fund for a demonstrative legacy has been used to pay debts and taxes but something is left over, divide that amount proportionally among the beneficiaries entitled to receive a demonstrative legacy from that fund.

> A will directed the executor to sell the testator's house and give the testator's daughter $50,000 and the testator's grandson $75,000 from the proceeds. The executor sold the house but had to use most of the proceeds to pay debts. Only $15,000 was left over. The executor therefore paid the daughter $6000 and the grandson $9000 (because $6000 is proportionally to $9000 as $50,000 is to $75,000).

If a will gives a gift of cash but does not identify a specific fund out of which the gift is to be paid, the gift is a **general legacy**. General legacies are paid out of what is left after specific devises, specific legacies and demonstrative legacies have been paid. If there's nothing left over after they've been paid, the beneficiary of the general legacy gets nothing. If the money for general legacies has been partly used up to pay debts and taxes, divide whatever's left proportionally among the beneficiaries who are entitled to receive general legacies.

> A testator left an estate of $160,000, including a house worth $100,000. His will said, "I leave my house to my daughter. To my sister I leave $40,000 and to my nephew I leave $20,000." There were debts of $30,000. After the executor transferred the house to the daughter and paid the debts, $30,000 was left in the estate. The executor paid the sister $20,000 and the nephew $10,000 (because $20,000 is proportionally to $10,000 as $40,000 is to $20,000).

Finally, here's a slightly different problem. A will may direct the executor to divide a particular category of property among a group of beneficiaries without providing any specific instructions. For example, it is very common for wills to instruct the executor to divide the testator's personal belongings equally among his children. The family members may be able to agree on the division of this property, but very often there are serious arguments.

TIP: Here's an approach you can take: Value the various items (if the beneficiaries cannot agree on what the different items are worth, you may have to get a professional valuation). Once all of the items are valued, the beneficiaries can take turns choosing an item until each has a group of items of equal value.

Problems That Can Arise with Beneficiaries

Even if the gifts are all right, there may be something wrong with a beneficiary.

A Beneficiary Who Has Died

If the testator gave a gift (whether real property, personal property or cash) to a named beneficiary and the beneficiary died before the testator, the gift fails (the legal term is **lapses**). The gift does not pass to the beneficiary's heirs but becomes part of the **residue** (see below) of the estate. (However, in some provinces, by statute gifts to certain categories of relatives—usually a child, grandchild, brother or sister—do not lapse. They go instead to that relative's spouse and/or children.) A testator can prevent a gift from failing completely by leaving the property to someone else as an alternative (this is called a **gift-over**).

If the will says, "I leave my diamond cufflinks to my friend Richard," but Richard died before the testator, the gift lapses, and the cufflinks become part of the residue of the estate. They do not go to Richard's only son John. On the other hand, if the will says, "I leave my diamond cufflinks to my friend Richard, but if he predeceases me, I leave my diamond cufflinks to my cousin George," George gets the cufflinks if Richard is dead.

If a beneficiary died after the testator, the property goes to the beneficiary's estate.

A Beneficiary Who Witnessed the Will

In all provinces, a person who witnesses a will is not allowed to receive any gifts under the will. So if a beneficiary was one of the witnesses to the will, the gift to that beneficiary fails. In most provinces a gift to a beneficiary also fails if the beneficiary's spouse witnessed the will. The purpose of the rule is to prevent a beneficiary from forcing the testator to make a will that favours the beneficiary—but when a beneficiary does witness a will, it is usually simply because of ignorance, and not because the beneficiary was strong-arming the testator. An executor may be tempted to ignore the rule, and simply give the beneficiary the gift in the will. If the executor does this, however, she can be sued by the other beneficiaries, whose share of the estate would be greater if that beneficiary got nothing. The executor cannot give the beneficiary the gift without getting the consent of all the other beneficiaries. In some provinces the beneficiary can apply to the court for an order allowing the gift. He will have to satisfy the court that he did not use her dominance over the testator to persuade or force the testator to make the gift.

A Beneficiary Who Is a Minor

Money or property cannot be given directly to a beneficiary who is under the age of majority (18 or 19 depending on the province). Most wills contain a provision that money or property left to minors is to be held in trust for them until they reach at least the age of majority. The executor is usually named the trustee for this money or property. See below at p. 248 for more about ongoing trusts.

Distribution of the Residue

The residue of the estate is what's left after all of the debts and taxes of the estate have been paid and the legacies and devises have been distributed. The people entitled to receive the residue are called the **residuary beneficiaries**.

Dividing the Residue

Often the residue is divided equally among the various residuary beneficiaries, but other times the beneficiaries are left shares of different sizes and the executor must determine the size of each share and divide the residue accordingly. Dividing up the residue is easy enough if the executor has converted all the assets of the estate into cash, but many wills give the executor the discretion to distribute some or all of the residue **in specie**— to distribute the assets in their existing form (which might be, for example, some cash, a bond, a car, the furniture, the china and silverware, the pots and pans). If the will allows distribution of the estate in specie, the executor must value the various items and can give each beneficiary a combination of cash and other property, as long as the total value of property given to each beneficiary amounts to her correct share. If the beneficiaries cannot agree on what the different items are worth, you may have to get a professional valuation.

The Beneficiaries

The residue may be left to one or more beneficiaries named in the will (for example, the testator might leave the residue to "my wife, Elaine" or "my brothers Jeffrey and David"), or it may be left to a category of beneficiaries (for example, the testator might leave the residue to "all of my children"). If the residuary beneficiaries are not individually named, the executor must be sure to identify all of the beneficiaries who are included in the group.

If any of the residuary beneficiaries died before the testator, the executor should talk to a lawyer to find out what happens to the dead beneficiary's share. It may be difficult to tell from reading the will...even if you understand the following discussion about distribution per stirpes and per capita. The will may state that the residue is to be divided among the testator's issue in equal shares **per stirpes**. This means that if a beneficiary dies before the testator, the beneficiary's descendants divide the beneficiary's share.

A testator left the residue of her estate to her issue in equal shares per stirpes. The testator had two sons and one daughter. The first son had one child, the second son had one child, and the daughter had three children. If the second son and the daughter died before the testator, the estate would be divided as follows:

- the first son (who is the only surviving child) will get one-third of the estate, and his child will get nothing
- the second son's one-third share goes to his child
- the daughter's one-third share will be divided equally among her three children —each of these grandchildren will get a one-ninth share of the residue

It may help to see this example in a chart:

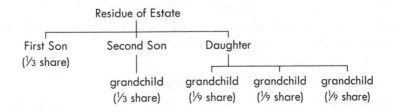

Alternatively, the will may state that the residue is to be divided among the beneficiaries **per capita**. In that case, if one of the beneficiaries died before the testator, that beneficiary's share goes back into the residue to be divided among the surviving beneficiaries—unless the provincial law on inheritance says the dead beneficiary's share should go to his own heirs. If the will says nothing about a beneficiary who dies before the testator—if it doesn't say "per capita" or "per stirpes," or make some other arrangement—then the residue is divided per capita.

IF THERE IS NO WILL

Every province has a statute that sets out how the assets in the estate of a person who died without a will are to be distributed. Below we've set out the general rules that are common to the various statutes, but the complete rules are somewhat different in each province. We recommend that you get advice from your lawyer about how to distribute the estate.

- If the person who died had a spouse but no children or other close relatives, the spouse gets everything. If the person who died had a spouse and also had surviving parents, siblings, nieces or nephews, the spouse will still get everything, except in Québec, where these relatives will get a share of the estate. Note that in some provinces a "spouse" must be a legally married spouse—an unmarried partner is not entitled to receive anything if his partner dies without making a will.

- If the person who died had children and no spouse, the estate is divided equally among the issue per stirpes (if a child died before the parent, the child's children divide the child's share equally).

- If the person who died had both a spouse and children, the estate is divided among the spouse and the children. In some provinces the spouse gets a larger share than the children and in other provinces the children get the larger share. In yet other provinces the spouse gets a fixed amount (sometimes called a **preferential share**) and then the balance is divided among the children per stirpes. In certain provinces, the spouse may be entitled to receive the family home instead of a preferential share.

- If the person who died had no spouse and no children, then the estate goes to other relatives, usually in the following order:

  - to surviving parents

  - to surviving brothers and sisters (**siblings**)

  - to more distant surviving relatives such as grandparents, aunts, uncles nieces, nephews and cousins

- If there are no surviving relatives, then the money goes (the legal term is **escheats**) to the provincial government.

The administrator must take reasonable steps to find the relatives of the person who died, and that may include questioning family and friends, advertising in the personal column of a newspaper, or even hiring a private investigator.

If any beneficiary is under the age of majority (18 or 19 depending on the province), the administrator can't just pay the money to the beneficiary. In some provinces, the administrator has to pay the money to a government official (often called the **Public Trustee**) who will handle the money until the beneficiary comes of age; in others, the administrator must apply to the court for a decision about who will take care of the money.

ACCOUNTING TO THE BENEFICIARIES

As the personal representative of an estate, you are a trustee for all of the beneficiaries of the estate, and as such, have a duty to account fully to them. You must account for

- all of the assets that came to the estate from the person who died
- all of the money the estate received as income or profits
- all of the money paid out of the estate, and all of the property distributed
- the compensation that you claim

If there are no questions concerning claims against the estate and all of the beneficiaries are over the age of majority, you may simply circulate the accounts (your records of the money and property received and the money spent and the property distributed on behalf of the estate) among the beneficiaries and ask them to approve the accounts, approve the amount you claim for compensation, and sign a statement releasing you personally from any claims arising from your administration of the estate. No court proceeding is required if all of the beneficiaries agree that it is unnecessary.

You may have to have your accounts approved by the courts in a formal proceeding called a **passing of accounts**, where the personal representative asks the court to approve of the way she has administered the estate. A formal passing of accounts is required if

- there are any claims by creditors that the personal representative disputes
- any beneficiary is under the age of majority
- any beneficiary disputes the accounts, or applies to the court for an order compelling the personal representative to pass the accounts
- (in some provinces) the personal representative had to post security with the court and is now asking the court to release the security

The personal representative has to serve anyone with an interest in the estate (all beneficiaries and creditors) with a copy of the accounts. If no one objects to the accounts, the personal representative or his lawyer attends before a court officer who reviews the accounts and may ask questions about them. If there is a problem with the form that the accounts are in, the court officer might ask the personal representative to redo them. If the accounts show that the personal representative did something wrong, he may have to face more court proceedings. If anyone with an interest raises an objection to the accounts, there will be a formal hearing with the personal representative or his lawyer present as well as the objector, and those present will have a chance to express their concerns. During a passing of accounts, the court fixes the amount of the personal representative's compensation and can rule on disputed creditors' claims. If the court approves the accounts, it confirms that all of the payments to creditors and beneficiaries were correct.

On a formal passing of accounts, you should hire a lawyer. (Even on an informal accounting you may want a lawyer or accountant to help you.) Your accounts must be in the form required by the court—speak to the court office or your lawyer.

FINAL DETAILS

After you've made the final distribution and passed your accounts, you may have to attend to a few other matters before you are totally finished with your work as the personal representative:

- Check whether the estimate of the value of the estate that you gave to the court when you applied for probate was in fact correct. If the value of the estate was higher than your estimate, you have a duty to notify the court and pay any additional probate fees. If the value of the estate was lower than your estimate, notify the court because you may be entitled to a partial refund of probate fees.

- If you were required to give security to the court when you received your letters probate or letters of administration, apply to the court for release of the security.

ONGOING TRUSTS

Wills often state that a certain portion of the estate is to be held **in trust** for one or more beneficiaries, and name the executor as **trustee**. (This happens most often when a beneficiary is a minor.) It means that the property is to be held and looked after by the executor for the benefit of the beneficiary on the terms and conditions set out in the will. For example, a will may direct the executor to hold the residue of the estate and to keep it invested for the testator's daughter until she reaches the age of 18, at which time the residue is to be given to the daughter.

If the will created a trust of this kind and appointed the executor to be trustee of the trust, the executor's responsibilities continue until the trust ends—until final distribution of the estate to the beneficiary or beneficiaries of the trust. During the term of the trust, the executor will have to

- keep the assets of the estate invested

- make payments out of the estate to the beneficiaries as directed by the will

- file annual income tax returns on behalf of the estate

- account to the beneficiaries on a continuing basis

Depending on the terms of the trust and the age of the beneficiaries, the executor's responsibilities can continue for many years.

PART VII

LEGAL DETOURS

22 YOU AND YOUR LAWYER

You thought this book was about death and dying—so you've probably been surprised by the number of times we've told you to see a lawyer instead of a doctor! In this chapter we're going to give you advice about finding and dealing with the lawyers we keep referring you to, and getting your money's worth out of them.

WHEN DO YOU NEED A LAWYER?

Throughout this book we have tried to provide you with some legal background to help you decide whether you should try to act as your own lawyer or whether you should get professional help. We have also told you when we think a lawyer is essential. To review, here are some of the situations where a lawyer might be useful or even essential:

- preparing a will or a living will
- preparing a power of attorney
- becoming a guardian or committee of an incompetent person
- getting a mentally or physically incapable family member out of a contract

- looking over a contract with an extended care facility
- probating a will
- paying debts and dealing with tax issues
- distributing the estate
- defending or prosecuting a lawsuit against or by the estate

Some of these things you can do yourself; for example, trying to negotiate your family member out of a bad contract, administering a simple estate, or suing in small claims court; but even here, we recommend that you see a lawyer if difficulties arise. And don't wait too long. If a lawyer is needed, the sooner she gets involved, the better—and usually the cheaper in the long run.

CAN YOU GET LEGAL HELP WITHOUT HAVING TO GET A LAWYER?

Sometimes you can get free or inexpensive legal information and advice from government and private sources. You can get kits to make a will or a living will, or you may be able to get help with some matters from a community legal clinic or a student legal clinic. The court office that handles wills and estates will be able to give you a certain amount of advice. Government departments can also give you information…if you can get past their voice mail. Keep in mind, however, that when you go looking for free legal advice, you may end up getting exactly what you pay for.

In many provinces non-lawyers offer a number of legal services. These people may call themselves **paralegals**, **legal consultants** or **legal services providers**. You might be tempted to use their services because they are cheaper than lawyers. But you should know that in most provinces, the paralegal industry is totally unregulated—there are no educational or liability insurance requirements. While some paralegals have many years of experience, others have none at all. If a paralegal does a bad job for you, there may be nobody to complain to, and it may not be worth your while to sue if the paralegal is not insured.

More important than that, in virtually every province the law only allows paralegals to represent clients on limited matters before certain lower courts, such as small claims court, residential landlord and tenant court and provincial offences court, and before some administrative boards and agencies, such as licensing commissions. It is against the law for paralegals to give legal advice or do legal work in other matters, although many openly advertise their services in these areas because the law is rarely enforced. (When the law is enforced it's the paralegal, not the client, who will get into trouble.) One of the things that paralegals are not allowed to do is prepare wills. But you're probably not saving money by having a paralegal draft a will anyway. Most lawyers look on wills as "loss leaders" and don't usually charge very much to draft a straightforward will. They expect to make their money on the will after the testator dies—very often the executor asks the lawyer who prepared the will to look after the estate as well.

WHAT KIND OF LAWYER DO YOU WANT?

All lawyers are not created equal. When you are deciding which one you want, you should consider
• the area or areas of law in which you need expertise
• the size of law firm
• the personality of the individual lawyer

Area of Expertise

A lawyer who is expert in drafting wills normally also handles estate administration matters. But a wills and estates lawyer doesn't usually know all that much about civil litigation if the estate is sued or if the executor wants to start a lawsuit. And a litigation lawyer doesn't usually know much about the tax laws relating to complex estate planning—a tax lawyer does. But forget about all of them if the problem involves guardianship of children or the marriage of a person who suffers from mental confusion. For those matters, you need a family law lawyer. It's very important to get the right lawyer for the right job. If you start off with a lawyer who's a general practitioner, he should refer you to a specialist when it's necessary. If you're worried that a specialist may charge a higher hourly rate than a general practitioner, don't fixate on that. A specialist can often solve a problem quickly because she is familiar with it.

Size of Law Firm

Law firms range in size from sole practitioners to large international firms employing hundreds of lawyers.

People often go to a sole practitioner because the location is convenient (a sole practitioner may be in the neighbourhood rather than downtown), and because they get more personal contact with the lawyer—rather than with secretaries, clerks and junior lawyers—and because fees tend to be lower than at large law firms. Sole practitioners often carry on a general practice and many have lots of experience in wills and estates. They refer clients to specialists when the need arises, but keep track of what's going on in the whole matter.

The other end of the spectrum from a small practitioner is the big well-known firm with dozens, if not hundreds, of lawyers. There is some prestige in being represented by the biggest firm in the city, and big firms are usually full-service, with experts in many fields (lawyers at a big firm are usually specialists rather than general practitioners). Whether you get personal attention from your lawyer or deal with a clerk or a junior lawyer will depend on the firm. Big law firms usually charge higher fees than smaller or one-person law offices.

In between these two extremes are small to mid-size firms, usually made up of lawyers who specialize in different areas of the law. The smaller size of the firm allows one lawyer to have a personal relationship with you, and there may be specialists there in other areas you need. Legal fees of small to mid-size firms may be a bit higher than those of sole practitioners but will usually be lower than those of the big firms.

Personality

You can also let a lawyer's personality sway your choice. After all, you may end up spending a lot of time with your lawyer. You may feel more comfortable if you have a formal, strictly business relationship, or you may prefer a more casual relationship. While there are exceptions, the general rule is that the larger the firm, the more formal the lawyers will be.

Whether your relationship is formal or casual, you want to feel that you can talk freely to your lawyer about your problems. You want a lawyer whose judgment you trust. And perhaps most important, you should have absolutely no doubt about the honesty and integrity of your lawyer.

HOW DO YOU FIND THE RIGHT LAWYER?

There are three main steps in finding a lawyer:
- get several recommendations
- investigate the recommended lawyers and narrow your choices
- interview the finalists before making your decision

   Get several recommendations by
- asking friends or relatives for the names of lawyers who have done similar work for them (for example, who have drafted a will or power of attorney, or acted in estate matters or in family law or civil litigation)
- asking organizations familiar with the kinds of problems you are having for the name of a lawyer they have dealt with (for example the Alzheimer Society, Advocacy Centre for the Elderly in Toronto, an AIDS resource

centre, a community organization that is knowledgeable about care in a facility)

- asking your provincial law society for a list of lawyers in your area who specialize in the field you need (for example, a general practitioner, a wills and estates lawyer, a tax lawyer, a civil litigation lawyer, a lawyer who deals with landlord and tenant law)

   Investigate the recommended lawyers by

- finding out the size of the firm each lawyer practises in

- comparing the fees of each lawyer

- finding out the location of each lawyer's office

   Once you have narrowed down your choices, meet with each lawyer to find out:

- how much experience the lawyer has in the area you need help in

- what the lawyer's rates are

- whether your work will be handled by the lawyer personally or by others (other partners or associates, articling students, law clerks)

- whether you can work comfortably with this person

HOW DO LAWYERS CHARGE FOR THEIR SERVICES?

Lawyers can charge for their services in different ways. They can

- bill at an hourly rate for the time they spend working for you

- charge a flat rate for a particular matter

- charge a contingency fee (in some provinces)

However their fees are calculated, lawyers are required to charge GST (or HST where applicable).

   In addition to their fees, lawyers also bill for disbursements—for example, long distance telephone calls, photocopies, document filing fees, experts' reports, and travel, among many possibilities. (A warning about photocopy fees: lawyers usually charge a lot more per page than your local copy shop.) Some disbursements are also subject to GST or HST. Be aware that disbursements can add up to a significant amount of money.

If you feel that you have been overcharged either for fees or disbursements, don't just gulp and get on with your life. Don't ignore the bill either—your lawyer will sue you, and may have the right to refuse to give you some of the documents received or prepared in the matter. Instead, speak or write to your lawyer. He should be able to explain why the bill is as high as it is, or may be willing to reduce the amount. If you are not satisfied after a discussion with your lawyer about the bill, you have the right to have the bill reviewed by an officer of the court in a procedure called an **assessment** or **taxation**. If the officer agrees that you have been overcharged, the bill will be reduced. In estate matters, the court may review the legal fees as part of the passing of accounts.

Billing at an Hourly Rate

When you hire a lawyer, ask what the hourly rate will be: you have the right to know. If you think the hourly rate is unreasonably high, you can try to negotiate a lower rate, or you can take your business elsewhere. If your lawyer later wishes to raise the stated hourly rate, you must be advised of the change in advance, and must agree to it. If your lawyer raises the hourly rate without telling you or without your consent, the account will be reduced to the original hourly rate if you have the bill assessed or taxed. You may want to ask your lawyer to set out her hourly rate in writing.

Before any work is done on a particular matter, if you are being billed at an hourly rate you should ask your lawyer for an estimate of how many hours the work will take. If it later turns out that the work is going to take longer than estimated, your lawyer must tell you before proceeding further.

Your lawyer will bill you for everything done, including meetings and telephone conversations with you and with others on your behalf, drafting of documents, and preparation of letters to you and others. The lawyer will also bill you for reading letters and documents received from you or others, doing research, reviewing the **file** (reading through the file folders that hold all the documents related to your case to remember what's there before actually getting down to work) and returning telephone calls—even when the other party isn't there to answer. If you have a conversation with your lawyer, you may be billed for the length of the entire conversation, even the time spent chatting about how the funeral went or how the family is getting along now (especially if you're the one who wants to chat). Lawyers divide every hour into tenths (six-minute segments), and may bill for as little as 0.1 of an hour. A phone call to your voice mail would be billed as 0.1.

Before your lawyer does any work for you, he will usually ask for a **retainer**, which is a deposit to be applied against the bill. The requested retainer is usually enough money to cover either all of the estimated work or a substantial part of it. The lawyer must hold the money in a special trust account until the work is done and a bill has been prepared for you. If the retainer is used up before the work is finished, you will be asked for a further retainer. There's no legal limit to the number of times your lawyer can ask you for a further retainer, so it's a good idea to get a written estimate before your lawyer starts the work.

> When billing at an hourly rate, your lawyer should give you an account that shows not just the total number of hours but also a detailed breakdown of how the time billed was spent. If the bill does not contain enough detail, ask for more.

Charging a Flat Rate

Lawyers are willing to quote a flat fee for certain kinds of work such as preparing a will or power of attorney, or acting on a house sale, and other kinds of work where they can predict how long the work will take. For some kinds of work, there is a **tariff** (a set list of fees) that all the lawyers in the county charge by. Disbursements will usually be charged over and above the flat fee. Sometimes disbursements can really add up, so be sure to ask how much they will cost. Your lawyer will ask for a retainer when charging a flat rate, just as when billing at an hourly rate.

Contingency Fee

In some provinces a lawyer is allowed to charge a **contingency fee** for suing someone on your behalf (for example, you might be able to arrange a contingency fee for collecting a debt owed to the estate or bringing a wrongful death lawsuit). The lawyer's fee will be a stated percentage of the amount of money you collect from the other party to the lawsuit. If you don't win or if you win and don't collect any money, you don't have to pay the lawyer's fees, although you usually still have to pay the disbursements. A lawyer will only agree to a contingency fee if you have a good chance of winning and collecting. A contingency fee allows a client with a good case but no money to start a lawsuit.

> If you have a good case but no money, and you live in a province where contingency fees are not allowed, many lawyers will agree to postpone billing you until after your case is finished. They may or may not require you to pay disbursements as the case proceeds. You'll have to pay legal fees even if you lose, but they won't be as high as if you win.

WHAT SHOULD YOU EXPECT
OF YOUR LAWYER?

Lawyers in all provinces are governed by rules of professional conduct that require them to

- act with honesty
- perform any legal services competently and promptly and make sure that anyone who assists the lawyer is also competent
- keep confidential all information about the client and the client's affairs
- represent only the interests of the client and avoid any conflicts of interest
- keep the client thoroughly advised of all work being done and all developments in the matter
- act only on the client's instructions

In addition, because lawyers are in a service industry you should expect good service. Your lawyer should

- not keep you waiting for appointments
- return your telephone calls within 24 hours
- generally treat you with courtesy and respect

You should feel confident that you are getting good quality legal services at a reasonable price and that you are being well treated. If you don't, you should find another lawyer.

HOW DO YOU GET THE MOST
OUT OF YOUR LAWYER?

There are things you can do that will help your lawyer do a better job for you, and there are also things you can do that will help keep your legal fees down.

To help your lawyer do the best possible job for you:

- Consult your lawyer sooner rather than later. In some situations problems can be prevented altogether if you get the right legal advice at the right time. Even after problems arise, they can often be solved much more quickly and at a lower cost if dealt with early.
- Tell your lawyer the absolute truth. Your lawyer has to know the full story (including weaknesses) in order to work for you properly.
- Collect *all* the information and documents that have to do with the matter in question: only you know what information you have. Not everything may turn out to be relevant, but let your lawyer be the judge of that.

- Make yourself available to the lawyer. You must be easily reachable by telephone and you must answer telephone calls and letters promptly. Sometimes your physical presence may also be required, so if you're in the middle of legal proceedings, don't leave town without consulting your lawyer first. To minimize the amount of time you spend waiting for your lawyer to get back to you, ask if there's a certain time of day when he usually returns calls. Or make sure you have a way for the lawyer to get a detailed message to you, such as e-mail, fax or voice-mail.

You want your lawyer to do a good job for you, but you also want the job done efficiently so that your legal fees are kept down. Here is how you can help your lawyer work efficiently:

- Do your homework. If you understand something about the law concerning your particular matter, you will be better able to identify what facts and documents are relevant and to talk about them in a logical manner. Also, the more you know about the law, the less time your lawyer will have to spend explaining it all to you. This book may help you to understand some legal issues.

- Give clear instructions. Your lawyer cannot do anything without them. It is your lawyer's job to tell you what your options are and what the consequences of different courses of action might be, and perhaps even to recommend a particular course of action, but only *you* can make the final decision. Once you've made the decision, be sure to tell your lawyer exactly what you have decided—don't assume she will know what you want done.

- Keep copies of any documents you give to or receive from your lawyer. Then you won't have to ask to be provided with additional copies, and you won't need to be reminded of what's already been done or decided.

- Make the best use of telecommunications. Many clients call their lawyers and leave messages that simply say "please call" without explaining why. If it takes several attempts for your lawyer to contact you, your legal bill will rise. (Remember you may be charged for each telephone call—even if you can't be reached.) More importantly, your lawyer won't be able to do what you want before connecting with you. It is far better to leave a detailed message in the first place—either with a secretary or law clerk or on voice-mail or by fax or e-mail. Some clients are reluctant to discuss their business with a secretary, but the secretary will be working on your file and will know all about it anyway. In addition, all employees are required by their law firms to keep client information confidential.

WHAT IF YOU'RE NOT HAPPY
WITH YOUR LAWYER?

If you've chosen your lawyer carefully, you shouldn't run into too many problems. But if, as time goes by, you become unhappy with any aspect of your relationship, what should you do?

If you are generally pleased with your lawyer's work, discuss problems as they come up—talk about phone calls that are not returned in a reasonable time or a bill that you don't fully understand. But if you've lost confidence in your lawyer, or no longer feel comfortable working with him, you should find another lawyer. It's wise to choose the new one before parting ways with the old one. Your new lawyer should be able to smooth over transitional matters like getting your file so that you never have to confront the lawyer you're firing.

If your concerns are of a more serious nature, such as professional negligence or misconduct, you should seek advice from another lawyer or contact your provincial law society. Lawyers are insured against their own professional negligence, so if a lawyer's mistake has cost you money, you should be able to recover something from the lawyer's insurer. Lawyers can be disciplined by the provincial law society if they are guilty of professional misconduct such as never returning your phone calls or answering your letters, or lying to you about what's going on with your matter. The law society has the power to reprimand lawyers, suspend them from practice for a time, or even disbar them. In serious cases of deliberate misconduct, such as taking your money and gambling it away, lawyers may also be subject to criminal charges. In addition, provincial law societies have a compensation fund available to clients who have suffered losses because of their lawyer's deliberate (rather than negligent) misconduct.

GOING TO COURT

With everything else you have to deal with in looking after your family member and handling the estate, we're certain that the last thing you want to think about is getting mixed up in a lawsuit and going to court. But after reading through this book, you know that court proceedings may be a possibility at different times—for example, to have yourself appointed property guardian of your family member, to sue for compensation if your family member was injured by someone, to be appointed administrator, to collect money owed to the estate.

Sometimes you don't have a choice about starting a court action to get what you want. But if you do have a choice, there are a number of things you should consider:

- How likely are you to win?

- How much will it cost to take the matter to court? Court proceedings can be expensive.

- What will you get if you win—something that makes the financial cost and the vexation worthwhile?

- Can you afford to lose? You'll still have legal bills to pay if the decision goes against you. In matters involving the estate of someone who is mentally incapacitated or dead, the estate is often ordered to pay costs of all the parties. But even if that happens, do you want the estate used up on legal costs?

- If you're suing for money, what are your chances of collecting it if you win? If the other party doesn't have enough money or property to pay the court judgment, the judgment isn't worth the paper it's written on.

- Do you have the time and emotional energy to be involved in a lawsuit? Not all court proceedings take up a lot of time, but many people find them very stressful in *any* court, especially if the proceedings arise out of a family dispute.

Sometimes you don't have a choice about being involved in a court action because you're the one being sued. If someone sues you, your family member or the estate you are administering, you should speak to a lawyer immediately because you only have a limited time to show that you're going to defend the action.

Being involved in legal proceedings doesn't necessarily mean going to court. Some matters involving the estate only require documents to be given to the court. But even if it's a full-blown lawsuit, there are other ways of resolving the dispute. You can try to negotiate a settlement with the other party, either on your own or with the help of a lawyer. Or you can choose **mediation**, a procedure where a neutral mediator will meet with you and the other party to help you try to reach an agreement. A mediator doesn't take sides and doesn't judge who is right and who is wrong, but helps the parties to try to find a solution that satisfies everyone.

Below we'll give you an idea about what goes on if you get involved in some common legal proceedings.

SMALL CLAIMS COURT

You might end up in small claims court if you are trying to collect a small debt or are being sued for payment by a creditor. Small claims court handles disputes involving from up to $3000 to up to $10,000, depending on the province, and its procedure is designed so that parties can handle their own cases (although many parties still choose to be represented by a lawyer or by a paralegal or other agent).

An action in a small claims court is started by the plaintiff writing a claim on a court form. The claim sets out, in a page or two, the facts of the matter and what the plaintiff wants the court to do—for example, order the defendant to pay a bill. If documents are involved, such as a contract or a bill or a letter, in most provinces the court requires them to be attached to the claim. The small claims court usually takes care of serving the claim on the defendant, who then writes a defence on a court form. The defendant explains why the plaintiff is not entitled to get what she is asking the court for, and normally ends the defence by asking the court to **dismiss** the plaintiff's case. The parties can try to settle the dispute before it goes to trial, but apart from that there is usually little contact between them before the trial. In some provinces, the parties are required to attend a pre-trial conference where a neutral (and often rather impatient—he has heard it all before, many times) third person, sometimes a retired judge, discusses the possibility of settlement with them.

When you receive notice from the court of your trial date, start organizing yourself. Practise what you plan to say; write some notes so you won't forget anything when you're standing up in the courtroom. You'll want to state in a calm and logical way what has happened and what you want the judge to do about it. If you plan to bring to court witnesses who have first-hand knowledge of the matter, talk to them about what *they're* going to say. You don't want to be surprised in front of the judge and the other party.

On the trial date, you'll probably find that the courtroom is very crowded, and you may have to wait a long time before your case is heard. You may even have to come back another day. When your case is called, stand whenever you speak to the judge, speak slowly and clearly (that's hard when you're nervous), and be respectful to the judge and polite (grrr!) to the other party.

It is not necessary to have a lawyer or a paralegal act for you at any stage of a small claims court proceeding, but some people prefer to have the entire case handled by someone with experience in going to court. Others ask for advice about writing the claim or the defence, or ask a lawyer or paralegal to do the talking at the trial. There are also self-help books available with information about writing a claim or a defence and about preparing for the trial.

SUPERIOR COURT

If you sue or are sued over a larger debt, or you want compensation because your family member was badly injured or killed because of someone else's **negligence** (carelessness), the lawsuit will be in the superior court of your province. This court has a different name in almost every province, and in yours it may be called the Supreme Court, the High Court, Queen's Bench, General Division, or Provincial Court (that's in Québec). The procedure in a superior court is not designed for parties to look after their own cases, and it is very wise to be represented by a lawyer. Paralegals or other agents are not usually allowed to appear in these courts.

Starting an Action

The person who starts the lawsuit is called the **plaintiff**. If your family member has the right to sue someone—for example, to get compensation for injuries in a car accident—but is not mentally capable of giving instructions to a lawyer about the lawsuit, you will probably have to start the lawsuit on your family member's behalf by applying to the court to be made your family member's **litigation guardian** or **guardian ad litem** (Latin, meaning "for the lawsuit"). Your family member will still be named as plaintiff. If your family member has died and you are the executor or administrator of her estate and are suing on behalf of the estate, the estate may be named as the plaintiff, or you may be named as the plaintiff in your capacity as executor or administrator—it depends on the province.

The plaintiff's lawyer drafts a document called a **statement of claim** that names the person or organization being sued (the **defendant**) and sets out the nature of the plaintiff's claim, the amount of **damages** (compensation requested) or other remedy being asked for, and the facts on which the claim is based. In some provinces the plaintiff's lawyer must first prepare a **writ of summons**, which is a formal statement that a lawsuit has been started. The lawsuit actually starts when the plaintiff pays a fee to the court to have the statement of claim **issued** (registered with the court). The writ of summons or statement of claim must then be **served** on the defendant, usually by having a court officer, or a private professional who specializes in delivering court documents, hand it to the defendant personally.

Defending the Action

After being served with the statement of claim, the defendant's lawyer has a limited period of time—usually a few weeks—in which to defend the action by preparing and then serving a **statement of defence** on the plaintiff's lawyer and also filing it at the court office. The statement of defence sets out the nature of the defence and the facts on which the defence is based. In some provinces the defendant's lawyer files an **appearance** before or at the same time as filing the statement of defence. An appearance simply states that the defendant will be defending the action. If the defendant does not serve and file a statement of defence within the time limit, the plaintiff can get a **default judgment** against the defendant. That means the plaintiff has won the lawsuit, although a defendant with a reasonable explanation can usually have the default judgment set aside so that the lawsuit continues.

Mandatory Mediation

After the statement of defence has been filed, in some provinces the parties may be required to meet with each other and a mediator. If mediation doesn't settle the matter, the lawsuit continues.

Discovery

The plaintiff and the defendant have the right to find out details of each other's case, including the documents and evidence the other party intends to rely upon. The parties are entitled to **discovery of documents,** meaning that each party must give the other party a list of all documents she has concerning the case, and let the other party look at those documents on request. In addition, each party has the right to have a lawyer question the other party either orally in person (**examination for discovery**) or in writing (**discovery by interrogatories**). The party answers the questions under an oath to tell the truth. An examination for discovery takes place before an official reporter who takes down the questions and answers word for word, and then prepares a written record (a **transcript**) of the session. In discovery by interrogatories, one party's lawyer sends written questions to the other party, who must answer those questions in writing.

Requesting a Trial Date

When all of the discoveries have been completed, the plaintiff's lawyer notifies the court that the matter is ready to go to trial, and asks the court to assign a trial date for the case. That date will probably be months away, so you'll either be annoyed that things aren't happening faster, or relieved that you don't have to see the inside of a courtroom just yet.

Pre-Trial Conference

Once a trial date has been requested, either party may request a **pre-trial conference.** In some provinces, the court will schedule one automatically. At a pre-trial conference, the lawyers for the parties and often the parties themselves appear before a judge who tries to help them settle the case. If the case cannot be settled, the judge will see whether the parties can agree on any matters that might shorten the length of the trial (for example, some of the facts about what happened, or the amount of money that the plaintiff lost or had to spend).

Trial and Judgment

The trial usually takes place before a judge only, but in some provinces may take place before a judge and a jury if one of the parties requests it.

At trial, the parties have to prove the facts set out in their own statement of claim or defence. The plaintiff's lawyer presents the plaintiff's case by calling witnesses to **testify** (give evidence under oath by telling what they know about those facts). After each witness testifies, the defendant's lawyer may **cross-examine** the witness to try to weaken the witness's evidence or get the witness to give additional evidence that might help the defendant's case instead. A cross-examination can occasionally look like a third-degree interrogation if the defendant's lawyer thinks the witness is not telling the truth or is hiding something, and neither the plaintiff's lawyer nor the judge is allowed to help the witness very much. The defendant's lawyer then presents the defendant's case in the same way, and the plaintiff's lawyer is allowed to cross-examine the defendant's witnesses. After the witnesses for both sides are finished, the lawyers make a presentation to the judge to summarize the evidence that has been given and to explain the law that applies to the case. In a jury case, the lawyers briefly tell the jury why their side should win, and then the judge gives the jury his own summary of the evidence and explanation of the law. A court reporter (just like at the examination for discovery) takes every single word down as it is said, the whole way through the trial.

At the end of the case, the judge gives **judgment**—that is, says who won and how much the loser has to pay. (If it's a jury case, the judge doesn't make the decision; the jury does instead by giving a **verdict**). If the plaintiff wins, the defendant has to pay the plaintiff something; if the defendant wins, the plaintiff gets nothing. The court usually orders the losing party to pay some of the other party's legal fees—but both sides will still have lawyers' bills. A successful plaintiff often has to use some of the money awarded by the court to pay the lawyer.

Enforcing the Judgment

A judgment for damages or an order to pay the costs of the winning party tells the losing party to pay money to the winning party. If the losing party does not pay voluntarily, it is up to the party who won to try to collect the money. The winning party has the right to question the losing party about her income and property, and can try to get some of that income and property by doing such things as **garnishing** the loser's wages (requiring the loser's employer to pay a portion of the loser's wages to the winning party) and seizing the loser's real property (a home, a cottage, business premises) and personal property (investments, cash in a bank account, a car, equipment). There are people who will help with this business; for example, the county sheriff's office, or a **bailiff** (a professional collector and repossessor).

If the loser lives out of the province or out of the country, the winner must work a little harder to collect the money awarded. The winner may be able simply to register the judgment with the court office where the loser lives and then enforce it as we outlined above. In some cases, the winner will have to start a lawsuit where the loser lives to enforce the original judgment.

Generally speaking, other provinces and other countries will assist the winner rather than protect the loser.

STREAMLINED ACTIONS

If you have to go to court for certain matters—for example, to have the court make a finding that your family member's power of attorney or living will has come into effect, to have yourself appointed as your family member's property guardian or guardian of the person, to have your appointment as administrator approved, or to resolve claims made by creditors or dependants to be paid money by the estate—you won't have to go through the whole rigamarole of a superior court action. You might still be in the superior court, or in some provinces in a special estate court called Probate Court, Surrogate Court or Wills and Estates Court.

The court proceeding in these matters is often called an **application**, and the person who starts the application is called the **applicant**. The applicant's lawyer prepares a document, also called an **application** (or **notice of application**), which sets out the nature of the applicant's claim and what the applicant wants the court to do. The applicant's lawyer also has to prepare an **affidavit**, which is a written statement containing evidence about the matter, and the person who provided the evidence (often the applicant) has to swear under oath that the affidavit contains the truth. The applicant must pay a fee to the court to have the application issued; and the application and the affidavit must be served on interested parties (the **respondents**), who then have a limited period of time to defend the application by serving affidavits of their own on the applicant's lawyer.

The applicant and respondent(s) usually have the right to have their lawyers **cross-examine** the person who provided the information for the affidavit. The cross-examination takes place, like an examination for discovery, before an official reporter who prepares a transcript setting out every question and answer. The parties may also have the right to know about and look at each other's documents that are related to the application. After cross-examinations are finished, the parties' lawyers appear before a judge who makes a decision based on the affidavits and transcripts of the cross-examinations. The judge may make a final decision right away. However, if the problem is complicated or sometimes even just if the respondents oppose what the applicant wants, the judge may order the matter to go to trial. When that happens, the application in effect turns into a superior court action and the next step is to have discoveries (see above at p. 267).

WHAT IF YOU DON'T AGREE WITH THE JUDGE'S DECISION?

A losing party who thinks the judge (or jury) was wrong may be able to appeal the decision within a limited period of time to a higher court. Small claims court decisions are usually appealed to the superior court, and superior court decisions are usually appealed to the provincial Court of Appeal. An appeal is expensive, especially to the Court of Appeal. Sometimes you need the court's permission to appeal. Even if you've got the money and the permission—and the time, because appeals aren't usually heard very quickly—an appeal court only overturns a trial decision if it believes that the judge made a serious mistake about how the law applied to the facts of the case. If you want to appeal a decision of the Court of Appeal, you have to go to the Supreme Court of Canada. That's even more expensive than going to the Court of Appeal, and you have to have the Supreme Court's permission to bring the appeal.

24

CONCLUSION

$\mathbf{W}$e wish that reaching the end of this book meant that you were coming to the end of your troubles, but we know it doesn't.

We also wish that we could do something to make your troubles go away, but we know we can't. You're going to have to live through some very unpleasant times. At least, though, if you've looked through this book, you won't live through them totally unaware of what's actually going on and how you're supposed to act and react. Now you have some idea of the importance of planning ahead whenever possible to smooth a difficult road, of why people don't have to die in pain, of how to avoid arranging the world's most expensive funeral, of the possibility of getting tax relief when some extra cash will be very useful...and many more things that may, over time, save you one crushing headache out of every two you're facing. And perhaps more importantly, having all this information and having it in one place may help you to find some extra time—time you've been using to try to figure out what to do now and what's going to come next—to spend with your family member or remembering your family member.

INDEX

CONTACTING US

If you have comments or suggestions, or are interested in having us give a presentation to your group or association, please contact us through one of the methods below:

Through our publisher   John Wiley & Sons Canada, Ltd.
22 Worcester Road
Etobicoke, Ontario
M9W 1L1

Or by e-mail   joann.kurtz@senecac.on.ca

Or visit our website at   www.kerr-and-kurtz.com